DATE DUE

DEC 9 1991	
ILL 7-01-92	
JAN. — 3 1994	
MAY 1 8 1994	
JUN. 0 7 1994	

ZUÑI
FOLK
TALES

FRANK HAMILTON CUSHING

ZUÑI
FOLK
TALES

Foreword by
JOHN WESLEY POWELL

Introduction by
MARY AUSTIN

THE UNIVERSITY OF ARIZONA PRESS

TUCSON

About the Author

FRANK HAMILTON CUSHING (1857 – 1900) began his researches into Native American lifeways at the age of nine, when he began a collection of Indian arrowheads that later became part of the permanent collection of the Smithsonian Institution. At the age of twenty-two, he was hired by Major John Wesley Powell, the famed explorer of the American West, as a field collector for the Bureau of American Ethnology. Powell posted Cushing to Zuñi Pueblo, in western New Mexico, where he lived for five years as an honorary member of the Zuñi people. He later served as head of the Hemenway Archaeological Expedition of 1886 – 88. Among his posthumous publications are *Zuñi Folk Tales* (1901), *Zuñi Breadstuff* (1974), and *Zuñi* (1979).

THE UNIVERSITY OF ARIZONA PRESS

First printing 1986
Manufactured in the U.S.A.

Library of Congress Cataloging-in-Publication Data

Cushing, Frank Hamilton, 1857 – 1900.
Zuñi folk tales.

Reprint. Previously published: New York : Knopf, 1931.
With new introd.
1. Zuni Indians—Legends. 2. Zuni Indians—Folklore.
3. Indians of North America—New Mexico—Legends.
4. Indians of North America—New Mexico—Folklore.
I. Title.
E99.Z9C92   1986   398.2′08997   85-28960

ISBN 0-8165-0986-7 (alk. paper)

LIST OF TALES

List of Tales

INTRODUCTION

IT is instructive to compare superstition with science. Mythology is the term used to designate the superstitions of the ancients. Folk-lore is the term used to designate the superstitions of the ignorant of today. Ancient mythology has been carefully studied by modern thinkers for purposes of trope and simile in the embellishment of literature, and especially of poetry; then it has been investigated for the purpose of discovering its meaning in the hope that some occult significance might be found, on the theory that the wisdom of the ancients was far superior to that of modern men. Now, science has entered this field of study to compare one mythology with another, and preeminently to compare mythology with science itself, for the purpose of discovering stages of human opinion.

When the mythology of tribal men came to be studied, it was found that their philosophy was also a mythology in which the mysteries of the universe were explained in a collection of tales told by wise men, prophets, and priests. This lore of the wise among savage men is of the same origin and has the same significance as the lore of Hesiod and Homer. It is thus a mythology in the early sense of that term. But the mythology of tribal men is devoid of that glamour and witchery born of poetry; hence it seems rude and savage in comparison, for example, with the mythology of the *Odyssey*, and to rank no higher as philosophic thought than the tales of the ignorant and superstitious which are called folk-lore ; and gradually such mythology has come to be called folk-lore. Folk-lore is a discredited mythology—a mythology once held as a philosophy. Nowadays the tales of savage men, not being credited by civilized and enlightened men with that wisdom which is held to belong to philosophy, are called folk-lore, or sometimes folk-tales.

The folk-tales collected by Mr. Cushing constitute a charming exhibit of the wisdom of the Zuñis as they believe, though it may be but a charming exhibit of the follies of the Zuñis as we believe.

The wisdom of one age is the folly of the next, and the opinions of tribal men seem childish to civilized men. Then why should we seek to discover their thoughts ? Science, in seeking to know the truth about the universe, does not expect to find it in mythology or folk-lore, does not even consider it as a paramount end that it should be used as an embellishment of literature, though it serves this purpose well. Modern science now considers it of profound importance to know the course of the evolution of the humanities ; that is, the evolution of pleasures, the evolution of industries, the evolution of institutions, the evolution of languages, and, finally, the evolution of opinions. How opinions grow seems to be one of the most instructive chapters in the science of psychology. Psychologists do not go to the past to find valid opinions, but to find stages of development in opinions; hence mythology or folk-lore is of profound interest and supreme importance.

Under the scriptorial wand of Cushing the folk-tales of the Zuñis are destined to become a part of the living literature of the world, for he is a poet although he does not write in verse. Cushing can think as myth-makers think, he can speak as prophets speak, he can expound as priests expound, and his tales have the verisimilitude of ancient lore; but his sympathy with the mythology of tribal men does not veil the realities of science from his mind.

The gods of Zuñi, like those of all primitive people, are the ancients of animals, but we must understand and heartily appreciate their simple thought if we would do them justice. All entities are animals — men, brutes, plants, stars, lands, waters, and rocks—and all have souls. The souls are tenuous existences—mist entities, gaseous creatures inhabiting firmer bodies of matter. They are ghosts that own bodies. They can leave their bodies, or if they discover bodies that have been vacated they can take possession of them. Force and mind belong to souls; fixed form, firm existence belong. to matter, while bodies and souls constitute the world. The world is a universe of animals. The stars are animals compelled to travel around the world by magic. The plants are animals under a spell of enchantment, so that usually they cannot travel. The waters are animals sometimes under the spell of enchantment. Lakes writhe in waves, the sea travels in circles about the earth, and the streams run over the lands. Mountains and hills tremble in pain, but cannot wander about; but rocks and hills and mountains sometimes travel about by night.

These animals of the world come in a flood of generations, and the first-born are gods and are usually called the ancients, or the first ones; the later-born generations are descendants of the gods, but alas, they are degenerate sons.

The theatre of the world is the theatre of necromancy, and the gods are the primeval wonder-workers; the gods still live, but their descendants often die. Death itself is the result of necromancy practised by bad men or angry gods.

In every Amerindian language there is a term to express this magical power. Among the Iroquoian tribes it is called *orenda ;* among the Siouan tribes some manifestations of it are called *wakan* or *wakanda*, but the generic term in this language is *hube*. Among the Shoshónean tribes it is called *pokunt*. Let us borrow one of these terms and call it "orenda." All unexplained phenomena are attributed to orenda. Thus the venom of the serpent is orenda, and this orenda can pass from a serpent to an arrow by another exercise of orenda, and hence the arrow is charmed. The rattle-snake may be stretched beside the arrow, and an invocation may be performed that will convey the orenda from the snake to the arrow, or the serpent may be made into a witch's stew and the arrow dipped into the brew.

No man has contributed more to our understanding of the doctrine of orenda as believed and practised by the Amerindian tribes than Cushing himself. In other publications he has elaborately discussed this doctrine, and in his lectures he was wont to show how forms and decorations of implements and utensils have orenda for their motive.

When one of the ancients—that is, one of the gods—of the Iroquois was planning the streams of earth by his orenda or magical power, he determined to have them run up one side and down the other; if he had done this men could float up or down at will, by passing from one side to the other of the river, but his wicked brother interfered and made them run down on both sides; so orenda may thwart orenda.

The bird that sings is universally held by tribal men to be exercising its orenda. And when human beings sing they also exercise orenda; hence song is a universal accompaniment of Amerindian worship. All their worship is thus fundamentally terpsichorean, for it is supposed that they can be induced to grant favors by pleasing them.

All diseases and ailments of mankind are attributed by tribal men to orenda, and all mythology is a theory of magic. Yet many of the tribes, perhaps all of them, teach in their tales of some method of introducing death and disease into the world, but it is a method by which supernatural agencies can cause sickness and death.

The prophets, who are also priests, wonderworkers, and medicine-men, are called shamans in scientific literature. In popular literature and in

frontier parlance they are usually called medicine-
men. Shamans are usually initiated into the guild,
and frequently there are elaborate tribal ceremonies for the purpose. Often individuals have
revelations and set up to prophesy, to expel diseases, and to teach as priests. If they gain a following they may ultimately exert much influence
and be greatly revered, but if they fail they may
gradually be looked upon as wizards or witches,
and they may be accused of black art, and in ex-
treme cases may be put to death. All Amerin-
dians believe in shamancraft and witchcraft.

The myths of cosmology are usually called creation myths. Sometimes all myths which account
for things, even the most trivial, are called creation
myths. Every striking phenomenon observed by
the Amerind has a myth designed to account for
its origin. The horn of the buffalo, the tawny
patch on the shoulders of the rabbit, the crest of
the blue-jay, the tail of the magpie, the sheen of
the chameleon, the rattle of the snake,—in fact,
everything that challenges attention gives rise to a
myth. Thus the folk-tales of the Amerinds seem
to be inexhaustible, for in every language, and
there are hundreds of them, a different set of myths
is found.

In all of these languages a strange similarity
in cosmology is observed, in that it is a cosmology
of regions or worlds. About the home world of
the tribe there is gathered a group of worlds, one
above, another below, and four more : one at every
cardinal point ; or we may describe it as a central

world, an upper world, a lower world, a northern world, a southern world, an eastern world, and a western world. All of the animals of the tribes, be they human animals, tree animals, star animals, water animals (that is, bodies of water), or stone animals (that is, mountains, hills, valleys, and rocks), have an appropriate habitation in the zenith world, the nadir world, or in one of the cardinal worlds, and their dwelling in the center world is accounted for by some myth of travel to this world. All bodies and all attributes of bodies have a home or proper place of habitation; even the colors of the clouds and the rainbow and of all other objects on earth are assigned to the six regions from which they come to the midworld.

We may better understand this habit of thought by considering the folk-lore of civilization. Here are but three regions: heaven, earth, and hell. All good things come from heaven, and all bad things from hell. It is true that this cosmology is not entertained by scholarly people. An enlightened man thinks of moral good as a state of mind in the individual, an attribute of his soul, and a moral evil as the characteristic of an immoral man; but still it is practically universal for even the most intelligent to affirm by a figure of speech that heaven is the place of good, and hell the place of evil. Now, enlarge this conception so as to assign a place as the proper region for all bodies and attributes, and you will understand the cosmological concepts of the Amerinds.

The primitive religion of every Amerindian

tribe is an organized system of inducing the ancients to take part in the affairs of men, and the worship of the gods is a system designed to please the gods, that they may be induced to act for men, particularly the tribe of men who are the worshipers. Time would fail me to tell of the multitude of activities in tribal life designed for this purpose, but a few of them may be mentioned. The first and most important of all are terpsichorean ceremonies and festivals. Singing and dancing are universal, and festivals are given at appointed times and places by every tribe. The long nights of winter are devoted largely to worship, and a succession of festival days are established, to be held at appropriate seasons for the worship of the gods. Thus there are festival days for invoking rain, there are festival days for thanksgiving—for harvest homes. In lands where the grasshopper is an important food there are grasshopper festivals. In lands where corn is an important food there are green-corn festivals; where the buffalo constituted an important part of their aliment there were buffalo dances. So there is a bear dance or festival, and elk dance or festival, and a multitude of other festivals as we go from tribe to tribe, all of which are fixed at times indicated by signs of the zodiac. In the higher tribes elaborate calendars are devised from which we unravel their picture-writings.

The practice of medicine by the shamans is an invocation to the gods to drive out evil spirits from the sick and to frighten them that they may leave.

By music and dancing they obtain the help of the ancients, and by a great variety of methods they drive out the evil beings. Resort is often had to scarifying and searing, especially when the sick man has great local pains. All American tribes entertain a profound belief in the doctrine of signatures,—*similia, similibus curantur*,—and they use this belief in procuring charms as medicine to drive out the ghostly diseases that plague their sick folk.

Next in importance to terpsichorean worship is altar worship. The altar is a space cleared upon the ground, or a platform raised from the ground or floor of the kiva or assembly-house of the people. Around the altar are gathered the priests and their acolytes, and here they make prayers and perform ceremonies with the aid of altar-pieces of various kinds, especially tablets of picture-writings on wood, bone, or the skins of animals. The altar-pieces consist of representatives of the thing for which supplication is made : ears of corn or vases of meal, ewers of water, parts of animals designed for food, cakes of grasshoppers, basins of honey, in fine any kind of food ; then crystals or fragments of rock to signify that they desire the corn to be hard, or of honeydew that they desire the corn to be sweet, or of corn of different colors that they desire the corn to be of a variety of colors. That which is of great interest to students of ethnology is the system of picture-writing exhibited on the altars. In this a great variety of things which they desire and a great variety of the characteristics of these things are represented in pictographs, or modeled in clay, or carved from wood and bone. The graphic art, as painting and sculpture, has its origin with tribal men in the development of altar-pieces. So also the drama is derived from primeval worship, as the modern practice of medicine has been evolved from necromancy.

There is another method of worship found in savagery, but more highly developed in barbarism, —the worship of sacrifice. The altar-pieces and the dramatic supplications of the lower stage gradually develop into a sacrificial stage in the higher culture. Then the objects are supposed to supply the ancients themselves with food and drink and the pleasures of life. This stage was most highly developed in Mexico, especially by the Nahua or Aztec, where human beings were sacrificed. In general, among the Amerinds, not only are sacrifices made on the altar, but they are also made whenever food or drink is used. Thus the first portions of objects designed for consumption are dedicated to the gods. There are in America many examples of these pagan religions, to a greater or less extent affiliated in doctrine and in worship with the religion of Christian origin.

In the early history of the association of white men with the Seneca of New York and Pennsylvania, there was in the tribe a celebrated shaman named Handsome Lake, as his Indian name is translated into English. Handsome Lake had a nephew who was taken by the Spaniards to Europe and educated as a priest. The nephew, on his return to America, told many Bible stories to his uncle, for he speedily relapsed into paganism. The uncle compounded some of these Bible stories with Seneca folk-tales, and through his eloquence and great influence as a shaman succeeded in establishing among the Seneca a new cult of doctrine and worship. The Seneca are now divided into two very distinct bodies who live together on the same reservation,—the one are " Christians," the other are " Pagans " who believe and teach the cult of Handsome Lake.

Mr. Cushing has introduced a hybrid tale into his collection, entitled " The Cock and the Mouse." Such tales are found again and again among the Amerinds. In a large majority of cases Bible stories are compounded with native stories, so that unwary people have been led to believe that the Amerinds are descendants of the lost tribes of Israel.

J. W. POWELL.

WASHINGTON CITY,
November, 1901.

INTRODUCTION
BY MARY AUSTIN

THE valley of Shiwina heads up into the high mesa country of northern New Mexico. The red cliffs and flattened shoulders of Thunder Mountain look southward upon the sole Pueblo of Zuñi, all that is left of the seven cities of Cibola, the false fame of whose wealth in silver and turquoise lured the adventurous Spaniard north into the *new* Mexico of the sixteenth century. But at the time a Franciscan *fraile* peered down upon the Middle Ant Heap of the World from the neighboring range, from which its pasteboard-colored mud walls appeared very like the then city of Mexico, there were easily seven of the populous house heaps strung along the north and south banks of Zuñi River, in which, when the snow was over the flat roofs, flame in the three-cornered fireplaces, and no snakes about, to run and tattle to the gods, the tales of this volume were being told in a manner surprisingly like that in which they are here related.

To understand why Frank Hamilton Cushing's collection of *Zuñi Folk Tales* is the first and still—throughout a considerable volume—the best-sustained translation of aboriginal American literature, the reader must realize that it is only since this volume first appeared, and was permitted to go out of print, that there has been even the beginning of an appreciation of the literary values in Amerind song or myth. Major Powell, in his introduction to the first edition, in his anxiety to have the Zuñi tales accepted for their reflective value on the evolution of opinion, unwittingly betrayed his own generation. He competently explains the use of the myth in worship, and that form of religious necromancy by which man's invisible environment is made to serve the tribal use; he mentions slightingly that mythology had also been used as an "embellishment to literature." But it did not occur to any ethnologist of thirty years ago that the Zuñi Folk Tales had proceeded directly out of that complex of intellectual perceptivity, emotional need, and æsthetic insight which is the matrix of all literatures. Nor even yet is the type of mentality which delights in the collection and collation of primitive lore invariably equipped for appreciating and evaluating literary quality. There are still in our institutions of learning men to whom it will come as a surprise that the sole reason for reprinting now, after a complete lapse from public attention, Cushing's Zuñi myths and tales is that he is the only American who notably brought to bear on that field adequate literary understanding.

I speak in the same sentence of myths and tales, since it is impossible to write intelligently of primitive literature without realizing that the myth is a special kind of tale, in which the unknown, the—for the time being—unknowable, is prefigured in the guise of the familiar: thunder as a great bird with clashing wings, God as the Father. Since, to the primitive, the unknowable is naturally charged with fearsomeness, the Myth of the Great Unknown takes on connotations of sanctity. It is the mistake of the unliterate to suppose that all primitive myth has this sacrosanct quality. To say that Indians believe so-and-so because so-and-so was discovered in an Indian tale is the most prolific source of misunderstanding of the Indian mind. The aboriginal American is not any more likely to believe his own tales literally than you are to agree that creatures with human figures and birds' wings once sang over the house-tops of Bethlehem, however ardently you may both trust in the something unknowable but true which gave rise to the imaginative concept.

Frank Hamilton Cushing was a man of such singular and penetrating insight into Indian life that he often skimmed on genius flashes over what were to the average ethnologist dark stretches of the unexplored. Nowhere in his writing does he make the explicit distinction which is here made for the lay reader, between the sacred myth and the secular tale; but everywhere he took it for granted.

Before it became a habit of mind with Frank Hamilton Cushing to assume, on the part of his readers, a knowledge of Indian folk ways which is not even yet native to more than a score or so of specialists, there had been one of the most singular histories of intellectual development that have occurred among men of science in the United States. Cushing was born in 1857, of native farmer stock in Pennsylvania, and grew up in the forest country of New York. He was of that physical constitution which a few hundred years earlier gave rise to the belief in changelings, so small and frail at birth that he spent his first three years on a pillow, and so phenomenally gifted that he seems to have remembered practically everything that happened to him from his first year. Being exempted, by his frailness, from the routine of public-school education, the boy Cushing practically grew up in the forest, where he developed an extraordinary sympathy with wild life, invented a vocabulary for himself and the creatures of the wood, and discovered an extraordinary aptitude for the vanished Indian life of the Lake Erie region. He could find Indian relics where no one would believe they could be found, and discovered such skill in fashioning, not only flints, but textiles, baskets, and Indian artifacts of every sort that he was actually able to recover many lost techniques and give a name and use to archæological finds which the best archæologists puzzled over. In 1879, at the age of twenty-two, he accompanied the Powell expedition to New Mexico, at that time almost totally unexplored. At his own request he was left at Zuñi Pueblo, the most significant and interesting of the Indian communal towns, where he spent altogether between five and six years. After mastering the Zuñi language, of which there is no other living example, he was adopted into the Macaw clan, under the sacred name Medicine-flower, which is never permitted to be borne by more than one person at a time. So sympathetically did he lend himself to every tribal requirement, including the faithful performance of the sacred ceremonial mysteries, that he became Priest of the Bow, living in the Governor's family and exercising important religious functions in the Pueblo. Thus his approach to tribal literature was more nearly that of an Indian than has been possible to any other recorder of Amerind myths and tales. The profound psychological insight which enabled him to redirect the whole American attitude toward Indian artifacts, and the same artistry which had controlled his reconstruction of them, went into the *Outlines of the Zuñi Creation Myth* and the *Zuñi Folk Tales*. Always it was present at the back of his mind, as it was in the minds of his Indian informants, that there existed a Sacred Myth, involving a cosmogony, a Creator, a company of Surpassing Beings, and profoundly mystical prototypes for every essential motion of man's soul. He knew also that, as in every Indian community, there was at Zuñi a considerable body of revered literature, in which the persons of the Great Myth more or less figured, shading off, as in all literatures, into the merely whimsical and entertaining. Of the epic Creation Myth of the Zuñi he made an outline and a partial translation, regrettably never finished. There is a reference in "The Serpent of the Sea" to the fact that this sacred myth, which is known in the other pueblos to require four hours for its recital, was never permitted to be related in installments, and never except by priests specially trained for it. The present collection he drew from the body of subsidiary narrative such as clusters about every great religious myth. Áhaiyúta and Mátsailéma, the Heavenly Twins of Pueblo mythology, are as popular in Pueblo fiction as Solomon or Samson and Delilah in the East. Readers brought up to believe that the walls of Jerico fell down when the Children of Israel trumpeted must not cavil at the necromancy of the Twins of Struggle and Chance. The dance of the revered and unbelievable in man's mind changes the figure at every turn of time and experience.

In primitive times, when so little was certainly known of the make-up of the world of visible things, and practically nothing understood of man's invisible environment, the attainment of magical power was the supreme achievement, the happy ending of every story; the matching of trick against trick the prevailing plot. But does the most popular of American magazines today ever miss printing at least one story in every number in which, in the world of politics or finance, the hero matches tricks with the villain? It is true that in the modern tale there is a tendency to overweight the story morally in favor of the hero—a tendency emergent in Zuñi tales, although mostly absent in older narratives. The creatures defeated or destroyed by the Divine Twins of Struggle and Chance are usually conceded by tribal judgment to have deserved killing.

The culture which produced the Zuñi tales lay on the hither side of complete primitivism. Town life was well ordered, civil government was beginning, and inter-tribal commerce creating its own precedent. Almost the only evidence we have that the sense of modern life had penetrated to the Middle Ant Heap where Cushing passed his four years of exile is the disposition of the narrator to explain occasionally that things were not quite as they are now in the days of our ancients. The inclusion of a European folk tale translated into Indian idiom witnesses the precise location of the cultural background between the Stone Age and ours.

To the long-ripened culture of Zuñi, perhaps the oldest within our land, is owed the preponderance of love and marriage as story elements, so much more in evidence here than in any other tribal collection yet made. The organization of Zuñi is matriarchal, and the place of woman and her interests more explicit. It was one of the few tribes in which a man's marriage had any direct relation to his place in the community, and therefore a determinative force in the social pattern.

Recently there has been an effort to classify the story of the Turkey Girl as a modern adaptation of the Cinderella motive, in which I cannot concur. The Turkey Girl is a favorite character in all Pueblo fiction; and if the Cinderella plot is an intrusion, what, then, shall we say of the dead bride, in a primitive village unvisited save by an occasional Catholic priest, who would hardly have found occasions for instructing his converts in the mysteries of Orpheus and Eurydice? To one familiar with the movements of the Amerind mind the Turkey Girl is a transcript of the experience of the loss of reality by indulgence in the day-dream, as the unkissed bride in the Land of Spirits derives from the dream of bereavement, in which the banquet disappears, the cup vanishes, the bride is drawn back to death as the act of appropriation is initiated.

It is in such revealing instances that the primitive function of story-telling is established. There is not much difference between the tribal notion of success in life, attained through the mysterious working of *orenda*, residing in the person of the hero or in a fetish in his possession, and the modern moron's dream of the way in which happiness and riches are arrived at, as revealed in the movies. *Orenda*, under the name of personality-plus, is still a marketable quality, and the immemorial business of fiction, Amerind or American, is to answer the question: plus *what?* Probably the oddly shaped pebble or the dried musk-rat's skin which the Amerind seeker adds to himself is no surer augury of success than some of the things that are peddled through the advertising pages of our literary magazines.

It is Cushing's fidelity to literary veracities like this that sustains his work above that of any of his contemporaries. Not only does he make no effort to popularize his Indian tales by conforming them to European folk-tale patterns; he never yields to that curious obsession of the American scholar which leads him to regard all æsthetic considerations as "embellishments," "figures of speech," "emotional interpretations." No one approaching the study of primitive literature under such an obsession can ever hope to understand that not only a single tale, but a complete cycle of tales, a whole literature, can and frequently does constitute a figure of speech for what is otherwise inexpressible.

Cushing never loses sight of this inclusiveness of the primitive tale, and this collection should not be read without the Creation Myth of which it is the corollary in the tribal mind. To do so would be like trying to understand English literature without a knowledge of the King James Bible. Many of the tales in this collection are as orthodoxly Indian as *Paradise Lost* is Christian; they have the same relation to the central myth as Milton's poem to the Old Testament; they are popular, fictionized versions of sacred story, but not themselves sacred, and not necessarily literally accepted.

After the ritual-epic, there will come renewed appreciation of the purely literary quality of Cushing's prose translations, the success with which he has kept the normal progressions, the rhythm clusters, of the original speech, as well as the purely formal notations of introduction and close. It is interesting to discover that "continued in our next" originated in the practice of "tying" the unfinished story so that none of its magical power might escape, and that the obligation to "read the Bible through" which troubled the youth of my generation may have originated in the impulse which forbids the priest chief to recite the esoteric version of the Great Myth in sections. One detects with chuckles in "The Boy Hunter" the original Sindbad dramatizing a personal experience. The formal keys to polite behavior in the Stone Age, such as "It is not thinking of nothing that a stranger comes to the house of a stranger," which permits the unexpected caller to open his business; the figures of speech; strange oaths—"By the delight of death" —all the color and gesture of the time so delightfully rendered, more than compensate for the occasional lapses of the translator, not a practiced *littérateur*, but instinctively familiar with the rhythms that subtend all literatures and make them akin.

Frank Hamilton Cushing died in 1900, the frail thread of his life snapped by a somewhat trivial accident. He died with much of his rare knowledge as yet uncommunicated, because of that strange stupidity of American life through which we appear to have money for everything but the perfection of scholarship, the development of our own cultural resources. Let it be known that in a corner of Europe an unknown epic scarcely inferior to Homer has been discovered, and American wealth would rise to it in a flood; but the announcement of the same sort of thing in our own land leaves us cold. And among us the discoverer, with his work of translation incomplete for plain lack of bread, dies chiefly of overwork and under-appreciation.

Zuñi Folk Tales and the unfinished *Creation Myth* were not all that came out of Cushing's genius. He wrote what is still the best account of Pueblo life before it was contaminated with modern Americanization; he wrote many interesting archæological papers, in which the charm of his writing contributes as much as the knowledge of the subject. While at Zuñi he gathered enough of tribal migration legend to point with certainty to the earlier and immensely more populous culture of the Gila River district as the source of the present New Mexican Indian culture. After he had lingered long enough at Zuñi to establish the historicity of the fabled Seven Cities of Cibola, he led the Hemingway expedition in 1888, unearthing the only really conclusive knowledge of the prehistory of a region so soon to be smothered in ebullient American prosperity. At the time of his death he was at work on his latest discovery, the extensive remains of a sea-dwelling pre-Columbian people on the coast of Florida. His work in redirecting archaeological interest was so explicitly rooted in his genius that it died with him. But his influence on the literary translation of aboriginal literature in the United States has barely begun. It has raised up no successors of his proportions; perhaps the combination of literary skill and sound knowledge of the kind required does not often occur. Perhaps he was, in fact, a changeling, a throw-back to the mysterious little people, traces of whose life, so close to the earth, make a network of fairy lore over ancestral Europe. He remains uniquely the only man not of their blood who understood competently the soul of such lore among the Amerinds of the West.

Santa Fe, New Mexico.
November, 1930.

ZUÑI
FOLK
TALES

THE TRIAL OF LOVERS:

OR THE MAIDEN OF MÁTSAKI AND THE RED FEATHER

(*Told the First Night*)

IN the days of the ancients, when Mátsaki was the home of the children of men, there lived, in that town, which is called " Salt City," because the Goddess of Salt made a white lake there in the days of the New, a beautiful maiden. She was passing beautiful, and the daughter of the priest-chief, who owned more buckskins and blankets than he could hang on his poles, and whose port-holes were covered with turquoises and precious shells from the ocean—so many were the sacrifices he made to the gods. His house was the largest in Mátsaki, and his ladder-poles were tall and decorated with slabs of carved wood—which you know was a great thing, for our grandfathers cut with the *ttmush* or flint knife, and even tilled their corn-fields with wooden hoes sharpened with stone and weighted with granite. That 's the reason why all the young men in the towns round about were in love with the beautiful maiden of Salt City.

Now, there was one very fine young man who lived across the western plains, in the Pueblo of the

Winds. He was so filled with thoughts of the maiden of Mátsaki that he labored long to gather presents for her, and looked not with favor on any girl of his own pueblo.

One morning he said to his fathers: "I have seen the maiden of Mátsaki; what think ye?"

"Be it well," said the old ones. So toward night the young man made a bundle of mantles and neck-laces, which he rolled up in the best and whitest buckskin he had. When the sun was setting he started toward Mátsaki, and just as the old man's children had gathered in to smoke and talk he reached the house of the maiden's father and climbed the ladder. He lifted the corner of the mat door and shouted to the people below—"*Shé!*"

"*Hai!*" answered more than a pair of voices from below.

"Pull me down," cried the young man, at the same time showing his bundle through the sky-hole.

The maiden's mother rose and helped the young man down the ladder, and as he entered the fire-light he laid the bundle down.

"My fathers and mothers, my sisters and friends, how be ye these many days?" said he, very carefully, as though he were speaking to a council.

"Happy! Happy!" they all responded, and they said also: "Sit down; sit down on this stool," which they placed for him in the fire-light.

"My daughter," remarked the old man, who was smoking his cigarette by the opposite side of the hearth-place, "when a stranger enters the house of a stranger, the girl should place before him food and cooked things." So the girl brought from the great vessel in the corner fresh rolls of *héwe*, or bread of corn-flour, thin as papers, and placed them in a tray before the young man, where the light would fall on them.

"Eat!" said she, and he replied, "It is well." Whereupon he sat up very straight, and placing his left hand across his breast, very slowly took a roll of the wafer bread with his right hand and ate ever so little; for you know it is not well or polite to eat much when you go to see a strange girl, especially if you want to ask her if she will let you live in the same house with her. So the young man ate ever so little, and said, "Thank you."

"Eat more," said the old ones; but when he replied that he was "past the naming of want," they said, "Have eaten," and the girl carried the tray away and swept away the crumbs.

"Well," said the old man, after a short time, "when a stranger enters the house of a stranger, it is not thinking of nothing that he enters."

"Why, that is quite true," said the youth, and then he waited.

"Then what may it be that thou hast come thinking of?" added the old man.

"I have heard," said the young man, "of your daughter, and have seen her, and it was with thoughts of her that I came."

Just then the grown-up sons of the old man, who had come to smoke and chat, rose and said to one another: "Is it not about time we should be going home? The stars must be all out." Thus saying, they bade the old ones to "wait happily until the morning," and shook hands with the young man who had come, and went to the homes of their wives' mothers.

"Listen, my child!" said the old man after they had gone away, turning toward his daughter, who was sitting near the wall and looking down at the beads on her belt fringe. "Listen! You have heard what the young man has said. What think you?"

"Why! I know not; but what should I say but 'Be it well,'" said the girl, "if thus think my old ones?"

"As you may," said the old man; and then he made a cigarette and smoked with the young man. When he had thrown away his cigarette he said to the mother: "Old one, is it not time to stretch out?"

So when the old ones were asleep in the corner, the girl said to the youth, but in a low voice: "Only possibly you love me. True, I have said 'Be it well'; but before I take your bundle and say 'thanks,' I would that you, to prove that you verily love me, should go down into my corn-field, among the lands of the priest-chief, by the side of the river, and hoe all the corn in a single morning. If you will do this, then shall I know you love me; then shall I take of your presents, and happy we will be together."

"Very well," replied the young man; "I am willing."

Then the young girl lighted a bundle of cedar

splints and showed him a room which contained a bed of soft robes and blankets, and, placing her father's hoe near the door, bade the young man "wait happily unto the morning."

So when she had gone he looked at the hoe and thought: "Ha! if that be all, she shall see in the morning that I am a man."

At the peep of day over the eastern mesa he roused himself, and, shouldering the wooden hoe, ran down to the corn-fields; and when, as the sun was coming out, the young girl awoke and looked down from her house-top, "Aha!" thought she, "he is doing well, but my children and I shall see how he gets on somewhat later. I doubt if he loves me as much as he thinks he does."

So she went into a closed room. Down in the corner stood a water jar, beautifully painted and as bright as new. It looked like other water jars, but it was not. It was wonderful, wonderful! for it was covered with a stone lid which held down many may-flies and gnats and mosquitoes. The maiden lifted the lid and began to speak to the little animals as though she were praying.

"Now, then, my children, this day fly ye forth all, and in the corn-fields by the river there shall ye see a young man hoeing. So hard is he working that he is stripped as for a race. Go forth and seek him."

"*Tsu-nu-nu-nu*," said the flies, and "*Tsi-ni-ni-ni*," sang the gnats and mosquitoes; which meant "Yes," you know.

"And," further said the girl, "when ye find him,

bite him, his body all over, and eat ye freely of his blood ; spare not his armpits, neither his neck nor his eyelids, and fill his ears with humming."

And again the flies said, " *Tsu-nu-nu-nu*," and the mosquitoes and gnats, " *Tsi-ni-ni-ni.*" Then, *nu-u-u*, away they all flew like a cloud of sand on a windy morning.

" Blood !" exclaimed the young man. He wiped the sweat from his face and said, " The gods be angry !" Then he dropped his hoe and rubbed his shins with sand and slapped his sides. "*Atu !*" he yelled ; "what matters — what in the name of the Moon Mother matters with these little beasts that cause thoughts ?" Whereupon, crazed and restless as a spider on hot ashes, he rolled in the dust, but to no purpose, for the flies and gnats and mosquitoes sang " *hu-n-n* " and " *tsi-ni-ni* " about his ears until he grabbed up his blanket and breakfast, and ran toward the home of his fathers.

"*Wa-ha ha! Ho o!*" laughed a young man in the Tented Pueblo to the north, when he heard how the lover had fared. "*Shoom !*" he sneered. " Much of a man he must have been to give up the maid of Mátsaki for may-flies and gnats and mosquitoes !" So on the very next morning, he, too, said to his old ones : " What a fool that little *boy* must have been. I will visit the maiden of Mátsaki. I 'll show the people of Pínawa what a Hámpasawan man can do. Courage !"—and, as the old ones said " Be it well," he went as the other had gone ; but, pshaw ! he fared no better.

After some time, a young man who lived in the River Town heard about it and laughed as hard as the youth of the Tented Pueblo had. He called the two others fools, and said that "girls were not in the habit of asking much when one's bundle was large." And as he was a young man who had everything, he made a bundle of presents as large as he could carry; but it did him no good. He, too, ran away from the may-flies and gnats and mosquitoes.

Many days passed before any one else would try again to woo the maiden of Mátsaki. They did not know, it is true, that she was a Passing Being; but others had failed all on account of mosquitoes and may-flies and little black gnats, and had been more satisfied with shame than a full hungry man with food. "That is sick satisfaction," they would say to one another, the fear of which made them wait to see what others would do.

Now, in the Ant Hill, which was named Hálonawan,[1] lived a handsome young man, but he was poor, although the son of the priest-chief of Hálonawan. He thought many days, and at last said to his grandmother, who was very old and crafty, '*Hó-ta ?* "

[1] The ancient pueblo of Zuñi itself was called Hálonawan, or the Ant Hill, the ruins of which, now buried beneath the sands, lie opposite the modern town within the cast of a stone. Long before Hálonawan was abandoned, the nucleus of the present structure was begun around one of the now central plazas. It was then, and still is, in the ancient songs and rituals of the Zuñis, *Hálona-ítiwana*, or the "Middle Ant Hill of the World," and was often spoken of in connection with the older town as simply the "Ant Hill."

" What sayest my *nána?* " said the old woman ; for, like grandmothers nowadays, she was very soft and gentle to her grandson.

" I have seen the maiden of Mátsaki and my thoughts kill me with longing, for she is passing beautiful and wisely slow. I do not wonder that she asks hard tasks of her lovers ; for it is not of their bundles that she thinks, but of themselves. Now, I strengthen my thoughts with my manliness. My heart is hard against weariness, and I would go and speak to the beautiful maiden."

" *Yo á !* my poor boy," said the grandmother. " She is as wonderful as she is wise and beautiful. She thinks not of men save as brothers and friends ; and she it is, I bethink me, who sends the may-flies and gnats and mosquitoes, therefore, to drive them away. They are but disguised beings, and beware, my grandson, you will only cover yourself with shame as a man is covered with water who walks through a rain-storm ! I would not go, my poor grandchild. I would not go," she added, shaking her head and biting her lips till her chin touched her nose-tip.

" Yes, but I must go, my grandmother. Why should I live only to breathe hard with longing ? Perhaps she will better her thoughts toward me."

" Ah, yes, but all the same, she will test thee. Well, go to the mountains and scrape bitter bark from the finger-root ; make a little loaf of the bark and hide it in your belt, and when the maiden sends you down to the corn-field, work hard at the hoeing until sunrise. Then, when your body is covered with sweat-drops, rub every part with the root-bark. The finger-root bark, it is bitter as bad salt mixed in with bad water, and the 'horn-wings' and 'long-beaks' and 'blue-backs' fly far from the salt that is bitter."

"Then, my gentle grandmother, I will try your words and thank you,"—for he was as gentle and good as his grandmother was knowing and crafty. Even that day he went to the mountains and gathered a ball of finger-root. Then, toward evening, he took a little bundle and went up the trail by the river-side to Mátsaki. When he climbed the ladder and shouted down the mat door: "*Shé!* Are ye within?" the people did not answer at once, for the old ones were angry with their daughter that she had sent off so many fine lovers. But when he shouted again they answered:

"*Hai*, and *Ée*, we are within. Be yourself within."

Then without help he went down the ladder, but he did n't mind, for he felt himself poor and his bundle was small. As he entered the fire-light he greeted the people pleasantly and gravely, and with thanks took the seat that was laid for him.

Now, you see, the old man was angry with the girl, so he did not tell her to place cooked things before him, but turned to his old wife.

"Old one," he began—but before he had finished the maiden arose and brought rich venison stew and flaky *héwe*, which she placed before the youth where the fire's brightness would fall upon it, with meat broth for drink; then she sat down

opposite him and said, "Eat and drink!" Whereupon the young man took a roll of the wafer-bread
and, breaking it in two, gave the girl the larger
piece, which she bashfully accepted.

The old man raised his eyebrows and upper lids,
looked at his old wife, spat in the fireplace, and
smoked hard at his cigarette, joining the girl in
her invitation by saying, "Yes, have to eat well."

Soon the young man said, "Thanks," and the
maiden quickly responded, "Eat more," and "Have
eaten."

After brushing the crumbs away the girl sat
down by her mother, and the father rolled a cigarette for the young man and talked longer with him
than he had with the others.

After the old ones had stretched out in the
corner and begun to "scrape their nostrils with
their breath," the maiden turned to the young
man and said: "I have a corn-field in the lands
of the priest-chief, down by the river, and if
you truly love me, I would that you should hoe
the whole in a single morning. Thus may you
prove yourself a man, and to love me truly; and if
you will do this, happily, as day follows day, will
we live each with the other."

"*Hai-i!*" replied the young man, who smiled
as he listened; and as the young maiden looked
at him, sitting in the fading fire-light with the
smile on his face, she thought: "Only possibly.
But oh! how I wish his heart might be strong,
even though his bundle be not heavy nor large.

"Come with me, young man, and I will show you

where you are to await the morning. Early take my father's hoe, which stands by the doorway, and go down to the corn-field long before the night shadows have run away from Thunder Mountain" —with which she bade him pass a night of contentment and sought her own place.

When all was still, the young man climbed to the sky-hole and in the starlight asked the gods of the woodlands and waters to give strength to his hands and power to his prayer-medicine, and to meet and bless him with the light of their favor; and he threw to the night-wind meal of the seeds of earth and the waters of the world with which those who are wise fail not to make smooth their trails of life. Then he slept till the sky of the day-land grew yellow and the shadows of the night-land grew gray, and then shouldered his hoe and went down to the corn-field. His task was not great, for the others had hoed much. Where they left off, there he fell to digging right and left with all his strength and haste, till the hard soil mellowed and the earth flew before his strokes as out of the burrows of the strongest-willed gophers and other digging creatures.

When the sun rose the maiden looked forth and saw that his task was already half done. But still she waited. As the sun warmed the day and the youth worked on, the dewdrops of flesh stood all over his body and he cast away, one after the other, his blanket and sash and even his leggings and moccasins. Then he stopped to look around. By the side of the field grew tall yellow-tops. He ran into the thicket and rubbed every part of his body, yea, even the hair of his head and his ear-tips and nostrils, with the bark of the finger-root. Again he fell to work as though he had only been resting, and wondered why the may-flies and gnats and mosquitoes came not to cause him thoughts as they had the others. Yet still the girl lingered; but at last she went slowly to the room where the jar stood.

"It is absurd," thought she, "that I should hope it or even care for it; it would indeed be great if it were well true that a young man should love me so verily as to hold his face to the front through such a testing." Nevertheless, she drew the lid off and bade her strange children to spare him no more than they had the others.

All hasty to feast themselves on the "waters of life," as our old grandfathers would say for blood, again they rushed out and hummed along over the corn-fields in such numbers that they looked more like a wind-driven sandstorm than ever, and "*tsi-ni-ni-i, tso-no-o*" they hummed and buzzed about the ears of the young man when they came to him, so noisily that the poor fellow, who kept at work all the while, thought they were already biting him. But it was only fancy, for the first may-fly that did bite him danced in the air with disgust and ex-claimed to his companions, "*Sho-o-o-m-m!*" and "*Us-á!*" which meant that he had eaten something nasty, that tasted as badly as vile odors smell. So not another may-fly in the throng would bite, although they all kept singing their song about his ears. And to this day may-flies are careful whom they bite, and dance a long time in the air before they do it.

Then a gnat tried it and gasped, " *Weh!* " which meant that his stomach had turned over, and he had such a sick headache that he reeled round and round in the air, and for that reason gnats always bite very quickly, for fear their stomachs will turn over, and they will reel and reel round and round in the air before doing it.

Finally, long-beak himself tried it, and, as long-beak hangs on, you know, longer than most other little beasts, he kept hold until his two hindlegs were warped out of shape ; but at last he had to let go, too, and flew straight away, crying, "*Yá kotchi!*" which meant that something bitter had burned his snout. Now, for these reasons mosquitoes always have bent-up hindlegs, which they keep lifting up and down while biting, as though they were standing on something hot, and they are apt to sing and smell around very cautiously before spearing us, and they fly straight away, you will notice, as soon as they are done.

Now, when the rest of the gnats and mosquitoes heard the words of their elder brothers, they did as the may-flies had done—did not venture, no, not one of them, to bite the young lover. They all flew away and settled down on the yellow-tops, where they had a council, and decided to go and find some prairie-dogs to bite. Therefore you will almost always find may-flies, gnats, and mosquitoes around prairie-dog holes in summer time when the corn is growing.

So the young man breathed easily as he hoed hard to finish his task ere the noonday, and when the maiden looked down and saw that he still labored there, she said to herself : " Ah, indeed he must love me, for still he is there ! Well, it *may be*, for only a little longer and they will leave him in peace." Hastily she placed venison in the cooking-pot and prepared fresh *héwe* and sweetened bread, "for *maybe*," she still thought, "and then I will have it ready for him."

Now, alas ! you do not know that this good and beautiful maiden had a sister, alas !—a sister as beautiful as herself, but bad and double-hearted ; and you know when people have double hearts they are wizards or witches, and have double tongues and paired thoughts—such a sister elder had the maiden of Mátsaki, alas !

When the sun had climbed almost to the middle of the sky, the maiden, still doubtful, looked down once more. He was there, and was working among the last hills of corn.

" Ah, truly indeed he loves me," she thought, and she hastened to put on her necklaces and bracelets of shells, her ear-rings as long as your fingers—of turquoises,—and her fine cotton mantles with borders of stitched butterflies of summer-land, and flowers of the autumn. Then she took a new bowl from the stick-rack in the corner, and a large many-colored tray that she had woven herself, and she filled the one with meat broth, and the other with the *héwe* and sweet-bread, and placing the bowl of meat broth on her head, she took the tray of *héwe* in her hand, and started down toward the corn-field by the river-side to meet her lover and to thank him.

Witches are always jealous of the happiness and good fortune of others. So was the sister of the beautiful maiden jealous when she saw the smile on her *hani's* face as she tripped toward the river.

"*Ho há!*" said the two-hearted sister. "*Tĕm-ithlokwa thlokwá! Wananí!*" which are words of defiance and hatred, used so long ago by demons and wizards that no one knows nowadays what they mean except the last one, which plainly says, "Just wait a bit!" and she hastened to dress herself, through her wicked knowledge, exactly as the beautiful maiden was dressed. She even carried just such a bowl and tray; and as she was beautiful, like her younger sister, nobody could have known the one from the other, or the other from the one. Then she passed herself through a hoop of magic yucca, which made her seem not to be where she was, for no one could see her unless she willed it.

Now, just as the sun was resting in the middle of the sky, the young man finished the field and ran down to the river to wash. Before he was done, he saw the maiden coming down the trail with the bowl on her head and the tray in her hand; so he made haste, and ran back to dress himself and to sit down to wait for her. As she approached, he said: "Thou comest, and may it be happily,"—when lo! there appeared two maidens exactly alike; so he quickly said, "Ye come."

"*E*," said the maidens, so nearly together that it sounded like one voice; but when they both placed the same food before him, the poor young man looked from one to the other, and asked:

"Alas! of which am I to eat?"

Then it was that the maiden suddenly saw her sister, and became hot with anger, for she knew her wicked plans. "Ah, thou foolish sister, why didst thou come?" she said. But the other only replied:

"Ah, thou foolish sister, why didst *thou* come?"

"Go back, for he is mine-to-be," said the maiden, beginning to cry.

"Go back, for he is mine-to-be," said the bad one, pretending to cry.

And thus they quarrelled until they had given one another smarting words four times, when they fell to fighting—as women always fight, by pulling each other's hair, and scratching, and grappling until they rolled over each other in the sand.

The poor young man started forward to part them, but he knew not one from the other, so thinking that the bad one must know how to fight better than his beautiful maiden wife, he suddenly caught up his stone-weighted hoe, and furiously struck the one that was uppermost on the head, again and again, until she let go her hold, and fell back, murmuring and moaning: "Alas! that thus it should be after all, after all!" Then she forgot, and her eyes ceased to see.

While yet the young man looked, lo! there was only the dying maiden before him; but in the air above circled an ugly black Crow, that laughed "*kawkaw, kawkaw, kawkaw!*" and flew away to its cave in Thunder Mountain.

Then the young man knew. He cried aloud and beat his breast; then he ran to the river and brought water and bathed the blood away from the maiden's temples; but alas! she only smiled and talked with her lips, then grew still and cold.

Alone, as the sun travelled toward the land of evening, wept the young man over the body of his beautiful wife. He knew naught but his sad thoughts. He took her in his arms, and placed his face close to hers, and again and again he called to her: "Alas, alas! my beautiful wife; I loved thee, I love thee. Alas, alas! Ah, my beautiful wife, my beautiful wife!"

When the people returned from their fields in the evening, they missed the beautiful maiden of Mátsaki; and they saw the young man, bending low and alone over something down in the lands of the priest-chief by the river, and when they told the old father, he shook his head and said:

"It is not well with my beautiful child; but as They (the gods) say, thus must all things be." Then he smiled — for the heart of a priest-chief never cries, — and told them to go and bring her to the plaza of Mátsaki and bury her before the House of the Sun; for he knew what had happened.

So the people did as their father had told them. They went down at sunset and took the beautiful maiden away, and wrapped her in mantles, and buried her near the House of the Sun.

2

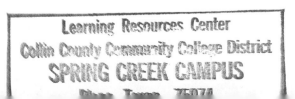

But the poor young man knew naught but his sad thoughts. He followed them; and when he had made her grave, he sat down by her earth bed and would not leave her. No, not even when the sun set, but moaned and called to her: "Alas, alas! my beautiful wife; I loved thee, I love thee; even though I knew not thee and killed thee. Alas! Ah, my beautiful wife!"

"*Shonetchi!*" ("There is left of my story.") And what there is left, I will tell you some other night.

(*Told the Second Night*)

"*Sonahtchi!*"

"*Sons shonetchi!*" ("There is left of my story";) but I will tell you not alone of the Maid of Mátsaki, because the young man killed her, for he knew not his wife from the other. It is of the Red Feather, or the Wife of Mátsaki that I will tell you this sitting.

Even when the sun set, and the hills and houses grew black in the shadows, still the young man sat by the grave-side, his hands rested upon his knees and his face buried in them. And the people no longer tried to steal his sad thoughts from him; but, instead, left him, as one whose mind errs, to wail out with weeping: "Alas, alas! my beautiful wife; I loved thee, I love thee; even though I knew not thee and killed thee! Alas! Ah, my beautiful wife!"

But when the moon set on the western hills, and

the great snowdrift streaked across the mid-sky, and the night was half gone, the sad watcher saw a light in the grave-sands like the light of the embers that die in the ashes. As he watched, his sad thoughts became bright thoughts, for the light grew and brightened till it burned the dark grave-sands as sunlight the shadows. Lo! the bride lay beneath. She tore off her mantles and raised up in her grave-bed. Then she looked at the eager lover so coldly and sadly that his bright thoughts all darkened, for she mournfully told him: " Alas! Ah, my lover, my husband knew not me from the other ; loved me not, therefore killed me ; even though I had hoped for love, loved me not, therefore killed me ! "

Again the young man buried his face in his hands and shook his head mournfully ; and like one whose thoughts erred, again he wailed his lament : " Alas, alas! my beautiful bride ! I do love thee ; I loved thee, but I did not know thee and killed thee ! Alas ! Ah, my beautiful bride, my beautiful bride ! "

At last, as the great star rose from the sky-land, the dead maiden spoke softly to the mourning lover, yet her voice was sad and strange : " Young man, mourn thou not, but go back to the home of thy fathers. Knowest thou not that I am another being ? When the sky of the day-land grows yellow and the houses come out of the shadows, then will the light whereby thou sawest me, fade away in the morn-light, as the blazes of late councils pale their red in the sunlight." Then her voice grew sadder as she said : " I am only a spirit ; for remember, alas ! ah, my lover, my husband knew not me from the other—loved me not, therefore killed me ; even though I had hoped for love, loved me not, therefore killed me."

But the young man would not go until, in the gray of the morning, he saw nothing where the light had appeared but the dark sand of the grave as it had been. Then he arose and went away in sorrow. Nor would he all day speak to men, but gazed only whither his feet stepped and shook his head sadly like one whose thoughts wandered. And when again the houses and hills grew black with the shadows, he sought anew the fresh grave and sat down by its side, bowed his head and still murmured : " Alas, alas ! my beautiful wife, I loved thee, though I knew not thee, and killed thee. Alas ! Ah, my beautiful wife ! "

Even brighter glowed the light in the grave-sands when the night was divided, and the maiden's spirit arose and sat in her grave-bed, but she only reproached him and bade him go. " For," said she, " I am only a spirit ; remember, alas ! ah, my lover, my husband knew not me from the other ; loved me not, therefore killed me ; even though I had hoped for love, loved me not, therefore killed me ! "

But he left only in the morning, and again when the dark came, returned to the grave-side.

When the light shone that night, the maiden, more beautiful than ever, came out of the grave-bed and sat by her lover. Once more she urged

him to return to his fathers; but when she saw
that he would not, she said: "Thou hadst better,
for I go a long journey. As light as the wind is,
so light will my feet be; as long as the day is, thou
canst not my form see. Know thou not that the
spirits are seen but in darkness? for, alas! ah, my
lover, my husband knew not me from the other;
loved me not, therefore killed me; even though I had
hoped for love, loved me not, therefore killed me!"

Then the young man ceased bemoaning his
beautiful bride. He looked at her sadly, and said:
"I do love thee, my beautiful wife! I do love
thee, and whither thou goest let me therefore go
with thee! I care not how long is the journey,
nor how hard is the way. If I can but see thee,
even only at night time, then will I be happy and
cease to bemoan thee. It was because I loved thee
and would have saved thee; but alas, my beautiful
wife! I knew not thee, therefore killed thee!"

"Alas! Ah, my lover; and Ah! how I loved
thee; but I am a spirit, and thou art unfinished.
But if thou thus love me, go back when I leave
thee and plume many prayer-sticks. Choose a
light, downy feather and dye it with ocher. Wrap
up in thy blanket a lunch for four daylights;
bring with thee much prayer-meal; come to me at
midnight and sit by my grave-side, and when in the
eastward the dayland is lighting, tie over my forehead the reddened light feather, and when with
the morning I fade from thy vision, follow only the
feather until it is evening, and then thou shalt see
me and sit down beside me."

So at sunrise the young man went away and gathered feathers of the summer birds, and cut many prayer-sticks, whereon he bound them with cotton, as gifts to the Fathers. Then he found a beautiful downy feather plucked from the eagle, and dyed it red with ocher, and tied to it a string of cotton wherewith to fasten it over the forehead of the spirit maiden. When night came, he took meal made from parched corn and burnt sweet-bread, and once more went down to the plaza and sat by the grave-side.

When midnight came and the light glowed forth through the grave-sands, lo! the maiden-spirit came out and stood by his side. She seemed no longer sad, but happy, like one going home after long absence. Nor was the young man sad or single-thoughted like one whose mind errs; so they sat together and talked of their journey till the day-land grew yellow and the black shadows gray, and the houses and hills came out of the darkness.

"Once more would I tell thee to go back," said the maiden's spirit to the young man; "but I know why thou goest with me, and it is well. Only watch me when the day comes, and thou wilt see me no more; but look whither the plume goeth, and follow, for thou knowest that thou must tie it to the hair above my forehead."

Then the young man took the bright red plume out from among the feathers of sacrifice, and gently tied it above the maiden-spirit's forehead.

As the light waved up from behind the great mountain the red glow faded out from the grave-

sands and the youth looked in vain for the spirit of
the maiden ; but before him, at the height of one's
hands when standing, waved the light downy
feather in the wind of the morning. Then the
plume, not the wife, rose before him, like the
plumes on the head of a dancer, and moved through
the streets that led westward, and down through
the fields to the river. And out through the streets
that led westward, and down on the trail by
the river, and on over the plains always toward the land of evening, the young man followed close the red feather ; but at last he began
to grow weary, for the plume glided swiftly before
him, until at last it left him far behind, and even
now and then lost him entirely. Then, as he
hastened on, he called in anguish :

"My beautiful bride ! My beautiful bride !
Oh, where art thou ?"

But the plume, not the wife, stopped and waited.
And thus the plume and the young man journeyed
until, toward evening, they came to the forests of
sweet-smelling piñons and cedars. As the night
hid the hills in the shadows, alas ! the plume disappeared, but the young man pressed onward, for
he knew that the plume still journeyed westward.
Yet at times he was so weary that he almost lost
the strength of his thoughts ; for he ran into trees
by the trail-side and stumbled over dry roots and
branches. So again and again he would call out
in anguish : "My beautiful wife ! My beautiful
bride ! Oh, where art thou ?"

At last, when the night was divided, to his joy

he saw, far away on the hill-top, a light that was red and grew brighter like the light of a camp-fire's red embers when fanned by the wind of the night-time. And like a star that is rising or setting, the red light sat still on the hill-top. So he ran hastily forward, until, as he neared the red light, lo! there sat the spirit of the beautiful maiden; and as he neared her, she said:

"Comest thou?" and "How hast thou come to the evening?"

As she spoke she smiled, and motioned him to sit down beside her. He was so weary that he slept while he talked to her; but, remember, she was a spirit, therefore she slept not.

Just as the morning star came up from the day-land, the maiden rose to journey on, and the young man, awaking, followed her. But as the hills came out of the shadows, the form of the maiden before him grew fainter and fainter, until it faded entirely, and only the red plume floated before him, like the plume on the head of a dancer. Far ahead and fast floated the plume, until it entered a plain of lava filled with sharp crags; yet still it went on, for the maiden's spirit moved over the barriers as lightly as the down of dead flowers in autumn. But alas! the young man had to seek his way, and the plume again left him far behind, until he was forced to cry out: "Ah, my beautiful bride, do wait for me, for I love thee, and will not turn from thee!" Then the plume stopped on the other side of the crags and waited until the poor young man came nearer, his feet and legs cut and bleeding, and his wind almost out. Then the trail was more even, and led through wide plains ; but even thus the young man could scarce keep the red plume in sight. But at night the maiden awaited him in a sheltered place, and they rested together beneath the cedars until daylight. Then again she faded out in the daylight, and the red plume led the way.

For a long time the trail was pleasant, but toward evening they came to a wide bed of cactus, and the plume passed over as swiftly as ever, but the young man's moccasins were soon torn and his feet and legs cruelly lacerated with the cactus spines ; yet still he pursued the red plume until the pain seemed to sting his whole body, and he gasped and wailed : "Ah, my beautiful wife, wait for me ; do wait, for I love thee and will not leave thee !" Then the plume stopped beyond the plain of cactus and waited until he had passed through, but not longer, for ere he had plucked all the needles of the cactus from his bleeding feet, it floated on, and he lifted himself up and followed until at evening the maiden again waited and bade him "Sit down and rest."

That night she seemed to pity him, and once more spoke to him : " *Yo á!* My lover, my husband, turn back, oh, turn back ! for the way is long and untrodden, and thy heart is but weak and is mortal. I go to the Council of Dead Ones, and how can the living there enter ? "

But the youth only wept, and begged that she let him go with her. " For, ah," said he, " my beautiful wife, my beautiful bride, I love thee and cannot turn from thee!"

And she smiled only and shook her head sadly as she replied: "*Yo á!* It shall be as thou willest. It may be thy heart will not wither, for tomorrow is one more day onward, and then down the trail to the waters wherein stands the ladder of others, shall I lead thee to wait me forever."

At mid-sun on the day after, the plume led the way straight to a deep cañon, the walls of which were so steep that no man could pass them alive. For a moment the red plume paused above the chasm, and the youth pressed on and stretched his hand forth to detain it; but ere he had gained the spot, it floated on straight over the dark cañon, as though no ravine had been there at all; for to spirits the trails that once have been, even though the waters have worn them away, still are.

Wildly the young man rushed up and down the steep brink, and despairingly he called across to the plume: "Alas! ah, my beautiful wife! Wait, only wait for me, for I love thee and cannot turn from thee!" Then, like one whose thoughts wandered, he threw himself over the brink and hung by his hands as if to drop, when a jolly little striped Squirrel, who was playing at the bottom of the cañon, happened to see him, and called out: "*Tsithl! Tsithl!*" and much more, which meant "*Ah hai! Wanani!*" "You crazy fool of a being! You have not the wings of a falcon, nor the hands of a Squirrel, nor the feet of a spirit, and if you drop you will be broken to pieces and the moles will eat up the fragments! Wait! Hold hard, and I will help you, for, though I am but a Squirrel, I know how to think!"

Whereupon the little chit ran chattering away and called his mate out of their house in a rock-nook: "Wife! Wife! Come quickly; run to our corn room and bring me a hemlock, and hurry! hurry! Ask me no questions; for a crazy fool of a man over here will break himself to pieces if we don't quickly make him a ladder."

So the little wife flirted her brush in his face and skipped over the rocks to their store-house, where she chose a fat hemlock and hurried to her husband who was digging a hole in the sand underneath where the young man was hanging. Then they spat on the seed, and buried it in the hole, and began to dance round it and sing,—

> "*Kiäthlä tsilu,*
> *Silokwe, silokwe, silokwe ;*
> *Ki'ai silu silu,*
> *Tsithl ! Tsithl !*"

Which meant, as far as any one can tell now (for it was a long time ago, and partly squirrel talk),

> " Hemlock of the
> Tall kind, tall kind, tall kind,
> Sprout up hemlock, hemlock,
> Chit ! Chit !"

And every time they danced around and sang the song through, the ground moved, until the fourth time they said " *Tsithl ! Tsithl !* " the tree sprouted forth and kept growing until the little Squirrel could jump into it, and by grabbing the topmost bough and bracing himself against the branches below, could stretch and pull it, so that in a short time he made it grow as high as the young man's feet, and he had all he could do to keep the poor youth from jumping right into it before it was strong enough to hold him. Presently he said " *Tsithl ! Tsithl !* " and whisked away before the young man had time to thank him. Then the sad lover climbed down and quickly gained the other side, which was not so steep ; before he could rest from his climb, however, the plume floated on, and he had to get up and follow it.

Just as the sun went into the west, the plume hastened down into a valley between the mountains, where lay a beautiful lake ; and around the borders of the lake a very ugly old man and woman, who were always walking back and forth across the trails, came forward and laughed loudly and greeted the beautiful maiden pleasantly. Then they told her to enter ; and she fearlessly walked into the water, and a ladder of flags came up out of the middle of the lake to receive her, down which she stepped without stopping until she passed under the waters. For a little — and then all was over — a bright light shone out of the water, and the sound of many glad voices and soft merry music came also from beneath it ; then the stars of the sky and the stars of the waters looked the same at each other as they had done before.

" Alas ! " cried the young man as he ran to the lake-side. " Ah, my beautiful wife, my beautiful wife, only wait, only wait, that I may go with thee ! " But only the smooth waters and the old man and woman were before him ; nor did the ladder come out or the old ones greet him. So he sat down on the lake-side wringing his hands and weeping, and ever his mind wandered back to his old lament : " Alas ! alas ! my beautiful bride, my beautiful wife, I love thee ; I loved thee, but I knew not thee and killed thee ! "

Toward the middle of the night once more he heard strange, happy voices. The doorway to the Land of Spirits opened, and the light shot up through the dark green waters from many windows, like sparks from a chimney on a dark, windless night. Then the ladder again ascended, and he saw the forms of the dead pass out and in, and heard the sounds of the *Kâkâ*, as it danced for the gods. The comers and goers were bright and beautiful, but their garments were snow-white cotton, stitched with many-colored threads, and their necklaces and bracelets were of dazzling white shells and turquoises unnumbered. Once he ventured to gain the bright entrance, but the water grew deep and chilled him till he trembled with fear and cold. Yet he looked in at the entrances, and lo ! as he gazed he caught sight of his beautiful bride all covered with garments and bright things. And there in the midst of the *Kâkâ* she sat at the head of the dancers. She seemed happy and smiled as she watched, and youths as bright and as happy came around her, and she seemed to forget her lone lover.

Then with a cry of despair and anguish he crawled to the lake-shore and buried his face in the sands and rank grasses. Suddenly he heard a low screech, and then a hoarse voice seemed to call him. He looked, and a great Owl flew over him, saying : "*Muhai ! Hu hu ! Hu hu !*"

"What wilt thou ?" he cried, in vexed anguish.

Then the Owl flew closer, and, lighting, asked : "Why weepest thou, my child ?"

He turned and looked at the Owl and told it part of his trouble, when the Owl suddenly twisted its head quite around—as owls do — to see if any-one were near ; then came closer and said : "I know all about it, young man. Come with me to my house in the mountain, and if thou wilt but follow my counsel, all will yet be well." Then the Owl led the way to a cave far above and bade him step in. As he placed his foot inside the opening, be-hold ! it widened into a bright room, and many Owl-men and Owl-women around greeted him hap-pily, and bade him sit down and eat.

The old Owl who had brought him, changed him-self in a twinkling, as he entered the room, and hung his owl-coat on an antler. Then he went away, but presently returned, bringing a little bag of medicine. "Before I give thee this, let me tell thee what to do, and what thou must promise," said he of the owl-coat.

The young man eagerly reached forth his hand for the magic medicine.

"Fool!" cried the being; "were it not well, for that would I not help thee. Thou art too eager, and I will not trust thee with my medicine of sleep. Thou shalt sleep here, and when thou awakest thou shalt find the morning star in the sky, and thy dead wife before thee on the trail toward the Middle Ant Hill. With the rising sun she will wake and smile on thee. Be not foolish, but journey preciously with her, and not until ye reach the home of thy fathers shalt thou approach her or kiss her; for if thou doest this, all will be as nothing again. But if thou doest as I counsel thee, all will be well, and happily may ye live one with the other."

He ceased, and, taking a tiny pinch of the medicine, blew it in the face of the youth. Instantly the young man sank with sleep where he had been sitting, and the beings, putting on their owl-coats, flew away with him under some trees by the trail that led to Mátsaki and the Ant Hill of the Middle.

Then they flew over the lake, and threw the medicine of sleep in at the windows, and taking the plumed prayer-sticks which the young man had brought with him, they chose some red plumes for themselves, and with the others entered the home of the *Kâkâ*. Softly they flew over the sleeping fathers and their children (the gods of the *Kâkâ* and the spirits) and, laying the prayer-plumes before the great altar, caught up the beautiful maiden and bore her over the waters and woodlands to where the young man was still sleeping. Then they hooted and flew off to their mountain.

As the great star came out of the dayland, the young man awoke, and lo! there before him lay his own beautiful wife. Then he turned his face away that he might not be tempted, and waited with joy and longing for the coming out of the sun. When at last the sun came out, with the first ray that brightened the beautiful maiden's face, she opened her eyes and gazed wildly around at first, but seeing her lonely lover, smiled, and said: "Truly, thou lovest me!"

Then they arose and journeyed apart toward the home of their fathers, and the young man forgot not the counsel of the Owl, but journeyed wisely, till on the fourth day they came in sight of the Mountain of Thunder and saw the river that flows by Salt City.

As they began to go down into the valley, the maiden stopped and said: "*Hahuá*, I am weary, for the journey is long and the day is warm." Then she sat down in the shadow of a cedar and said: "Watch, my husband, while I sleep a little; only a little, and then we will journey together again." And he said: "Be it well."

Then she lay down and seemed to sleep. She smiled and looked so beautiful to the longing lover that he softly rose and crept close to her. Then, alas! he laid his hand upon her and kissed her.

Quickly the beautiful maiden started. Her face was all covered with sadness, and she said, hastily and angrily: "Ah, thou shameless fool! I now know! Thou lovest me not! How vain that I should have hoped for thy love!"

With shame, indeed, and sorrow, he bent his
head low and covered his face with his hands.
Then he started to speak, when an Owl flew up
and hooted mournfully at him from a tree-top.
Then the Owl winged her way to the westward,
and ever after the young man's mind wandered.
Alas! alas! Thus it was in the days of the
ancients. Maybe had the young man not kissed
her yonder toward the Lake of the Dead, we
would never have journeyed nor ever have
mourned for others lost. But then it is well! If
men and women had never died, then the world
long ago had overflown with children, starvation,
and warring.

Thus shortens my story.

3

THE YOUTH AND HIS EAGLE

IN forgotten times, in the days of our ancients, at the Middle Place, or what is now Shiwina (Zuñi), there lived a youth who was well grown, or perfect in manhood. He had a pet Eagle which he kept in a cage down on the roof of the first terrace of the house of his family. He loved this Eagle so dearly that he could not endure to be separated from it; not only this, but he spent nearly all his time in caring for and fondling his pet. Morning, noon, and evening, yea, and even between those times, you would see him going down to the eagle-cage with meat and other kinds of delicate food. Day after day there you would find him sitting beside the Eagle, petting it and making affectionate speeches, to all of which treatment the bird responded with a most satisfied air, and seemed equally fond of his owner.

Whenever a storm came the youth would hasten out of the house, as though the safety of the crops depended upon it, to protect the Eagle. So, winter and summer, no other care occupied his attention. Corn-field and melon-garden was this bird to this youth; so much so that his brothers, elder and younger, and his male relatives generally, looked down upon him as negligent of all manly duties, and wasteful of their substance, which he helped not to earn in his excessive care of the bird. Naturally, therefore, they looked with aver-

sion upon the Eagle; and one evening, after a
hard day's work, after oft-repeated remonstrances
with the youth for not joining in their labors, they
returned home tired and out of humor, and, climbing the ladder of the lower terrace, passed the
great cage on their way into the upper house.
They stopped a moment before entering, and one
of the eldest of the party exclaimed: "We have
remonstrated in vain with the younger brother;
we have represented his duties to him in every
possible light, yet without effect. What remains
to be done? What plans can we devise to alienate
him from this miserable Eagle?"

"Why not kill the wretched bird?" asked one
of them. "That, I should say, would be the most
simple means of curing him of his infatuation."

"That is an excellent plan," exclaimed all of the
brothers as they went on into the house; "we
must adopt it."

The Eagle, apparently so unconscious, heard all
this, and pondered over it. Presently came the
youth with meat and other delicate food for his
beloved bird, and, opening the wicket of the gate,
placed it within and bade the Eagle eat. But the
bird looked at him and at the food with no apparent
interest, and, lowering its head on its breast, sat
moody and silent.

"Are you ill, my beloved Eagle?" asked the
youth, "or why is it that you do not eat?"

"I do not care to eat," said the Eagle, speaking
for the first time. "I am oppressed with much
anxiety."

"Do eat, my beloved Eagle," said the youth. "Why should you be sad? Have I neglected you?"

"No, indeed, you have not," said the Eagle. "For this reason I love you as you love me; for this reason I prize and cherish you as you cherish me; and yet it is for this very reason that I am sad. Look you! Your brothers and relatives have often remonstrated with you for your neglect of their fields and your care for me. They have often been angered with you for not bearing your part in the duties of the household. Therefore it is that they look with reproach upon you and with aversion upon me, so much so that they have at last determined to destroy me in order to do away with your affection for me and to withdraw your attention. For this reason I am sad,—not that they can harm me, for I need but spread my wings when the wicket is opened, and what can they do? But I would not part from you, for I love you. I would not that you should part with me, for you love me. Therefore am I sad, for I must go tomorrow to my home in the skies," said the Eagle, again relapsing into moody silence.

"Oh, my beloved bird! my own dear Eagle, how could I live without you? How could I remain behind when you went forward, below when you went upward?" exclaimed the youth, already beginning to weep. "No! Go, go, if it need be, alas! but let me go with you," said the youth.

"My friend! my poor, poor youth!" said the Eagle, "you cannot go with me. You have not wings to fly, nor have you knowledge to guide your course through the high skies into other worlds that you know not of."

" Let me go with you," cried the youth, falling on his knees by the side of the cage. " I will comfort you, I will care for you, even as I have done here; but live without you I cannot!"

" Ah, my youth," said the Eagle, " I would that you could go with me, but the end would not be well. You know not how little you love me that you wish to do this thing. Think for a moment! The foods that my people eat are not the foods of your people; they are not ripened by fire for our consumption, but whatever we capture abroad on our measureless hunts we devour as it is, asking no fire to render it palatable or wholesome. You could not exist thus."

" My Eagle! my Eagle!" cried the youth. " If I were to remain behind when you went forward, or below when you went upward, food would be as nothing to me; and were it not better that I should eat raw food, or no food, than that I should stay here, excessively and sadly thinking of you, and thus never eat at all, even of the food of my own people? No, let me go with you!"

" Once more I implore you, my youth," said the Eagle, " not to go with me, for to your own un-doing and to my sadness will such a journey be undertaken."

" Let me go, let me go! Only let me go!" implored the youth.

" It is said," replied the Eagle calmly. " Even

as you wish, so be it. Now go unto your own home for the last time ; gather large quantities of sustaining food, as for a long journey. Place this food in strong pouches, and make them all into a package which you can sling upon your shoulder or back. Then come to me tomorrow morning, after the people have begun to descend to their fields."

The youth bade good-night to his Eagle and went into the house. He took of parched flour a great quantity, of dried and pulverized wafer-bread a large bag, and of other foods, such as hunt-ers carry and on which they sustain themselves long, he took a good supply, and made them all into a firm package. Then, with high hopes and much thought of the morrow, he laid himself to rest. He slept late into the morning, and it was not until his brothers had departed for their fields of corn that he arose ; and, eating a hasty breakfast, slung the package of foods over his shoulders and descended to the cage of the Eagle. The great bird was waiting for him. With a smile in its eyes it came forth when he opened the wicket, and, settling down on the ground, spread out its wings and bade the youth mount.

" Sit on my back, for it is strong, oh youth ! Grasp the base of my wings, and rest your feet above my thighs, that you may not fall off. Are you ready ? Ah, well. And have you all needful things in the way of food ? Good. Let us start on our journey."

Saying this, the Eagle rose slowly, circling wider

and wider as it went up, and higher and higher, until it had risen far above the town, going slowly. Presently it said : " My youth, I will sing a farewell song to your people for you and for me, that they may know of our final departure." Then, as with great sweeps of its wings it circled round and round, going higher and higher, it sang this song :

" Huli-i-i— Huli-i-i—
Pa shish lakwa-a-a—
U-u-u-u—
U-u-u-u-a !

Pa shish lakwa-a-a—

U-u-u-u—
U-u-u-u-a ! "

As the song floated down from on high, " Save us ! By our eyes !" exclaimed the people. " The Eagle and the youth ! They are escaping ; they are leaving us !"

And so the word went from mouth to mouth, and from ear to ear, until the whole town was gazing at the Eagle and the youth, and the song died away in the distance, and the Eagle became smaller and smaller, winding its way upward until it was a mere speck, and finally vanished in the very zenith.

The people shook their heads and resumed their work, but the Eagle and the youth went on until at last they came to the great opening in the zenith of the sky. In passing upward by its endless cliffs they came out on the other side into the sky-world ; and still upward soared the Eagle,

until it alighted with its beloved burden on the
summit of the Mountain of Turquoises, so blue
that the light shining on it paints the sky blue.

"*Huhua!*" said the Eagle, with the weariness
that comes at the end of a long journey. "We
have reached our journey's end for a time. Let
us rest ourselves on this mountain height of my
beloved world."

The youth descended and sat by the Eagle's
side, and the Eagle, raising its wings until the
tips touched above, lowered its head, and catching
hold of its crown, shook it from side to side, and
then drew upon it, and then gradually the eagle-
coat parted, and while the youth looked and wondered in love and joy, a beautiful maiden was
uncovered before him, in garments of dazzling
whiteness, softness, and beauty. No more beautiful maiden could be conceived than this one, —
bright of face, clear and clean, with eyes so dark
and large and deep, and yet sharp, that it was be-
wildering to look into them. Such eyes have
never been seen in this world.

"Come with me, my youth—you who have loved
me so well," said she, approaching him and reaching
out her hand. "Let us wander for a while on this
mountain side and seek the home of my people."

They descended the mountain and wound round
its foot until, looking up in the clear light of the
sky-world, they beheld a city such as no man has
ever seen. Lofty were its walls,—smooth, gleaming, clean, and white; no ladders, no smoke, no
filth in any part whatsoever.

" Yonder is the home of my people," said the maiden, and resuming her eagle-dress she took the youth on her back again, and, circling upward, hovered for a moment over this home of the Eagles, then, through one of the wide entrances which were in the roof, slowly descended. No ladders were there, inside or outside ; no need of them with a people winged like the Eagles, for a people they were, like ourselves—more a people, indeed, than we, for in one guise or the other they might appear at will.

No sooner had the Eagle-maiden and the youth entered this great building than those who were assembled there greeted them with welcome assurances of joy at their coming. " Sit ye down and rest," said they.

The youth looked around. The great room into which they had descended was high and broad and long, and lighted from many windows in its roof and upon its walls, which were beautifully white and clean and finished, as no walls in this world are, with many devices pleasing to the eye. Starting out from these walls were many hooks or pegs, suspended from which were the dresses of the Eagles who lived there, the forms of which we know.

" Yea, sit ye down and rest and be happy," said an old man. Wonderfully fine he was as he arose and approached the couple and said, spreading abroad his wings : " Be ye always one to the other wife and husband. Shall it be so ? "

And they both, smiling, said " Yes." And so the youth married the Eagle-maiden.

After a few days of rest they found him an eagle-coat, fine as the finest, with broad, strong wings, and beautiful plumage, and they taught him how to comform himself to it and it to himself. And as Eagles would teach a young Eagle here in this world of ours, so they taught the youth gradually to fly. At first they would bid him poise himself in his eagle-form on the floor of their great room, and, laying all over it soft things, bid him open his wings and leap into the air. Anxious to learn, he would spread his great wings and with a powerful effort send himself high up toward the ceiling; but untaught to sustain himself there, would fall with many a flap and tumble to the floor. Again and again this was tried, but after a while he learned to sustain and guide himself almost wholly round the room without once touching anything; and his wife in her eagle-form would fly around him, watching and helping, and whenever his flight wavered would fan a strong wind up against his wings with her own that he might not falter, until he had at last learned wholly to support himself in the air. Then she bade him one day come out with her to the roof of the house, and from there they sailed away, away, and away over the great valleys and plains below, ever keeping to the northward and eastward; and whenever he faltered in his flight she bore his wings up with her own wings, teaching him how, this way and that, until, when they returned to the roof, those who watched them said : " Now, indeed, is he learned in the ways of our people. How good it is that this is so ! " And they were very happy, the youth and the Eagle-maiden and their people.

One day the maiden took the youth out again into the surrounding country, and as they flew along she said to him : " You may wonder that we never fly toward the southward. Oh, my youth, my husband ! never go yonder, for over that low range of mountains is a fearful world, where no mortal can venture. If you love me, oh, if you truly love me, never venture yonder!" And he listened to her advice and promised that he would not go there. Then they went home.

One day there was a grand hunt, and he was invited to join in it. Over the wide world flew this band of Eagle hunters to far-away plains. Whatsoever they would hunt, behold ! below them somewhere or other might the game be seen, were it rabbit, mountain sheep, antelope, or deer, and each according to his wish captured the kind of game he would, the youth bringing home with the rest his quarry. Of all the game they captured he could eat none, for in that great house of the Eagles, so beautiful, so perfect, no fire ever burned, no cooking was ever done. And after many days the food which the youth brought with him was diminished so that his wife took him out to a high mountain one day, and said : "As I have told you before, the region beyond those low mountains is fearful and deadly; but yonder in the east are other kinds of people than those whom you should dread. Not far away is the home of the Pelicans and Storks, who, as you know, eat food that has been cooked, even as your people do. When you grow hungry, my husband, go to them, and as they are your grandparents they will feed you and give you of their abundance of food, that you may bring it here, and thus we shall do well and be happy."

The youth assented, and, guided part of the way by his faithful, loving wife, he went to the home of the Storks. No sooner had he appeared than they greeted him with loud assurances of welcome and pleasure at his coming, and bade him eat. And they set before him bean-bread, bean-stews, beans which were baked, as it were, and mushes of beans with meat intermixed, which seemed as well cooked as the foods of our own people here on this mortal earth. And the youth ate part of them, and with many thanks returned to his home among the Eagles. And thus, as his wife had said before, it was all well, and they continued to live there happily.[1]

Between the villages of the Eagles and the Storks the youth lived; so that by-and-by the Storks became almost as fond of him as were the Eagles, addressing him as their beloved grandchild. And in consequence of this fondness, his

[1] This curious conception of the food of the storks and cranes and pelicans, for of such birds the folk-tale tells, is interesting. It is doubtless an attempt to explain what has been observed with relation to the pelicans and the storks especially : that they consume their food raw, and, as the Indian believes, cook it, as it were, in their own bodies, and then withdraw it, either for their young or for their final consumption. As this semi-digested food of such birds resembles very nearly the thick bean stews of the Zuñis, they have evidently taken from it the suggestion for the special kinds of food which were offered to the youth.

old grandfather and grandmother among the Storks especially called his attention to the fearful region lying beyond the range of mountains to the south, and they implored him, as his wife had done, not to go thither. " For the love of us, do not go there, oh, grandchild!" said they one day, when he was about to leave.

He seemed to agree with them, and spread his wings and flew away. But when he had gone a long distance, he turned southward, with this exclamation: " Why should I not see what this is? Who can harm me, floating on these strong wings of mine? Who can harm an Eagle in the sky?" So he flew over the edge of the mountains, and behold! rising up on the plains beyond them was a great city, fine and perfect, with walls of stone built as are the towns of our dead ancients. And the smoke was wreathing forth from its chimneys, and in the hazy distance it seemed teeming with life at the moment when the youth saw it, which was at evening time.

The inhabitants of that city saw him and sent messages forth to the town of the Eagles that they would make a grand festival and dance, and invited the Eagles to come with their friends to witness this dance. And when the youth returned to the home of his Eagle people, behold! already had this message been delivered there, and his wife in sorrow was awaiting him at the doorway.

" Alas! alas! my youth! my husband!" said she. " And so, regarding more your own curiosity than the love of your wife, you have been into that fearful country, and as might have been expected, you were observed. We are now invited to visit the city you saw and to witness a dance of the inhabitants thereof, which invitation we cannot refuse, and you must go with us. It remains to be seen, oh my youth, whom I trusted, if your love for me be so great that you may stand the test of this which you have brought upon yourself, by heedlessness of my advice and that of your grandparents, the Storks. Oh, my husband, I despair of you, and thus despairing, I implore you to heed me once more, and all may be well with you even yet. Go with us tonight to the city you saw, the most fearful of all cities, for it is the city of the damned, and wonderful things you will see; but do not laugh or even smile once. I will sit by your side and look at you. Oh, think of me as I do of you, and thus thinking you will not smile. If you truly love me, and would remain with me always, and be happy as I would be happy, do this one thing for me."

The youth promised over and over, and when night came he went with the Eagle people to that city. A beautiful place it was, large and fine, with high walls of stone and many a little window out of which the red firelight was shining. The smoke was going up from its chimneys, the sparks winding up through it, and, with beacon fires burning on the roofs, it was a happy, bustling scene that met the gaze of the youth as he approached the town. There were sounds and cries of life everywhere. Lights shone and merriment echoed from every street and room, and they were ushered into a great dance hall, or *kiwitsin*, where the audience was already assembled.

By-and-by the sounds of the coming dance were heard, and all was expectation. The fires blazed up and the lights shone all round the room, making it as bright as day. In came the dancers, maidens mostly, beautiful, and clad in the richest of ancient garments; their eyes were bright, their hair black and soft, their faces gleaming with merriment and pleasure. And they came joking down the ladders into the room before the place where the youth sat, and as they danced down the middle of the floor they cried out in shrill, yet not unpleasant voices, as they jostled each other, playing grotesque pranks and assuming the most laughter-stirring attitudes :

" *Hapa ! hapa ! is ! is ! is !* " (" Dead ! dead ! this ! this ! this !")—pointing at one another, and repeating this baleful expression, although so beautiful, and full of life and joy and merriment.

Now, the youth looked at them all through this long dance, and though he thought it strange that they should exclaim thus one to another, so lively and pretty and jolly they were, he was nevertheless filled with amusement at their strange antics and wordless jokes. Still he never smiled.

Then they filed in again and there were more dancers, merrier than before, and among them were two or three girls of surpassing beauty even in that throng of lovely women, and one of them looked in a coquettish manner constantly toward the youth, directing all her smiles and merriment to him as she pointed round to her companions, exclaiming: "*Hapa! hapa! is! is! is!*"

The youth grew forgetful of everything else as he leaned forward, absorbed in watching this girl with her bright eyes and merry smiles. When, finally, in a more amusing manner than before, she jostled some merry dancer, he laughed outright and the girl ran forward toward him, with two others following, and reaching out, grasped his hands and dragged him into the dance. The Eagle-maiden lifted her wings and with a cry of woe flew away with her people. But ah, ah! the youth minded nothing, he was so wild with merriment, like the beautiful maidens by his side, and up and down the great lighted hall he danced with them, joining in their uncouth postures and their exclamations, of which he did not yet understand the true meaning—"*Hapa! hapa! is! is! is!*"

By-and-by the fire began to burn low, and the maidens said to him: "Come and pass the night with us all here. Why go back to your home? Are we not merry companions? Ha! ha! ha! ha! *Hapa! hapa! is! is! is!*" They began to laugh and jostle one another again. Thus they led the youth, not unwillingly on his part, away into a far-off room, large and fine like the others, and there on soft blankets he lay himself down, and these maidens gathered round him, one pillowing his head on her arm, another smiling down into his face, another sitting by his side, and soon he fell asleep. All became silent, and the youth slept on.

In the morning, when broad daylight had come, the youth opened his eyes and started. It seemed as though there were more light than there should be in the house. He looked up, and the room which had been so fine and finished the night before was tottering over his head; the winds shrieked through great crevices in the walls; the windows were broken and wide open; sand sifted through on the wind and eddied down into the old, barren room. The rafters, dried and warped with age, were bending and breaking, and pieces of the roof fell now and then when the wind blew more strongly. He raised himself, and clammy bones fell from around him; and when he cast his eyes about him, there on the floor were strewn bones and skulls. Here and there a face half buried in the sand, with eyes sunken and dried and patches of skin clinging to it, seemed to glare at him. Fingers and feet, as of mummies, were strewn about, and it was as if the youth had entered a great cemetery, where the remains of the dead of all ages were littered about. He lifted himself still farther, and where the head of one maiden had lain or the arms of another had entwined with his, bones were clinging to him. One by one he picked them off stealthily and laid them down, until at last he freed himself, and, rising, cautiously stepped between the bones which were lying around, making no noise until he came to the broken-down doorway of the place. There, as he passed out, his foot tripped against a splinter of bone which was embedded in the debris of the ruin, and as a sliver sings in the wind, so this sang

4

out. The youth, startled and terrorized, sprang
forth and ran for his life in the direction of the
home of the Storks. Shrieking, howling, and
singing like a slivered stick in the wind, like creak-
ing boughs in the forest, with groans and howls
and whistlings that seemed to freeze the youth as
he ran, these bones and fragments of the dead
arose and, like a flock of vampires, pursued him
noisily.

He ran and ran, and the great cloud of the dead
were coming nearer and nearer and pressing round
him, when he beheld one of his grandparents, a
Badger, near its hole. The Badger, followed by
others, was fast approaching him, having heard this
fearful clamor, and cried out: "Our grandson!
Let's save him!" So they ran forward and, catching him up, cast him down into one of their
holes. Then, turning toward the uncanny crowd and
bristling up, with sudden emotion and mighty effort
they cast off that odor by which, as you know, they
may defile the very winds. *Thlitchiii!* it met
the crowd of ghosts. *Thliwooo!* the whole host
of them turned with wails and howls and gnashings
of teeth back toward the City of the Dead, whence
they had come. And the Badgers ran into the
hole where lay the youth, lifted him up, and
scolded him most vigorously for his folly.

Then they said: "Sit up, you fool, for you are
not yet saved! Hurry!" said they, one to another.
"Heat water!" And, the water being heated, nau-
seating herbs and other medicines were mingled
with it, and the youth was directed to drink of that.

He drank, not once, but four times. *Ukch, usa !*
—and after he had been thus treated the old Badgers
asked him if he felt relieved or well, and the youth
said he was very well compared with what he had
been.

Then they stood him up in their midst and said
to him : "You fool and faithless lout, why did
you go and become enamored of Death, however
beautiful? It is only a wonder that with all our
skill and power we have saved you thus far. It
will be a still greater wonder, O foolish one, if she
who loved you still loves you enough after this
faithlessness to save the life which you have forfeited. Who would dance and take joy in Death?
Go now to the home of your grandparents, the
Storks, and there live. Your plumage gone, your
love given up, what remains? You can neither descend to your own people below without wings,
nor can you live with the people of the Eagles
without love. Go, therefore, to your grandparents !"

And the youth got up and dragged himself away
to the home of the Storks ; but when he arrived
there they looked at him with downcast faces and
reproached him over and over, saying : "There is
small possibility of your regaining what you have
forfeited,— the love and affection of your wife."

"But I will go to her and plead with her," said
the youth. "How should I know what I was
doing?"

"We told you not to do it, and you heeded not
our telling."

So the youth lagged away to the home of the

Eagles, where, outside that great house with high walls, he lingered, moping and moaning. The Eagles came and went, or they gathered and talked on the housetop, but no word of greeting did they offer him; and his wife, at last, with a shiver of disgust, appeared above him and said: "Go back! go back to your grandparents. Their love you may not have forfeited; mine you have. Go back! for we never can receive you again amongst us. Oh, folly and faithlessness, in you they have an example!"

So the youth sadly returned to the home of the Storks. There he lingered, returning ever and anon to the home of the Eagles; but it was as though he were not there, until at last the elder Eagles, during one of his absences, implored the Eagle-maid to take the youth back to his own home.

"Would you ask me, his wife, who loved him, now to touch him who has been polluted by being enamored of Death?" asked she.

But they implored, and she acquiesced. So, when the youth appeared again at the home of the Eagles, she had found an old, old Eagle dress, many of the feathers in it broken; ragged and disreputable it was, and the wing-feathers were so thin that the wind whistled through them. Descending with this, she bade him put it on, and when he had done so, she said: "Come with me now, according to the knowledge in which we have instructed you."

And they flew away to the summit of that blue

mountain, and, after resting there, they began to descend into the sky which we see, and from that downward and downward in very narrow circles.

Whenever the youth, with his worn-out wings, faltered, the wife bore him up, until, growing weary in a moment of remembrance of his faithlessness, she caught in her talons the Eagle dress which sustained him and drew it off, bade him farewell forever, and sailed away out of sight in the sky. And the youth, with one gasp and shriek, tumbled over and over and over, fell into the very center of the town in which he had lived when he loved his Eagle, and utterly perished.

Thus it was in the times of the ancients ; and for this reason by no means whatsoever may a mortal man, by any alliances under the sun, avoid Death. But if one would live as long as possible, one should never, in any manner whatsoever, remembering this youth's experience, become enamored of Death.

Thus shortens my story.

THE POOR TURKEY GIRL

LONG, long ago, our ancients had neither sheep nor horses nor cattle; yet they had domestic animals of various kinds—amongst them Turkeys.

In Mátsaki, or the Salt City, there dwelt at this time many very wealthy families, who possessed large flocks of these birds, which it was their custom to have their slaves or the poor people of the town herd in the plains round about Thunder Mountain, below which their town stood, and on the mesas beyond.

Now, in Mátsaki at this time there stood, away out near the border of the town, a little tumble-down, single-room house, wherein there lived alone a very poor girl,—so poor that her clothes were patched and tattered and dirty, and her person, on account of long neglect and ill-fare, shameful to look upon, though she herself was not ugly, but had a winning face and bright eyes; that is, if the face had been more oval and the eyes less oppressed with care. So poor was she that she herded Turkeys for a living; and little was given to her except the food she subsisted on from day to day, and perhaps now and then a piece of old, worn-out clothing.

Like the extremely poor everywhere and at all times, she was humble, and by her longing for kindness, which she never received, she was made kind even to the creatures that depended upon her, and lavished this kindness upon the Turkeys she drove to and from the plains every day. Thus, the Turkeys, appreciating this, were very obedient. They loved their mistress so much that at her call they would unhesitatingly come, or at her behest go whithersoever and whensoever she wished.

One day this poor girl, driving her Turkeys down into the plains, passed near Old Zuñi,—the Middle Ant Hill of the World, as our ancients have taught us to call our home,— and as she went along, she heard the herald-priest proclaiming from the house-top that the Dance of the Sacred Bird (which is a very blessed and welcome festival to our people, especially to the youths and maidens who are permitted to join in the dance) would take place in four days.

Now, this poor girl had never been permitted to join in or even to watch the great festivities of our people or the people in the neighboring towns, and naturally she longed very much to see this dance. But she put aside her longing, because she re-flected : " It is impossible that I should watch, much less join in the Dance of the Sacred Bird, ugly and ill-clad as I am." And thus musing to herself, and talking to her Turkeys, as was her custom, she drove them on, and at night returned them to their cages round the edges and in the plazas of the town.

Every day after that, until the day named for the dance, this poor girl, as she drove her Turkeys out in the morning, saw the people busy in cleaning and preparing their garments, cooking delicacies, and otherwise making ready for the festival to

which they had been duly invited by the other villagers, and heard them talking and laughing merrily at the prospect of the coming holiday. So, as
she went about with her Turkeys through the day,
she would talk to them, though she never dreamed
that they understood a word of what she was
saying.

It seems that they did understand even more
than she said to them, for on the fourth day, after
the people of Mátsaki had all departed toward
Zuñi and the girl was wandering around the
plains alone with her Turkeys, one of the big Gob-
blers strutted up to her, and making a fan of his
tail, and skirts, as it were, of his wings, blushed with
pride and puffed with importance, stretched out
his neck and said: " Maiden mother, we know
what your thoughts are, and truly we pity you, and
wish that, like the other people of Mátsaki, you
might enjoy this holiday in the town below. We
have said to ourselves at night, after you have
placed us safely and comfortably in our cages:
'Truly our maiden mother is as worthy to enjoy
these things as any one in Mátsaki, or even Zuñi.'
Now, listen well, for I speak the speech of all the
elders of my people: If you will drive us in early
this afternoon, when the dance is most gay and
the people are most happy, we will help you to
make yourself so handsome and so prettily dressed
that never a man, woman, or child amongst all
those who are assembled at the dance will know
you ; but rather, especially the young men, will
wonder whence you came, and long to lay hold of

your hand in the circle that forms round the altar to dance. Maiden mother, would you like to go to see this dance, and even to join in it, and be merry with the best of your people?"

The poor girl was at first surprised. Then it seemed all so natural that the Turkeys should talk to her as she did to them, that she sat down on a little mound, and, leaning over, looked at them and said: " My beloved Turkeys, how glad I am that we may speak together! But why should you tell me of things that you full well know I so long to, but cannot by any possible means, do?"

" Trust in us," said the old Gobbler, " for I speak the speech of my people, and when we begin to call and call and gobble and gobble, and turn toward our home in Mátsaki, do you follow us, and we will show you what we can do for you. Only let me tell you one thing: No one knows how much happiness and good fortune may come to you if you but enjoy temperately the pleasures we enable you to participate in. But if, in the excess of your enjoyment, you should forget us, who are your friends, yet so much depend upon you, then we will think: ' Behold, this our maiden mother, though so humble and poor, deserves, forsooth, her hard life, because, were she more prosperous, she would be unto others as others now are unto her.' "

" Never fear, O my Turkeys," cried the maiden, —only half trusting that they could do so much for her, yet longing to try,—" never fear. In everything you direct me to do I will be obedient as you always have been to me."

The sun had scarce begun to decline, when the Turkeys of their own accord turned homeward, and the maiden followed them, light of heart. They knew their places well, and immediately ran to them. When all had entered, even their bare-legged children, the old Gobbler called to the maiden, saying : " Enter our house." She therefore went in. " Now, maiden, sit down," said he, " and give to me and my companions, one by one, your articles of clothing. We will see if we cannot renew them."

The maiden obediently drew off the ragged old mantle that covered her shoulders and cast it on the ground before the speaker. He seized it in his beak, and spread it out, and picked and picked at it ; then he trod upon it, and lowering his wings, began to strut back and forth over it. Then taking it up in his beak, and continuing to strut, he puffed and puffed, and laid it down at the feet of the maiden, a beautiful white embroidered cotton mantle. Then another Gobbler came forth, and she gave him another article of dress, and then another and another, until each garment the maiden had worn was new and as beautiful as any possessed by her mistresses in Mátsaki.

Before the maiden donned all these garments, the Turkeys circled about her, singing and singing, and clucking and clucking, and brushing her with their wings, until her person was as clean and her skin as smooth and bright as that of the fairest maiden of the wealthiest home in Mátsaki. Her hair was soft and wavy, instead of being an ugly, sun-burnt shock ; her cheeks were full and dimpled, and her eyes dancing with smiles,—for she now saw how true had been the words of the Turkeys.

Finally, one old Turkey came forward and said : " Only the rich ornaments worn by those who have many possessions are lacking to thee, O maiden mother. Wait a moment. We have keen eyes, and have gathered many valuable things,—as such things, being small, though precious, are apt to be lost from time to time by men and maidens."

Spreading his wings, he trod round and round upon the ground, throwing his head back, and laying his wattled beard on his neck ; and, presently beginning to cough, he produced in his beak a beautiful necklace ; another Turkey brought forth earrings, and so on, until all the proper ornaments appeared, befitting a well-clad maiden of the olden days, and were laid at the feet of the poor Turkey girl.

With these beautiful things she decorated herself, and, thanking the Turkeys over and over, she started to go, and they called out : " O maiden mother, leave open the wicket, for who knows whether you will remember your Turkeys or not when your fortunes are changed, and if you will not grow ashamed that you have been the maiden mother of Turkeys ? But we love you, and would bring you to good fortune. Therefore, remember our words of advice, and do not tarry too long."

" I will surely remember, O my Turkeys ! " answered the maiden.

Hastily she sped away down the river path toward Zuñi. When she arrived there, she went in at the western side of the town and through one of the long covered ways that lead into the dance court. When she came just inside of the court, behold, every one began to look at her, and many murmurs ran through the crowd,— murmurs of astonishment at her beauty and the richness of her dress,— and the people were all asking one another, " Whence comes this beautiful maiden ? "

Not long did she stand there neglected. The chiefs of the dance, all gorgeous in their holiday attire, hastily came to her, and, with apologies for the incompleteness of their arrangements,— though these arrangements were as complete as they possibly could be,—invited her to join the youths and maidens dancing round the musicians and the altar in the center of the plaza.

With a blush and a smile and a toss of her hair over her eyes, the maiden stepped into the circle, and the finest youths among the dancers vied with one another for her hand. Her heart became light and her feet merry, and the music sped her breath to rapid coming and going, and the warmth swept over her face, and she danced and danced until the sun sank low in the west.

But, alas ! in the excess of her enjoyment, she thought not of her Turkeys, or, if she thought of them, she said to herself, " How is this, that I should go away from the most precious consideration to my flock of gobbling Turkeys ?   I will stay a while longer, and just before the sun sets I will run back to them, that these people may not see who I am, and that I may have the joy of hearing them talk day after day and wonder who the girl was who joined in their dance."

So the time sped on, and another dance was called, and another, and never a moment did the people let her rest; but they would have her in every dance as they moved around the musicians and the altar in the center of the plaza.

At last the sun set, and the dance was well-nigh over, when, suddenly breaking away, the girl ran out, and, being swift of foot,— more so than most of the people of her village,— she sped up the river path before any one could follow the course she had taken.

Meantime, as it grew late, the Turkeys began to wonder and wonder that their maiden mother did not return to them. At last a gray old Gobbler mournfully exclaimed, " It is as we might have expected. She has forgotten us; therefore is she not worthy of better things than those she has been accustomed to. Let us go forth to the mountains and endure no more of this irksome captivity, inasmuch as we may no longer think our maiden mother as good and true as once we thought her."

So, calling and calling to one another in loud voices, they trooped out of their cage and ran up toward the Cañon of the Cottonwoods, and then round behind Thunder Mountain, through the Gateway of Zuñi, and so on up the valley.

All breathless, the maiden arrived at the open wicket and looked in. Behold, not a Turkey was there! Trailing them, she ran and she ran up the

valley to overtake them; but they were far ahead,
and it was only after a long time that she came
within the sound of their voices, and then, re-
doubling her speed, well-nigh overtook them, when
she heard them singing this song:

> " *K'yaanaa, to! to!*
> *K'yaanaa, to! to!*
> *Ye ye!*
> *K'yaanaa, to! to!*
> *K'yaanaa, to! to!*
> *Yee huli huli!*

> " *Hon awen Tsita*
> *Itiwanakwïn*
> *Otakyaan aaa kyaa;*
> *Lesna akyaaa*
> *Shoya-k'oskwi*
> *Teyäthltokwïn*
> *Hon aawani!*

> " *Ye yee huli huli,*
> *Tot-tot, tot-tot, tot-tot,*
> *Huli huli!*
> *Tot-tot, tot-tot, tot-tot,*
> *Huli huli!*" [1]

> " Up the river, *to! to!*
> Up the river, *to! to!*
> Sing *ye ye!*
> Up the river, *to! to!*
> Up the river, *to! to!*
> Sing *yee huli huli!*

> " Oh, our maiden mother
> To the Middle Place
> To dance went away;

[1] This, like all the folk-songs, is difficult of translation; and that which is
given is only approximate.

Therefore as she lingers,
To the Cañon Mesa
And the plains above it
We all run away !

" Sing *ye yee huli huli,*
Tot-tot, tot-tot, tot-tot,
Huli huli !
Tot-tot, tot-tot, tot-tot,
Huli huli !"

Hearing this, the maiden called to her Turkeys ; called and called in vain. They only quickened their steps, spreading their wings to help them along, singing the song over and over until, indeed, they came to the base of the Cañon Mesa, at the borders of the Zuñi Mountains. Then singing once more their song in full chorus, they spread wide their wings, and *thlakwa-a-a, thlakwa-a-a*, they fluttered away over the plains above.

The poor Turkey girl threw her hands up and looked down at her dress. With dust and sweat, behold ! it was changed to what it had been, and she was the same poor Turkey girl that she was before. Weary, grieving, and despairing, she returned to Mátsaki.

Thus it was in the days of the ancients. Therefore, where you see the rocks leading up to the top of Cañon Mesa (Shoya-k'oskwi), there are the tracks of turkeys and other figures to be seen. The latter are the song that the Turkeys sang, graven in the rocks ; and all over the plains along the borders of Zuñi Mountains since that day turkeys have been more abundant than in any other place.

After all, the gods dispose of men according as men are fitted; and if the poor be poor in heart and spirit as well as in appearance, how will they be aught but poor to the end of their days?

Thus shortens my story.

HOW THE SUMMER BIRDS CAME

IN the days of the ancients, in the town under Thunder Mountain called K'iákime, there lived a most beautiful maiden. But one thing which struck the people who knew her was that she seldom came forth from her room, or went out of her house ; never seemed to care for the people aroun⁴ her, never seemed to care to see the young men when they were dancing.

Now, this was the way of it. Through the roof of her room was a little skylight, open, and when it rained, one of the Gods of the Rain descended in the rain-drops and wooed this maiden, and married her all unknown to her people ; so that she was in his company every time it rained, and when the dew fell at night, on his ladder of water descending he came, and she was very happy, and cared not for the society of men. By-and-by, behold! to the utter surprise of the people, whose eyes could not see this god, her husband, there was a little boy born to her.

Now, he was the child of the gods, and, therefore, before he was many days old, he had begun to run about and speak, and had wonderful intelligence and wonderful strength and vivacity. He was only a month or two old when he was like a child of five or six or eight years of age, and he would climb to the house-top and run down into the plaza and out around the village hunting birds

5

or other small animals. With only his fingers and little stones for weapons, he never failed to slay and bring home these little creatures, and his mother's house was supplied more than any other house in the town with plumes for sacrifice, from the birds which he captured in this way.

Finally he observed that the older men of the tribe carried bows and arrows, and that the arrows went more swiftly and straighter than the stones he threw; and though he never failed to kill small animals, he found he could not kill the larger ones in that way. So he said to his mother one night: "Oh, mother, where does the wood grow that they make bows of, and where do they get sticks for their arrows? I wish you would tell me."

But the mother was quite silent; she did n't like to tell him, for she thought it would lead him away from the town and something would happen to him. But he kept questioning her until at last, weary with his importunities, she said: "Well, my little boy, if you go round the cliff here to the eastern side, there is a great hollow in the rocks, and down at the bottom of that hollow is a great cave. Now, around that shelter in the rocks are growing the trees out of which bows are made, and there also grow the bushes from which arrows are cut; they are so plentiful that they could supply the whole town, and furnish all the hunters here with bows and arrows; but they cannot get them, because in the cave lives a great Bear, a very savage being, and no one dares go near there to get timber for the bows or sticks for the arrows, because the Bear would surely devour whoever ventured there.   He has devoured many of our people; therefore you must not go there to get these arrows."

" No, indeed," said the boy.   But at night he lay down with much in his mind, and was so thoughtful that he hardly slept the whole night.   He was planning what he would do in the morning.

The next morning his mother was busy about her work, and finally she went down to the spring for some water, and the little boy slipped out of the house, ran down the ladder, went to the riverside, stooped down, and crawled along the bank of the river, until he could get around on the side of the cliff where the little valley of the spring that flows under Thunder Mountain lies.   There he climbed up and up until he came to the shelter in the rocks round on the eastern side of Thunder Mountain.   The mouth of this hollow was entirely closed with fine yellow-wood and oak, the best timber we have for bows, and straight sprouts were growing everywhere out of which arrows could be made.

"Ah, this must be the place," said the boy, as he looked at it.   "I don't see any Bear.   I think I will climb up and see if there is anything to be afraid of, and try if I can cut a stick before the Bear comes out."

He started and climbed into the mouth of the cavern, and his father, one of the Gods of the Rain, threw a tremendous shaft of lightning, and it thundered, and the cave closed together.

"Ha!" cried the boy. "What in the world is the meaning of this?" Then he stood there a moment, and presently the clouds finished and the cave opened, and all was quiet. He started to go in once more, and down came the lightning again, to remind him that he should not go in there.

"Ha!" cried the boy again. "What in the world does it mean?" And he rubbed his eyes,— it had rather stunned him,—and so soon as it had cleared away he tried again, and again for the fourth time.

Finally the god said, "Ah! I have reminded him and he does not heed. He must go his own way." So the boy climbed into the cave.

No sooner had he got in than it began to get dark, and *Wah!* came the Bear on his hind legs and grabbed the boy and began to squeeze him very tight.

"O my! O my!" cried he. "Don't squeeze me so hard! It hurts; don't squeeze me so hard! My mother is one of the most beautiful women you ever saw!"

"Hollo!" exclaimed the Bear. "What is that you say?"

"My mother is one of the most beautiful women you ever saw!"

"Indeed!" said the Bear, as he relaxed his hold. "My son, sit down. What did you come to my house for? I am sure you are very welcome."

"Why," said the boy, "I came to get a piece of wood for a bow and sticks for arrows."

Said the Bear, "I have looked out for this timber for a long time. There is none better in the whole country. Let me tell you what I will do. You don't look very strong. You haven't anything to cut the trees down with. I will go myself and cut down a tree for you. I will pick out a good one for a bow; not only that, but I will get fine sticks for arrows, too."

So he stalked off into the forest, and crack, crack, he smashed the trees down, and, picking out a good one, gnawed off the ends of it and brought it to the boy, then gathered a lot of fine straight sticks for arrow-shafts and brought them.

"There," said he, "take those home. Do you know how to make a bow, my son?"

"No, I don't very well," replied he.

"Well," said the Bear, "I have cut off the ends; make it about that length. Now take it home, and shave down the inside until it is thin enough to bend quickly at both ends, and lay it over the coals of fire so it will get hard and dry. That is the way to make a good bow."

"All right," said the boy; and as he took up the bundle of sticks and the stave for the bow, he said: "Just come along toward night and I will introduce you to my mother."

"All right," said the old Bear; "I will be along just about sunset. Then I can look at your bow and see whether you have made it well or not."

So the boy trudged home with his bundle of sticks and his bow stave, and when he arrived there his mother happened to be climbing out, and saw him coming.

"You wretched boy," she said, "I told you not to go out to the cave! I warrant you have been there where the Bear stays!"

"Oh, yes, my mother; just see what I have brought," said the boy. "I sold you to the Bear. He will be here to get you this evening. See what I have brought!" and he laid out his bow-timber and arrow-shafts.

"Oh," said she, "you are the most wretched and foolish of little boys; you pay no attention to what any one says to you; your mother's word is nothing but wind in your ears."

"Just see what I have brought home," said he. He worked as hard as he could to make his bow, stripped the arrow-shafts, smoothed and straightened them before the fire, and made the points of obsidian—very black it is; very hard and sharp were the points when he placed them on the arrows. Now, after placing the feathers on the arrows, he stood them up on the roof of the house against the parapet in the sunlight to dry; and he had his bow on the other side of the house against the other parapet to dry. He was still at work, toward sunset, when he happened to look up and saw the Bear coming along, slowly, comfortably, rolling over the sand.

"Ah!" said he, "the old man is coming." He paid no attention to him, however.

Presently the Bear came close to the ladder, and shook it to see if it was strong enough to hold him.

"Thou comest?" asked the boy.

"Yes," said the Bear.   "How have you been all day?"

"Happy," said the boy.

"How is your mother?"

"Happy," said the boy, "expecting you."

So the old Bear climbed up.   "Ah, indeed," said he, as he got over the edge of the house, "have you made the bow?"

"Yes, after a fashion."

So the Bear went over, raised himself on his hind feet, looked at the bow, pulled it, and said, as he laid it down: "It is a splendid bow.   What is this black stuff on these arrows?"

"Obsidian," answered the boy.

"These points are nothing but black coals," said the Bear.

"I tell you," said the boy, "they are good, black, flint arrow-heads, hard and sharp as any others."

"No," said the other, "nothing but coals."

"Now, suppose you let me try one of those coals on you," said the boy.

"All right," said the Bear.   He walked over to the other side of the roof and stood there, and the boy took one of the arrows, fitted it to the bow, and let go.   It went straight into the heart of the Bear, and even passed through him entirely.

"Wah!" uttered the Bear, as he gave a great snort and rolled over on the house-top and died.

"Ha, ha!" shouted the boy, "what you had intended to do unto me, thus unto you!   Oh, mother!" called he, as he ran to the sky-hole, "here is your husband; come and see him.   I have killed him;

but, then, he would have me make the experiment," said the boy.

"Oh, you foolish, foolish, disobedient boy!" said the mother. "What have you been doing now? Are we safe?"

"Oh, yes," said he; "my step-father is as passive as if he were asleep." And he went on and skinned his once prospective step-father, and then took out his heart and hung it to the cross-piece of the ladder as a sign that the people could go and get all the bow-timber and arrows they pleased.

That night, after the evening meal was over, the boy sat down with his mother, and he said: "By the way, mother, are there any monsters or fearful creatures anywhere round about this country that kill people and make trouble?"

"No," said the mother, "none whatever."

"I don't know about that; I think there must be," said the boy.

"No, there are none whatever, I tell you," answered the mother.

The boy began to tumble on the floor, rolling about, playing with his mother's blankets, and throwing things around, and once in a while he would ask her again the same question, until finally she got very cross with him and said: "Yes, if you want to know, down there in the valley, beyond the great plains of sagebrush, is a den of *Misho* Lizards who are fearful and deadly to every one who goes near them. Therefore you had better be careful how you run round the valley."

"What makes them so fearful?" asked he.

"Well," said she, "they are venomous; they have a way of throwing from their mouths or breath a sort of fluid which, whenever it strikes a person, burns him, and whenever it strikes the eyes it blinds them. A great many people have perished there. Whenever a man arrives at their den they are very polite and greet him most courteously; they say: 'Come in; sit down right here in the middle of the floor before the fire.' But as soon as the person is seated in their house they gather round the walls and throw this venom on him, and he dies almost immediately."

"Is it possible?" responded the little boy; and for some reason or other he began to grow sleepy, and said: "Now, let us go to sleep, mother."

So he lay down and slept. Just as soon as it was light the next morning he aroused himself, dressed, took his bow and arrows, and, placing them in a corner near the ladder, said: "Oh, mother, give me my breakfast; I want to go and shoot some little birds. I would like to have some roasted birds for dinner."

She gave him his breakfast as quickly as she could, and he ran down the ladder and went to shooting at the birds, until he happened to see that his mother and others were out of sight; then he skulked into the sagebrush and went as straight as he could for the den of the *Misho* Lizards. There happened to be two young ones sunning themselves outside, and they said:

"Ah, my fine little fellow, glad to see you this morning. Come in, come in; the old ones will be very much pleased to entertain you. Come in!"

"Thank you," said the boy. He walked in, but he felt under his coat to see if a huge lump of rock salt he had was still there.

"Sit right down here," said the old people. The whole den was filled with these *Misho* Lizards, and they were excessively polite, every one of them.

The boy sat down, and the old *Misho* said to the young ones: "Hurry up, now; be quick!" And they began to throw their venom at him, and continued until he was all covered with it; but, knowing beforehand, and being the child of the gods, he was prepared and protected, and it did him no harm.

"Thank you, thank you," said the boy. "I will do the same thing. Then he pulled out the salt and pushed it down into the fire, where it exploded and entirely used up the whole council of *Misho* Lizards.

"There!" cried the boy. "Thus would you have done unto me, thus unto you."

He took two fine ones and cut out their hearts, then started for home. When he arrived there, he climbed the ladder and suspended the two hearts beside that of the Bear and went down into the house, saying, "Well, mother, is dinner ready?"

"There now," said she, "I know it. I saw you hang those hearts up. You have been down there."

"Yes," said he, "they are all gone—every solitary one of them."

"Oh, you foolish, foolish, disobedient fellow! I

am all alone in the world, and if you should go to some of those fearful places some time and not come back, who would hunt for me? What should I do?" said the mother.

"Don't be troubled, mother, now," said the boy. "I don't think I will go any more. There is nothing else of that kind around, is there, mother?"

"No, there is not," she replied; "not a thing. There may be somewhere in the world, but there is not anywhere here."

In the evening, as he sat with his mother, the boy kept questioning and teasing her to tell him of some other monsters—pulling on her skirts and repeating his questions.

"I tell you," she said, "there are no such creatures."

"Oh, mother, I know there are," said he, "and you must tell me about them."

So he continued to bother her until her patience gave out, and she told him of another monster. Said she : "If you follow that cañon down to the southeast, there is a very, very, very high cliff there, and the trail that goes over that cliff runs close by the side of a precipice. Now, that has been for ages a terrible place, for there is a Giant living there, who wears a hair-knot on his forehead. He lies there at length, sunning himself at his ease. He is very good-natured and very polite. His legs stretch across the trail on which men have to go who pass that way, and there is no other way to get by. And whenever a man tries to go by that trail, he says : 'Pass right along, pass right along; I am glad to see you. Here is a fresh trail; some one has just passed. Don't disturb me; I am sunning myself.' Down below is the den where his children live, and on the flesh of these people he feeds them."

"Mercy!" exclaimed the boy. "Fearful! I never shall go there, surely. That is too terrible! Come, let us go to sleep; I don't want to hear anything more about it."

But the next morning, just as soon as daylight appeared, he got up, dressed himself, and snatched a morsel of food.

His mother said to him: "Where are you going? Are you thinking of that place I told you about?"

"No," said he; "I am going to kill some prairie-dogs right here in sight. I will take my war-club."

So he took his war-club, and thrust it into his belt in front, ran down the hill on which the village stood, and straightway went off to the place his mother had told him of. When he reached the top of the rocks he looked down, and there, sure enough, lay the Giant with the forehead knot.

The Giant looked up and said: "Ah, my son, glad to see you this morning; glad to see you coming so early. Some one just passed here a little while ago; you can see his tracks there."

"Well," said the boy, "make room for me."

"Oh, just step right over," said the old man; "step right over me."

"I can't step over your great legs," said the boy; "draw them up."

"All right," said the old Demon. So he drew his knees up. "There, now, there is plenty of room; pass right along, my son."

Just as the boy got near the place, he thrust out his leg suddenly that way, to kick him off the cliff; but the boy was too nimble for him, and jumped aside.

"Oh, dear me," cried the Monster; "I had a stitch in my leg; I had to stretch it out."

"Ah," said the boy, "you tried to kick me off, did you?"

"Oh, no," said the old villain; "I had a terrible stitch in my knee,"—and he began to knead his knee in the most vehement manner. "Just pass right along; I trust it won't happen again."

The boy again attempted to pass, and the same thing happened as before.

"Oh, my knee! my knee!" exclaimed the Monster.

"Yes, your knee, your knee!" said the boy, as he whipped out his war-club and whacked the Giant on the head before he had time to recover himself. "Thus unto me you would have done, thus unto you!" said the boy.

No sooner had the Giant fallen than the little Top-knots gathered round him and began to eat; and they ate and ate and ate,—there were many of them, and they were voracious—until they came to the top-knot on the old fellow's head, and then one of them cried; "Oh, dear, alas and alas! this is our own father!"

And while they were still crying, the boy cut

out the Giant's heart and slung it over his
shoulder; then he climbed down the cliff to where
the young Top-knots were, and slew them all except
two,—a pair of them. Then he took these two,
who were still young, like little children, and grasping one by the throat, wrung its neck and threw
it into the air, when it suddenly became a winged
creature, and spread out its wings and soared
away, crying: "Peep, peep, peep," just as the falcons of today do. Then he took the other one
by the neck, and swung it round and round, and
flung it into the air, and it flew away with a heavy
motion, and cried: "Boohoo, boohoo, boohoo!"
and became an owl.

"Ah," said the boy, "born for evil, changed for
good! Ye shall be the means whereby our children in the future shall sacrifice to the gods
themselves."

Then he trudged along home with the Giant's
heart, and when he got there, he hung it on the
cross-piece of the ladder by the side of the other
hearts. It was almost night then.

"There, now!" said his mother, as he entered
the house; "I have been troubled almost to death
by your not coming home sooner. You went off
to the place I told you of; I know you did!"

"Ha!" said he, "of course I did. I went up
there, and the poor fellows are all dead."

"Why will you not listen to me?" said she.

"Oh, it is all right, mother," said the boy. "It
is all right." She went on scolding him in the
usual fashion, but he paid no attention to her.

As soon as she had sat down to her evening tasks, he asked : " Now, is there any other of these terrible creatures ? "

" Well, I shall tell you of nothing more now," said she.

" Why, is there anything more ? " asked the boy.

" No, there is not," replied she.

" Ah, mother, I think there must be."

" No ; there is nothing more, I tell you."

" Ah, mother, I think there must be."

And he kept bothering and teasing until she told him again (she knew she would have to) : " Yes, away down in the valley, some distance from here, near the little Cold-making Hill, there lives a fearful creature, a four-fold Elk or Bison, more enormous than any other living thing. *Awiteli Wakashi* he is called, and no one can go near him. He rushes stamping and bellowing about the country, and people never pass through that section from fear."

" Ah," said the boy ; " don't tell me any more ; he must be a fearful creature, indeed."

" Yes ; but you will be sure to go there," said she.

" Oh, no, no, mother ; no, indeed ! "

But the next morning he went earlier than ever, carrying with him his bows and arrows. He was so filled with dread, however, or pretended to be, that as he went along the trail he began to cry and sniffle, and walk very slowly, until he came near the hole of an old Gopher, his grandfather. The old fellow was working away, digging another cellar, throwing the dirt out, when he heard this crying. Said he : " That is my grandson ; I wonder what he is up to now." So he ran and stuck his nose out of the hole he was digging, and said : " Oh, my grandchild, where are you going ? "

The boy stopped and began to look around.

" Right here ! right here ! " cried the grand-father, calling his attention to the hole. " Come, my boy."

The boy put his foot in, and the hole enlarged, and he went down into it.

" Now, dry your eyes, my grandchild, and tell me what is the matter."

" Well," said the boy, " I was going to find the four-fold Bison. I wanted to take a look at him, but I am frightened ! "

" Why, what is the matter ? Why do you not go ? " said the Gopher.

" Well, to tell you the truth, I thought I would try to kill him," he answered.

" Well, I will do what I can to help ; you had better not try to do it alone. Sit here com-fortably ; dry your eyes, and I will see what I can do."

The old Gopher began to dig, dig, dig under the ground for a long way, making a fine tunnel, and packed it hard on the top and sides so that it would not fall in. He finally came to hear the " thud, thud, thud " of the heart of this creature, where it was lying, and dug the hole up to that spot. When he got there he saw the long layers of hair on its body, where no arrow could penetrate, and he cut the hair off, so that the skin showed white. Then he silently stole back to where the boy was and said : " Now, my boy, take your bow and arrows and go along through this hole until you get to where the tunnel turns upward, and then, if you look well, you will see a light patch. That is the skin next the heart of the four-fold Bison. He is sleeping there. You will hear the 'thud, thud, thud' of his heart. Shoot him exactly in the middle of that place, and then, mind you, turn around and run for your life, and the moment you get to my hole, tumble in, headforemost or any way."

So the boy did as he was told—crawled through the tunnel until he came to where it went upward, saw the light patch, and let fly an arrow with all his might, then rushed and scrambled back as hard as he could. With a roar that shook the earth the four-fold Bison fell over, then struggled to his feet, snorted, bellowed, and stuck his great horn into the tunnel, and like a flash of fire ripped it from end to end, just as the boy came tumbling into the deeper hole of his grandfather.

" Ah ! " exclaimed the Gopher.

" He almost got me," said the boy.

" Sit still a moment and rest, my grandson," said the Gopher. " He did n't catch you. I will go and see whether he is dead."

So the Gopher stuck his nose out of the hole and saw there a great heap of flesh lying. He went out, nosed around, and smelt, jumped back, and went forward again until he came to the end

6

of the creature, and then he took one of his nails and scratched out an eye, and there was no sign of life. So he ran back to the boy, and said : " Yes, he breathes no more ; you need not fear him longer."

" Oh, thank you, my grandfather ! " said the boy. And he climbed out, and laid himself to work to skin the beast. He took off its great thick skin, and cut off a suitable piece of it, for the whole pelt was so large and heavy that he could not carry it ; then he took out the animal's great heart, and finally one of the large intestines and filled it with blood, then started for home. He went slowly, because his load was so heavy, and when he arrived he hung the heart on the ladder by the side of the others, and dragged the pelt to the sky-hole, and nearly scared the wits out of his mother by dropping it into the room.

" Oh, my child, now, here you are ! Where have you been ? " cried she. " I warned you of the place where the four-fold Bison was ; I wonder that you ever came home."

" Ah, the poor creature ! " said the boy ; " he is dead. Just look at this. He is n't handsome any more ; he is n't strong and large any more."

" Oh, you wretched, wretched boy ! You will be the death of me, as well as of yourself, some time," said the mother.

" No, mother," said the boy ; " that is all nonsense."

That evening the boy said to his mother : " Now, mother, is there anything else of this kind left ? If there is, I want to know it. Now, don't disappoint me by refusing to tell."

" Oh, my dear son," said she, " I wish you would n't ask me ; but indeed there is.   There are terrible birds, great Eagles, fearful Eagles, living over on Shuntekia.   In the very middle of an enormous cliff is a hollow place in the rocks where is built their nest, and there are their young ones. Day after day, far and near, they catch up children and young men and women, and carry them away, never more to be seen.   These birds are more terrible than all the rest, because how can one get near to slay them ?   My son, I do hope and trust that you will not go this time,—but, you foolish little boy, I see that you will go."

" Well, mother, let us go to sleep, and never mind anything about it," said the boy.

But after his mother had gone to sleep, he took the piece of rawhide he had skinned from the four-fold Bison, and, cutting it out, made himself a suit— a green rawhide suit, skin-tight almost, so that it was perfectly smooth.   Then he scraped the hair off, greased it all over, and put it away inside a blanket so that it would not dry.   In the morning, quite early, he took his weapons, and taking also his rawhide suit, and the section of the four-fold Bison's intestine which he had filled with blood, he ran into the inlet, and across it, and climbed the mesa near the Shuntekia cliff.   When he came within a short distance of the nest of the Eagles, he stopped and slipped on his rawhide suit, and tied the intestine of blood round his neck, like a sausage.

Then he began to cry and shake his head, and he cried louder than there was any need of his doing in reality; for presently the old father of the Eagles, who was away up in the sky, just a mere speck, heard and saw him and came swishing down in a great circle, winding round and round the boy, and the boy looked up and began to cry louder still, as if frightened out of his wits, and finally rolled himself up like a porcupine, and threw himself down into the trail, crying and howling with apparent fear. The Eagle swooped down on him, and tried to grasp him in his talons, and, *kopo kopooo*, his claws simply slipped off the rawhide coat. Then the Eagle made a fiercer grab at him and grew angry, but his claws would continually slip off, until he tore a rent in the intestine about the boy's neck, and the blood began to stream over the boy's coat, making it more slippery than ever. When the Eagle smelt the blood, he thought he had got him, and it made him fiercer than ever; and finally, during his struggling, he got one talon through a stitch in the coat, and he spread out his wings, and flew up, and circled round and round over the point where the young Eagles nest was, when he let go and shook the boy free, and the boy rolled over and over and came down into the nest; but he struck on a great heap of brush, which broke his fall. He lay there quite still, and the old Eagle swooped down and poised himself on a great crag of rock near by, which was his usual perching place.

"There, my children, my little ones," said he, "I have brought you food. Feast yourselves! Feast yourselves! For that reason I brought it."

So the little Eagles, who were very awkward, long-legged and short-winged, limped up to the boy and reached out their claws and opened their beaks, ready to strike him in the face. He lay there quite still until they got very near, and then said to them : "*Shhsht !*" And they tumbled back, being awkward little fellows, and stretched up their necks and looked at him, as Eagles will.

Then the old Eagle said : "Why don't you eat him ? Feast yourselves, my children, feast yourselves ! "

So they advanced again, more cautiously this time, and a little more determinedly too ; and they reached out their beaks to tear him, and he said : "*Shhsht !*" and, under his breath, "Don't eat me !" And they jumped back again.

"What in the world is the matter with you little fools ? " said the old Eagle. "Eat him ! I can 't stay here any longer ; I have to go away and hunt to feed you ; but you don't seem to appreciate my efforts much." And he lifted his wings, rose into the air, and sailed off to the northward.

Then the two young Eagles began to walk around the boy, and to examine him at all points. Finally they approached his feet and hands.

"Be careful, be careful, don't eat me ! Tell me about what time your mother comes home," said he, sitting up. "What time does she usually come ? "

"Well," said the little Eagles, "she comes home when the clouds begin to gather and throw their shadow over our nest." (Really, it was the shadow of the mother Eagle herself that was thrown over the nest.)

"Very well," said the boy; "what time does your father come home?"

"When the fine rain begins to fall," said they, meaning the dew.

"Oh," said the boy. So he sat there, and by-and-by, sure enough, away off in the sky, carrying something dangling from her feet, came the old mother Eagle. She soared round and round until she was over the nest, when she dropped her burden, and over and over it fell and tumbled into the nest, a poor, dead, beautiful maiden. The young boy looked at her, and his heart grew very hot, and when the old Eagle came and perched, in a moment he let fly an arrow, and struck her down and dashed her brains out.

"Ha, ha!" exclaimed the boy. "What you have done to many, thus unto you."

Then he took his station again, and by-and-by the old father Eagle came, bearing a youth, fair to look upon, and dropped him into the nest. The young boy shut his teeth, and he said: "Thus unto many you have done, and thus unto me you would have done; so unto you." And he drew an arrow and shot him. Then he turned to the two young Eagles and killed them, and plucked out all the beautiful colored feathers about their necks, until he had a large bundle of fine plumes with which he thought to wing his arrows or to waft his prayers.

Then he looked down the cliff and saw there was no way to climb down, and there was no way to climb up.   Then he began to cry, and sat on the edge of the cliff, and cried so loud that the old Bat Woman, who was gathering cactus-berries below, or thought she was, overheard the boy.

Said she : " Now, just listen to that.   I warrant it is my fool of a grandson, who is always trying to get himself into a scrape.   I am sure it must be so. Phoo ! phoo ! "

She spilled out all the berries she had found from the basket she had on her back, and then labored up to where she could look over the edge of the shelf.

" Yes, there you are," said she ; " you simpleton ! you wretched boy !   What are you doing here ? "

" Oh, my grandmother," said he, " I have got into a place and I cannot get out."

" Yes," said she ; " if you were anything else but such a fool of a grandson and such a hard-hearted wretch of a boy, I would help you get down ; but you never do as your mother and grandmother or grandfathers tell you."

" Ah, my grandmother, I will do just as you tell me this time," said the boy.

" Now, will you ? " said she.   " Now, can you be certain ?—will you promise me that you will keep your eyes shut, and join me, at least in your heart, in the prayer which I sing when I fly down ?   *Yan lehalliah kiana.*   Never open your eyes ; if you do, the gods will teach you a lesson, and your poor old grandmother, too."

" I will do just as you tell me," said he, as he reached over and took up his plumes and held them ready.

"Not so fast, my child," said she; "you must promise me."

"Oh, my grandmother, I will do just as you tell me," said he.

"Well, step into my basket, very carefully now. As I go down I shall go very prayerfully, depending on the gods to carry so much more than I usually carry. Do you not wink once, my grandson."

"All right; I will keep my eyes shut this time," said he. So he sat down and squeezed his eyes together, and held his plumes tight, and then the old grandmother launched herself forth on her skin wings. After she had struggled a little, she began to sing:

> "Ha ash tchaa ni,—Ha ash tchaa ni:
> Tche pa naa,—thlen-thle.
> Thlen! Thlen! Thlen!"

"Now, just listen to that," said the boy; "my old grandmother is singing one of those tedious prayers; it will take us forever to go down."

Then presently the old Bat Woman, perfectly unconscious of his state of mind, began to sing again:

> "Thlen thla kia yai na kia."

"There she goes again," said he to himself; "I declare, I must look up; it will drive me wild to sit here all this time and hear my old grandmother try to sing."

Then, after a little while, she commenced again:

> "Ha ash tchaa ni,—Ha ash tchaa ni:
> Tche pa naa,—thlen-thle.
> Thlen! Thlen! Thlen!"

The boy stretched himself up, and said: "Look here, grandmother! I have heard your '*Thlen! Thlen! Thlen!*' enough this time. I am going to open my eyes."

"Oh, my grandchild, never think of such a thing." Then she began again to sing:

> "Ha ash tchaa ni,—Ha ash tchaa ni:
> Tche pa naa,—thlen-thle.
> Thlen! Thlen! Thlen!"

She was not near the ground when she finished it the fourth time, and the boy would not stand it any more. Lo! he opened his eyes, and the old grandmother knew it in a moment. Over and over, boy over bat, bat over boy, and the basket between them, they went whirling and pitching down, the old grandmother tugging at her basket and scolding the boy.

"Now, you foolish, disobedient one! I told you what would happen! You see what you have done!" and so on until they fell to the ground. It fairly knocked the breath out of the boy, and when he got up again he yelled lustily.

The old grandmother picked herself up, stretched herself, and cried out anew: "You wretched, foolish, hard-hearted boy; I never will do anything for you again—never, never, never!"

"I know, my grandmother," said the boy, "but you kept up that '*Thlen! Thlen! Thlen!*' so much. What in the world did you want to spend so much time *thlening, thlening,* and buzzing round in that way for?"

"Ah, me!" said she, "he never did know any-thing—never will be taught to know anything."

"Now," said she to him, "you might as well come and eat with me. I have been gathering cactus-fruit, and you can eat and then go home." She took him to the place where she had poured out the contents of the basket, but there was scarcely a cactus-berry. There were cedar-berries, cones, sticks, little balls of dirt, coyote-berries, and everything else uneatable.

"Sit down, my grandson, and eat; strengthen yourself after your various adventures and exertions. I feel very weary myself," said she. And she took a nip of one of them; but the boy couldn't exactly bring himself to eat. The truth is, the old woman's eyes were bad, in the same way that bats' eyes are usually bad, and she couldn't tell a cactus-berry from anything else round and rough.

"Well, inasmuch as you won't eat, my grandson," said she, "why, I can't conceive, for these are very good, it seems to me. You had better run along home now, or your mother will be killing herself thinking of you. Now, I have only one direction to give you. You don't deserve any, but I will give you one. See that you pay attention to it. If not, the worst is your own. You have gathered a beautiful store of feathers. Now, be very careful. Those creatures who bore those feathers have gained their lives from the lives of living beings, and therefore their feathers differ from other feathers. Heed what I say, my grand-

son.   When you come to any place where flowers
are blooming,—where the sunflowers make the
field yellow,—walk round those flowers if you want
to get home with these feathers.   And when you
come to more flowers, walk round them.   If you
do not do that, just as you came you will go back
to your home."

"All right, my grandmother," said the boy.   So,
after bidding her good-by, he trudged away
with his bundle of feathers ; and when he came to
a great plain of sunflowers and other flowers he
walked round them ; and when he came to another large patch he walked round them, and then
another, and so on ; but finally he stopped, for it
seemed to him that there were nothing but fields
of flowers all the way home.   He thought he had
never seen so many before.

"I declare," said he, "I will not walk round
those flowers any more.   I will hang on to these
feathers, though."

So he took a good hold of them and walked in
amongst the flowers.   But no sooner had he entered the field than flutter, flutter, flutter, little
wings began to fly out from the bundle of feathers,
and the bundle began to grow smaller and smaller,
until it wholly disappeared.   These wings which
flew out were the wings of the Sacred Birds of
Summerland, made living by the lives that had
supported the birds which bore those feathers, and
by coming into the environment which they had so
loved, the atmosphere which flowers always bring
of summer.

Thus it was, my children, in the days of the ancients, and for that reason we have little jay-birds, little sparrows, little finches, little willow-birds, and all the beautiful little birds that bring the summer, and they always hover over flowers.

"My friends" [said the story-teller], "that is the way we live. I am very glad, otherwise I would not have told the story, for it is not exactly right that I should,—I am very glad to demonstrate to you that we also have books; only they are not books with marks in them, but words in our hearts, which have been placed there by our ancients long ago, even so long ago as when the world was new and young, like unripe fruit. And I like you to know these things, because people say that the Zuñis are dark people."[1]

Thus shortens my story.

[1] That is, people in the dark—having no knowledge.

THE SERPENT OF THE SEA

NOTE.—The priest of the K'iáklu or epic-ritual of Zuñi is never allowed to initiate the telling of short folk-stories. If he make such a beginning, he must complete the whole cycle before he ceases his recital or his listeners relax their attention. The following tale was told by an attendant Indian (not a priest), whose name is Waíhusiwa.

"*Son ah tehi!*" he exclaimed, which may be interpreted: "Let us abide with the ancients to-night."

The listeners reply: "*E-so*," or "*Tea-tu*." ("Certainly," or "Be it well.")

IN the times of our forefathers, under Thunder Mountain was a village called K'iákime ("Home of the Eagles"). It is now in ruins; the roofs are gone, the ladders have decayed, the hearths grown cold. But when it was all still perfect, and, as it were, new, there lived in this village a maiden, the daughter of the priest-chief. She was beautiful, but possessed of this peculiarity of character: There was a sacred spring of water at the foot of the terrace whereon stood the town. We now call it the Pool of the Apaches; but then it was sacred to Kólowissi (the Serpent of the Sea). Now, at this spring the girl displayed her peculiarity, which was that of a passion for neatness and cleanliness of person and clothing. She could not endure the slightest speck or particle of dust or dirt upon her clothes or person, and so she spent most of her time in washing all the things she used and in bathing herself in the waters of this spring.

Now, these waters, being sacred to the Serpent of the Sea, should not have been defiled in this

93

way. As might have been expected, Kólowissi became troubled and angry at the sacrilege committed in the sacred waters by the maiden, and he said: "Why does this maiden defile the sacred waters of my spring with the dirt of her apparel and the dun of her person? I must see to this." So he devised a plan by which to prevent the sacrilege and to punish its author.

When the maiden came again to the spring, what should she behold but a beautiful little child seated amidst the waters, splashing them, cooing and smiling. It was the Sea Serpent, wearing the semblance of a child,—for a god may assume any form at its pleasure, you know. There sat the child, laughing and playing in the water. The girl looked around in all directions—north, south, east, and west—but could see no one, nor any traces of persons who might have brought hither the beautiful little child. She said to herself: "I wonder whose child this may be! It would seem to be that of some unkind and cruel mother, who has deserted it and left it here to perish. And the poor little child does not yet know that it is left all alone. Poor little thing! I will take it in my arms and care for it."

The maiden then talked softly to the young child, and took it in her arms, and hastened with it up the hill to her house, and, climbing up the ladder, carried the child in her arms into the room where she slept.

Her peculiarity of character, her dislike of all dirt or dust, led her to dwell apart from the rest of her family, in a room by herself above all of the other apartments.

She was so pleased with the child that when she had got him into her room she sat down on the floor and played with him, laughing at his pranks and smiling into his face ; and he answered her in baby fashion with cooings and smiles of his own, so that her heart became very happy and loving. So it happened that thus was she engaged for a long while and utterly unmindful of the lapse of time.

Meanwhile, the younger sisters had prepared the meal, and were awaiting the return of the elder sister.

" Where, I wonder, can she be ? " one of them asked.

" She is probably down at the spring," said the old father ; " she is bathing and washing her clothes, as usual, of course ! Run down and call her."

But the younger sister, on going, could find no trace of her at the spring. So she climbed the ladder to the private room of this elder sister, and there found her, as has been told, playing with the little child. She hastened back to inform her father of what she had seen. But the old man sat silent and thoughtful. He knew that the waters of the spring were sacred. When the rest of the family were excited, and ran to behold the pretty prodigy, he cried out, therefore : " Come back ! come back ! Why do you make fools of your-selves ? Do you suppose any mother would leave her own child in the waters of this or any other spring ? There is something more of meaning than seems in all this."

When they again went and called the maiden to come down to the meal spread for her, she could not be induced to leave the child.

" See ! it is as you might expect," said the father. " A woman will not leave a child on any inducement ; how much less her own."

The child at length grew sleepy. The maiden placed it on a bed, and, growing sleepy herself, at length lay by its side and fell asleep. Her sleep was genuine, but the sleep of the child was feigned. The child became elongated by degrees, as it were, fulfilling some horrible dream, and soon appeared as an enormous Serpent that coiled itself round and round the room until it was full of scaly, gleaming circles. Then, placing its head near the head of the maiden, the great Serpent surrounded her with its coils, taking finally its own tail in its mouth.

The night passed, and in the morning when the breakfast was prepared, and yet the maiden did not descend, and the younger sisters became impatient at the delay, the old man said : " Now that she has the child to play with, she will care little for aught else. That is enough to occupy the entire attention of any woman."

But the little sister ran up to the room and called. Receiving no answer, she tried to open the door ; she could not move it, because the Serpent's coils filled the room and pressed against it. She pushed the door with all her might, but it could not be moved. She again and again called her sister's name, but no response came. Beginning now to be frightened, she ran to the skyhole over the room in which she had left the others and cried out for help. They hastily joined her,—all save the old father,—and together were able to press the door sufficiently to get a glimpse of the great scales and folds of the Serpent. Then the women all ran screaming to the old father. The old man, priest and sage as he was, quieted them with these words : " I expected as much as this from the first report which you gave me. It was impossible, as I then said, that a woman should be so foolish as to leave her child playing even near the waters of the spring. But it is not impossible, it seems, that one should be so foolish as to take into her arms a child found as this one was."

Thereupon he walked out of the house, deliberately and thoughtful, angry in his mind against his eldest daughter. Ascending to her room, he pushed against the door and called to the Serpent of the Sea : " Oh, Kólowissi ! It is I, who speak to thee, O Serpent of the Sea ; I, thy priest. Let, I pray thee, let my child come to me again, and I will make atonement for her errors. Release her, though she has been so foolish, for she is thine, absolutely thine. But let her return once more to us that we may make atonement to thee more amply." So prayed the priest to the Serpent of the Sea.

When he had done this the great Serpent

7

loosened his coils, and as he did so the whole building shook violently, and all the villagers became aware of the event, and trembled with fear.

The maiden at once awoke and cried piteously to her father for help.

"Come and release me, oh, my father! Come and release me!" she cried.

As the coils loosened she found herself able to rise. No sooner had she done this than the great Serpent bent the folds of his large coils nearest the doorway upward so that they formed an arch. Under this, filled with terror, the girl passed. She was almost stunned with the dread din of the monster's scales rasping past one another with a noise like the sound of flints trodden under the feet of a rapid runner, and once away from the writhing mass of coils, the poor maiden ran liké a frightened deer out of the doorway, down the ladder and into the room below, casting herself on the breast of her mother.

But the priest still remained praying to the Serpent; and he ended his prayer as he had begun it, saying: "It shall be even as I have said; she shall be thine!"

He then went away and called the two warrior priest-chiefs of the town, and these called together all the other priests in sacred council. Then they performed the solemn ceremonies of the sacred rites—preparing plumes, prayer-wands, and offerings of treasure.

After four days of labor, these things they ar-

ranged and consecrated to the Serpent of the Sea.
On that morning the old priest called his daughter
and told her she must make ready to take these
sacrifices and yield them up, even with herself,—
most precious of them all,—to the great Serpent
of the Sea ; that she must yield up also all thoughts
of her people and home forever, and go hence to the
house of the great Serpent of the Sea, even in the
Waters of the World. "For it seems," said he,
"to have been your desire to do thus, as mani-
fested by your actions. You used even the sacred
water for profane purposes ; now this that I have
told you is inevitable. Come ; the time when you
must prepare yourself to depart is near at hand."

She went forth from the home of her childhood
with sad cries, clinging to the neck of her mother
and shivering with terror. In the plaza, amidst
the lamentations of all the people, they dressed
her in her sacred cotton robes of ceremonial, embroidered elaborately, and adorned her with earrings, bracelets, beads,—many beautiful, precious
things. They painted her cheeks with red spots
as if for a dance ; they made a road of sacred meal
toward the Door of the Serpent of the Sea—a distant spring in our land known to this day as the
Doorway to the Serpent of the Sea—four steps
toward this spring did they mark in sacred terraces on the ground at the western way of the
plaza. And when they had finished the sacred
road, the old priest, who never shed one tear, although all the villagers wept sore,—for the maiden
was very beautiful,—instructed his daughter to go

forth on the terraced road, and, standing there, call
the Serpent to come to her.

Then the door opened, and the Serpent descended from the high room where he was coiled,
and, without using ladders, let his head and breast
down to the ground in great undulations. He
placed his head on the shoulder of the maiden,
and the word was given—the word : " It is time "—
and the maiden slowly started toward the west,
cowering beneath her burden ; but whenever she
staggered with fear and weariness and was like to
wander from the way, the Serpent gently pushed
her onward and straightened her course.

Thus they went toward the river trail and in it,
on and over the Mountain of the Red Paint ; yet
still the Serpent was not all uncoiled from the
maiden's room in the house, but continued to crawl
forth until they were past the mountain—when the
last of his length came forth. Here he began to
draw himself together again and to assume a new
shape. So that ere long his serpent form con-
tracted, until, lifting his head from the maiden's
shoulder, he stood up, in form a beautiful youth in
sacred gala attire ! He placed the scales of his
serpent form, now small, under his flowing mantle,
and called out to the maiden in a hoarse, hissing
voice : " Let us speak one to the other. Are you
tired, girl ? " Yet she never moved her head, but
plodded on with her eyes cast down.

" Are you weary, poor maiden ? "—then he said
in a gentler voice, as he arose erect and fell a little
behind her, and wrapped his scales more closely

in his blanket—and he was now such a splendid
and brave hero, so magnificently dressed! And
he repeated, in a still softer voice : " Are you still
weary, poor maiden ? "

At first she dared not look around, though the
voice, so changed, sounded so far behind her and
thrilled her wonderfully with its kindness. Yet
she still felt the weight on her shoulder, the weight
of that dreaded Serpent's head ; for you know after
one has carried a heavy burden on his shoulder or
back, if it be removed he does not at once know
that it is taken away ; it seems still to oppress and
pain him. So it was with her ; but at length she
turned around a little and saw a young man—a
brave and handsome young man.

" May I walk by your side ? " said he, catching
her eye. " Why do you not speak with me ? "

" I am filled with fear and sadness and shame,"
said she.

" Why ? " asked he. " What do you fear ? "

" Because I came with a fearful creature forth
from my home, and he rested his head upon my
shoulder, and even now I feel his presence there,"
said she, lifting her hand to the place where his head
had rested, even still fearing that it might be there.

" But I came all the way with you," said he, " and
I saw no such creature as you describe."

Upon this she stopped and turned back and
looked again at him, and said : " You came all the
way ? I wonder where this fearful being has gone ! "

He smiled, and replied : " I know where he has
gone."

"Ah, youth and friend, will he now leave me in peace," said she, "and let me return to the home of my people?"

"No," replied he, "because he thinks very much of you."

"Why not? Where is he?"

"He is here," said the youth, smiling, and laying his hand on his own heart. "I am he."

"You are he?" cried the maiden. Then she looked at him again, and would not believe him.

"Yea, my maiden, I am he!" said he. And he drew forth from under his flowing mantle the shrivelled serpent scales, and showed them as proofs of his word. It was wonderful and beautiful to the maiden to see that he was thus, a gentle being; and she looked at him long.

Then he said: "Yes, I am he. I love you, my maiden! Will you not haply come forth and dwell with me? Yes, you will go with me, and dwell with me, and I will dwell with you, and I will love you. I dwell not now, but ever, in all the Waters of the World, and in each particular water. In all and each you will dwell with me forever, and we will love each other."

Behold! As they journeyed on, the maiden quite forgot that she had been sad; she forgot her old home, and followed and descended with him into the Doorway of the Serpent of the Sea and dwelt with him ever after.

It was thus in the days of the ancients. Therefore the ancients, no less than ourselves, avoided using springs, except for the drinking of their water ; for to this day we hold the flowing springs the most precious things on earth, and therefore use them not for any profane purposes whatsoever.

Thus shortens my story.

THE MAIDEN OF THE YELLOW ROCKS

IN the days of the ancients, when our ancestors lived in the Village of the Yellow Rocks,[1] also in the Salt City,[2] also in the Village of the Winds,[3] and also in the Village of the White Flowering Herbs, and also in the Village of Odd Waters, where they come forth, when in fact all these broken-down villages were inhabited by our ancients, there lived in the Village of the Yellow Rocks a very beautiful maiden, the daughter of the high priest.

Although a woman, she was wonderfully endowed by birth with the magic knowledge of the hunt and with the knowledge of all the animals who contribute to the sustenance of man,—game animals. And, although a woman, she was also somewhat bad in her disposition, and selfish, in that, possessing this knowledge above all other men and women, she concluded she would have all these animals—the deer, antelope, rabbits — to herself. So, through her wonderful knowledge of their habits and language, she communicated with them and charmed them, and on the top of the mountain—where you will see to this day the ancient figures of the deer cut in the rock—she built a huge corral, and gathered one after another all the deer and antelope and other wild animals of that great country. And

---

[1] Situated about seven miles east of Zuñi.
[2] Mátsaki, now a ruin about three miles east of Zuñi.
[3] Pínawa, an ancient ruin about a mile and a half west of Zuñi.

the hunters of these villages hunted in vain; they trailed the deer and the antelope, but they lost their trails and always came home with nothing save the weapons they took with them.   But this maiden, whenever she wished for deer, would go to her corral and kill whatever animal she wanted; so she and her family always had plenty of meat, while others were without it; always had plenty of buckskins with which to make moccasins and apparel, while others were every day wearing out their old supply and never able to replenish it.

Now, this girl was surpassingly beautiful, and was looked upon by many a young man as the flower of his heart and the one on whom he would ultimately concentrate his thoughts for life.   Amongst these young men, the first to manifest his feelings was a youth from the Village of the Winds.

One day he said to his old people: "I am going courting."   And they observed that he made up a bundle of various precious things for women's dress and ornamentation—necklaces, snow-white buckskin moccasins and leggings, and embroidered skirts and mantles—and, taking his bundle on his shoulders, he started off for the Village of the Yellow Rocks.

When he reached the village he knew the home of the maiden by the beauty of the house.   Among other houses it was alone of its kind.   Attached to the ladder was the cross-piece carved as it is in these days, but depending from it was a fringe of black hair (not scalp-locks) with which they still ornament certain houses when they have sacred

ceremonies ; and among this fringe were hung hollow stalactites from a sacred cave on the Colorado
Chiquito, which sounded, when the wind blew
them together, like little bells. This fringe was
full of them, so that when a stranger came to
this important chief-priest's house he no sooner
touched the ladder-rung at the foot than the bells
tinkled, and they knew some one was coming.

As he placed his foot on the lowermost rung of
the ladder, *chi-la-li* sang the bells at the top.

Said the people within : " Some one is coming."

Step after step he went up, and still the bells
made music at the top, and as he stepped over on
the roof, *thud, thud*, his footsteps sounded as he
walked along ; and when he reached the door, those
within said : " Thou comest ? " And he replied :
" I come. Draw me in " ; by which expression he
meant that he had brought with him a present to
the family. Whenever a man has a bundle to
hand down, it is the place of the woman to take it ;
and that is called " drawing a man in," though she
only takes his bundle and he follows. In this case
he said " Draw me in," and the maiden came to
the top of the ladder and took the bundle and
dropped it on the floor. They knew by the appearance of the bundle what the object of the visit
was.

The old man was sitting by the fireplace,—it
was night-time,— and as the stranger entered,
said, " Thou hast come ? "

The young man answered : " Yes."

Said the old man : " It is not customary for a

stranger to visit the house of a stranger without saying something of what may be in his thoughts."

"It is quite true," said the youth ; "I come thinking of this maiden, your daughter. It has occurred to me that I might happily and without fear rest my thoughts and hopes on her ; therefore I come."

The daughter brought forth food for the young man and bade him eat. He reached forth his hand and partook of the food. She sat down and took a mouthful or two, whereby they knew she was favorably disposed. She was favorably disposed to all appearance, but not in reality. When he had finished eating, she said : "As you like, my father. You are my father." She answered to her own thoughts : "Yes, you have often reproached me for not treating with more gentleness those who come courting me."

Finally said the father : "I give ye my blessing and sacred speech, my children. I will adopt thee as my child."[1]

"My children," said the father, after a while, when he had smoked a little, "the stranger, now a son, has come a long distance and must be weary."

So the maiden led him to an upper chamber, and said : "Rest here ; you are not yet my husband. I would try you in the morning. Get up early, when the deer are most plentiful, and go forth and slay me a fine one, and then indeed shall we rest our hopes and thoughts on each other for life."

"It is well," said the youth ; and he retired to

[1] This, it may be explained, is all that the marriage ceremony consists of.

sleep, and in the morning arose early. The maiden gave into his hands the food for the day; he caught up his bows and arrows and went forth into the forests and mountains, seeking for the deer. He found a superb track and followed it until it suddenly disappeared, and though he worked hard and followed it over and over again, he could find nothing. While the young man was out hunting and following the tracks for nothing, the young girl went out, so as to be quite sure that none of her deer should get out; and what did she do? She went into the river and followed it against the current, through the water beyond the village and where the marked rocks stand, up the cañon to the place where her deer were gathered. They were all there, peaceful and contented. But there were no tracks of the girl; no one could follow where she went.

The young man hunted and hunted, and at night-time, all tired out and hungry, took his way back to the home of the maiden. She was there.

"Ha!" said she, "what good fortune today?"

And the young man with his face dragged down and his eyes not bright, answered: "I found no game today."

"Well," said the girl, "it is too bad; but under the circumstances we cannot rest our thoughts and hopes on each other for life."

"No, I suppose not," said the young man.

"Here is your bundle," said the girl. She raised it very carefully and handed it to him. He took it over his shoulder, and after all his weary work went on his way home.

The very next day a young man named Hálona, when he heard of this, said : " Ha ! ha ! What a fool he was ! He did n't take her enough presents ; he did n't please her. I am said to be a very pleasant fellow " (he was a very conceited young man) ; " I will take her a bundle that will make things all right."

So he put into a bundle everything that a woman could reasonably want, — for he was a wealthy young man, and his bundle was very heavy,—put on his best dress, and with fine paint on his face started for the home of the maiden. Finally, his foot touched the lowermost rung of the ladder ; the stalactites went jingling above as he mounted, and *thud* went his bundle as he dropped it on the roof.

"Somebody has come," said the people below. " Listen to that ! "

The maiden shrugged her shoulders and said : " Thou comest ? "

" Yes," answered the young man ; " draw me in."

So she reached up and pulled the huge bundle down into the room, placing it on the floor, and the young man followed it down.

Said the old man, who was sitting by the fire, for it was night : " Thou comest. Not thinking of nothing doth one stranger come to the house of another. What may be thy thoughts ? "

The young man looked at the maiden and said to himself : " What a magnificent creature she is ! She will be my wife, no fear that she will not." Then said he aloud : " I came, thinking of your daughter. I would rest my hopes and thoughts on her."

"It is well," said the old man. "It is the custom of our people and of all people, that they may possess dignity, that they may be the heads of households; therefore, young men and maidens marry and establish themselves in certain houses. I have no objection. What dost thou think, my daughter?"

"I have no objection," said the daughter.

"Ah, what did I tell you?" said the youth to himself, and ate with a great deal of satisfaction the meal placed before him.

The father laid out the corn-husks and tobacco, and they had a smoke; then he said to his daughter: "The stranger who is now my son has come a long way, and should not be kept sitting up so long."

As the daughter led him to another room, he thought: "What a gentle creature she is! How softly she steps up the ladder."

When the door was reached, she said: "Here we will say good-night."

"What is the matter?" he asked.

Said she: "I would like to know of my husband this much, that he is a good hunter; that I may have plenty of food all my days, and plenty of buckskins for my clothing. Therefore I must ask that in the morning you go forth and hunt the deer, or bring home an antelope for me.

The young man quickly recovered himself, and said: "It is well," and lay himself down to rest.

So the next morning he went out, and there was the maiden at the top of the house watching him. He could n't wait for daylight ; he wanted the Sun, his father, to rise before his time, and when the Sun did rise he jumped out of bed, tied his quiver to his belt, took his bow in his hand, and, with a little luncheon the maiden had prepared for him, started off.

As he went down the river he saw the maiden was watching him from the top of the house ; so he started forward and ran until he was out of sight, to show how fine a runner he was and how good a hunter ; because he was reputed to be a very strong and active young man. He hunted and hunted, but did not find any deer, nor even any tracks.

Meanwhile, the maiden went up the stream as before and kept watch of the corral ; and he fared as the other young man had fared. At night he came home, not quite so downcast as the other had been, because he was a young man of more self-reliance.

She asked, as she met him : "Have n't you got any deer today ?"

He answered : "No."

She said : "I am sorry, but under the circumstances I don't see how we can become husband and wife."

So he carried his bundle home.

The next day there was a young man in the City of Salt who heard of this,—not all of it, but he heard that day after day young men were going to the home of this maiden to court her, and she turned them all away. He said: "I dare say they did n't take enough with them." So he made up two bundles and went to the home of the maiden, and he said to himself: "This time it will be all right."

When he arrived, much the same conversation was gone through as before with the other young men, and the girl said, when she lighted him to the door of his room: "My young friend, if you will find a deer for me tomorrow I will become your wife and rest my hope only on you."

"Mercy on me!" thought the young man to himself, "I have always been called a poor hunter. What shall I do?"

The next morning he tried, but with the same results.

Now, this girl was keeping the deer and antelope and other animals so long closed up in the corral that the people in all the villages round about were ready to die of hunger for meat. Still, for her own gratification she would keep these animals shut up.

The young man came back at evening, and she asked him if he had found a deer for her.

"No," said he, "I could not even find the trail of one."

"Well," she said, "I am sorry, for your bundles are heavy."

He took them up and went home with them.

Finally, this matter became so much talked about that the two small gods on the top of Thunder Mountain, who lived with their grandmother where our sacrificial altar now stands, said : " There is something wrong here ; we will go and court this maiden."   Now, these gods were extremely ugly in appearance when they chose to be—mere pigmies who never grew to man's stature.   They were always boys in appearance, and their grandmother was always crusty with them ; but they concluded one night that they would go the next day to woo this maiden.

Said one to the other : " Suppose we go and try our luck with her."   Said he : " When I look at you, you are very handsome."

Said the other to him : " When I look at you, you are extremely handsome."

They were the ugliest beings in human form, but in reality were among the most magnificent of men, having power to take any form they chose.

Said the elder one : " Grandmother, you know how much talk there is about this maiden in the Village of the Yellow Rocks.   We have decided to go and court her."

" You miserable, dirty, ugly little wretches ! The idea of your going to court this maiden when she has refused the finest young men in the land ! "

" Well, we will go," said he.

" I don't want you to go," replied she.   " Your names will be in the mouths of everybody ; you will be laughed and jeered at."

" We will go," said they.   And, without paying the slightest attention to their grandmother, they made up their bundle—a very miserable bundle it was ; the younger brother put in little rocks and
8

sticks and bits of buckskins and all sorts of worthless things—and they started off.

"What are you carrying this bundle for?" asked Áhaiyúta, the elder brother.

"I am taking it as a present to the maiden," said Mátsailéma, the younger one.

"She does n't want any such trash as that," said the other. "They have taken very valuable presents to her before; we have nothing to take equal to what has been carried to her by others."

They decided to throw the bundle away altogether, and started out with absolutely nothing but their bows and arrows.

As they proceeded they began to kill wood-rats, and continued until they had slaughtered a large number and had a long string of them held up by their tails.

"There!" exclaimed the younger brother. "There is a fine present for the girl." They knew perfectly well how things were, and were looking out for the interests of their children in the villages round about.

"Oh, my younger brother!" said the elder. "These will not be acceptable to the girl at all; she would not have them in the house!"

"Oh, yes, she would," said the younger; "we will take them along as a present to her."

So they went on, and it was hardly noon when they arrived with their strings of rats at the white cliffs on the southern side of the cañon opposite the village where the maiden lived.

" Here, let us sit down in the shade of this cliff,"

said the elder brother, "for it is not proper to go courting until evening."

"Oh, no," said the younger, "let us go along now. I am in a hurry! I am in a hurry!"

"You are a fool!" said the elder brother; "you should not think of going courting before evening. Stay here patiently."

So they sat down in the shade of the cliff. But the younger kept jumping up and running out to see how the sun was all the afternoon, and he would go and smooth out his string of rats from time to time, and then go and look at the sun again. Finally, when the sun was almost set, he called out: "Now, come on!"

"Wait until it is wholly dark," said the other. "You never did have any patience, sense, or dignity about you."

"Why not go now?" asked the younger.

So they kept quarrelling, but the elder brother's wish prevailed until it was nearly dark, when they went on.

The elder brother began to get very bashful as they approached the village. "I wonder which house it is," said he.

"The one with the tallest ladder in front of it, of course," said the other.

Then the elder brother said in a low voice: "Now, do behave yourself; be dignified."

"All right!" replied the younger.

When they got to the ladder, the elder one said in a whisper: "I don't want to go up here; I don't want to go courting; let's go back."

"Go along up," said the younger.

"Keep still; be quiet!" said the elder one; "be dignified!"

They went up the ladder very carefully, so that there was not a tinkle from the bells. The elder brother hesitated, while the younger one went on to the top, and over the edge of the house.

"Now!" cried he.

"Keep still!" whispered the other; and he gave the ladder a little shake as he went, and the bells tinkled at the top.

The people downstairs said: "Who in the world is coming now?"

When they were both on the roof, the elder brother said: "You go down first."

"I will do nothing of the kind," said the other, "you are the elder."

The people downstairs called out: "Who comes there?"

"See what you have done, you simpleton!" said the elder brother. Then with a great deal of dignity he walked down the ladder. The younger one came tumbling down, carrying his string of rats.

"Throw it out, you fool; they don't want rats!" said the elder one.

"Yes, they do," replied the other. "The girl will want these; maybe she will marry us on account of them!"

The elder brother was terribly disturbed, but the other brought his rats in and laid them in the middle of the floor.

The father looked up, and said : "You come ?"

" Yes," answered the two odd ones.

" Sit down," said the old man. So they sat down, and food was placed before them.

" It seems," said the father, " that ye have met with luck today in hunting," as he cast his eyes on the string of rats.

" Yes," said the Two.

So the old priest went and got some prayer-meal, and, turning the faces of the rats toward the east, said a short prayer.

" What did I tell you ?" said the younger brother ; " they like the presents we have brought. Just see ! "

Presently the old man said : " It is not customary for strangers to come to a house without something in mind."

" Quite so," said the younger brother.

" Yes, my father," said the elder one ; " we have come thinking of your daughter. We understand that she has been wooed by various young men, and it has occurred to us that they did not bring the right kind of presents."

" So we brought these," said the younger brother.

" It is well," said the old man. " It is the custom for maidens and youths to marry. It rests with my daughter."

So he referred the matter to his daughter, and she said : " As you think, my father. Which one ?"

" Oh, take us both ! " said the younger brother.

This was rather embarrassing to the maiden, but she knew she had a safe retreat. So when the father admonished her that it was time to lead the two young men up into the room where the others had been placed, she told them the same story.

They said, " It is well."

They lay down, but instead of sleeping spent most of the night in speculating as to the future.

" What a magnificent wife we will have," said one to the other.

" Don't talk so loud ; every one will hear you ; you will be covered with shame ! "

After a while they went to sleep ; but were awake early the next morning.   The younger brother began to talk to the elder one, who said : " Keep quiet ; the people are not awake ; don't disturb them ! "

The younger one said : " The sun is rising."

" Keep quiet," said the other, "and when they are awake they will give us some luncheon to take with us."

But the younger one jumped up and went rushing about the house, calling out : " The sun is rising ; Get up ! "

The luncheon was provided, and when they started off the maiden went out on the house-top and asked them which direction they would take.

Said they : " We will go over to the south and will get a deer before long, although we are very small and may not meet with very good luck."

So they descended the ladder, and the maiden said to herself : " Ugly, miserable little wretches ; I will teach them to come courting me in this way ! "

The brothers went off to the cliffs, and, while pretending to be hunting, they ran back through the thickets near the house and waited to see what the maiden would do.

Pretty soon she came out. They watched her and saw that she went down the valley and presently ran into the river, leaving no trail behind, and took her course up the stream. They ran on ahead, and long before she had ascended the river found the path leading out of it up the mountain. Following this path, they came to the corral, and, looking over it, they saw thousands of deer, mountain-sheep, antelope, and other animals wandering around in the enclosure.

"Ha! here is the place!" the younger brother exclaimed. "Let us go at them now!"

"Keep quiet! Be patient! Wait till the maiden comes," said the elder one. "If we should happen to kill one of these deer before she comes, perhaps she has some magic power or knowledge by which she would deprive us of the fruits of our efforts."

"No, let us kill one now," said the other. But the elder one kept him curbed until the maiden was climbing the cliff, when he could restrain him no longer, and the youth pulled out his bow and let fly an arrow at the largest deer. One arrow, and the deer fell to the ground, and when the maiden appeared on the spot the deer was lying dead not far away.

The brothers said: "You come, do you? And here we are!"

She looked at them, and her heart went down and became as heavy as a stone, and she did not answer.

"I say, you come!" said the younger brother. "You come, do you?"

She said, "Yes." Then said she to herself: "Well, I suppose I shall have to submit, as I made the arrangement myself." Then she looked up and said: "I see you have killed a deer."

"Yes, we killed one; did n't have any difficulty at all," said the younger brother. "Come, and help us skin him; we are so little and hungry and tired we can't do it. Come on."

So the girl went slowly forward, and in a dejected way helped them skin the deer. Then they began to shoot more deer, and attempted to drag them out; but the men were so small they could not do it, and the girl had to help them. Then they cut up the meat and made it into bundles. She made a large one for herself, and they made two little ones for themselves.

"Now," said they, wiping their brows, "we have done a good day's work, have n't we?" and they looked at the maiden with twinkling eyes.

"Yes," said she; "you are great hunters."

"Shall we go toward home?" asked the younger brother of the maiden. "It would be a shame for you to take such a bundle as that. I will take it for you."

"You little conceited wretch!" cried the elder brother. "Have n't I tried to restrain you?—and now you are going to bury yourself under a bundle of meat!"

" No," said the younger brother, " I can carry it."

So they propped the great bundle of meat against a tree. The elder brother called on the maiden to help him; the younger one stooped down and received it on his back. They had no sooner let go of it than it fell on the ground and completely flattened the little man out.

" Mercy! mercy! I am dying; help me out of here!" cried he.

So they managed to roll the thing off, and he got up and rubbed his back, complaining bitterly (he was only making believe), and said: " I shall have to take my little bundle."

So he shouldered his little bundle, and the maiden took the large one; but before she started she turned to the animals and said, " Oh, my children! these many days, throwing the warm light of your favor upon me, you have rested contented to remain away from the sight of men. Now, hereafter you shall go forth whithersoever you will, that the earth may be covered with your offspring, and men may once more have of your flesh to eat and of your pelts to wear." And away went the antelope, the deer, the mountain-sheep, the elk, and the buffalo over all the land.

Then the young Gods of War turned to the maiden and said: " Now, shall we go home?"

" Yes," said she.

" Well, I will take the lead," said the younger brother.

" Get behind where you belong," said the other; " I will precede the party." So the elder brother went first, the maiden came next, and the younger brother followed behind, with his little bag of meat.

So they went home, and the maiden placed the meat to dry in the upper rooms of the house.

While she was doing this, it was yet early in the day. The two brothers were sitting together, and whispering: "And what will she say for herself now?"

"I don't see what she can say for herself."

"Of course, nothing can she say for herself."

And when the meat was all packed away in the house and the sun had set, they sat by themselves talking this over: "What can she say for herself?"

"Nothing whatever; nothing remains to be done."

"That is quite so," said they, as they went in to the evening meal and sat with the family to eat it.

Finally the maiden said: "With all your hunting and the labors of the day, you must be very weary. Where you slept last night you will find a resting-place. Go and rest yourselves. I cannot consent to marry you, because you have not yet shown yourselves capable of taking care of and dressing the buckskins, as well as of killing deer and antelope and such animals. For a long time buckskins have been accumulating in the upper room. I have no brothers to soften and scrape them; therefore, if you Two will take the hair off from all my buckskins tomorrow before sunset, and scrape the underside so that they will be thin and soft, I will consent to be the wife of one of you, or both."

And they said : " Oh mercy, it is too bad ! "

" We can never do it," said the younger brother.

" I don't suppose we can ; but we can try," said the elder.

So they lay down.

" Let us take things in time," said the elder one, after he had thought of it.   And they jumped up and called to the maiden : " Where are those buckskins ? "

" They are in the upper room," said she.

She showed them the way to the upper room. It was packed to the rafters with buckskins.   They began to make big bales of these and then took them down to the river.   When they got them all down there they said : " How in the world can we scrape so many skins ?   There are more here than we can clean in a year."

" I will tell you what," said the younger brother ; " we will stow away some in the crevices of the rocks, and get rid of them in that way."

" Always hasty, always hasty," said the elder. " Do you suppose that woman put those skins away without counting every one of them ?   We can't do that."

They spread them out in the water that they might soak all night, and built a little dam so they would not float away.   While they were thus engaged they heard some one talking, so they pricked up their ears to listen.

Now, the hill that stands by the side across from

the Village of the Yellow Rocks was, and still is, a favorite home of the Field-mice. They are very prolific, and have to provide great bundles of wool for their families. But in the days of the ancients they were terrible gamblers and were all the time betting away their nests, and the young Mice being perfectly bare, with no wool on them at all, died of cold. And still they kept on betting, making little figures of nests and betting these away against the time when they should have more. It was these Mice which the two gods overheard.

Said the younger brother: "Listen to that! Who is talking?"

"Some one is betting. Let us go nearer."

They went across the river and listened, and heard the tiny little voices calling out and shouting.

"Let us go in," said the younger brother. And he placed his foot in the hole and descended, followed by the other. They found there an enormous village of Field-mice in human form, their clothes, in the shape of Mice, hanging over the sides of the house. Some had their clothing all off down to their waists, and were betting as hard as they could and talking with one another.

As soon as the two brothers entered, they said: "Who comes?"

The Two answered: "We come."

"Come in, come in," cried the Mice,—they were not very polite. "Sit down and have a game. We have not anything to bet just now, but if you trust us we will bet with you."

"What had you in mind in coming?" said an old Field-mouse with a broken tail.

They answered that they had come because they heard voices.   Then they told their story.

"What is this you have to do?" asked the Mice.

"To clean all the hair off those pelts tomorrow."

The Mice looked around at one another; their eyes fairly sparkled and burned.

"Now, then, we will help you if you will promise us something," said they; "but we want your solemn promise."

"What is that?" asked the brothers.

"That you will give us all the hair."

"Oh, yes," said the brothers; "we will be glad to get rid of it."

"All right," said they; "where are the skins?" Then they all began to pour out of the place, and they were so numerous that it was like water, when the rain is falling hard, running over a rock.

When they had all run out the two War-gods drew the skins on the bank, and the Field-mice went to nibbling the hair and cleaning off the underside.   They made up little bundles of the flesh from the skins for their food, and great parcels of the hair.   Finally they said: "May we have them all?"

"No," said the brothers, "we must have eight reserved, four for each, so that we will be hard at work all day tomorrow."

"Well," said the Mice, "we can't consent to leaving even so many, unless you promise that you will gather up all the hair and put it somewhere so that we can get it."

The Two promised that, and said : " Be sure to leave eight skins, will you ? and we will go to bed and rest ourselves."

" All right, all right ! " responded the Field-mice.

So the brothers climbed up the hill to the town, and up the ladder, and slept in their room.

The next morning the girl said : " Now, remember, you will have to clean every skin and make it soft and white."

So they went down to the river and started to work. The girl had said to them that at midday she would go down and see how they were getting along. They were at work nearly all the forenoon on the skins. While the elder brother shaved the hair off, the younger one scraped them thin and softened them.

When the maiden came at noon, she said : " How are you getting along ? "

" We have finished four and are at work on the fifth."

" Remember," said she, " you must finish all of them today or I shall have to send you home."

So they worked away until a little before the sun set, when she appeared again. They had just finished the last. The Field-mice had carefully dressed all the others (they did it better than the men), and there they lay spread out on the sands like a great field of something growing, only white.

When the maiden came down she was perfectly overcome ; she looked and looked and counted and recounted. She found them all there. Then she got a long pole and fished in the water, but there were none.

Said she : " Yes, you shall be my husbands; I shall have to submit."

She went home with them, and for a long time they all lived together, the woman with her two husbands.   They managed to get along very comfortably, and the two brothers did n't quarrel any more than they had done before.

Finally, there were born little twin boys, exactly like their fathers, who were also twins, although one was called the elder and the other the younger.

After a time the younger brother said : " Now, let us go home to our grandmother.   People always go home to their own houses and take their families with them."

" No," said the elder one. " you must remember that we have been only pretending to be human beings.   It would not do to take the maiden home with us."

" Yes," said the other ; " I want her to go with us.   Our grandmother kept making fun of us; called us little, miserable, wretched creatures.   I want to show her that we amount to something !"

The elder brother could not get the younger one to leave the wife behind, and like a dutiful wife she said : " I will go with you."   They made up their bundles and started out.   It was a very hot day, and when they had climbed nearly to the top of Thunder Mountain, the younger brother said : " Ahem ! I am tired.   Let us sit down and rest."

"It will not do," said the elder brother. "You know very well it will not do to sit down ; our father, the Sun, has forbidden that we should be among mortals. It will not do."

"Oh, yes, it will ; we must sit down here," said the younger brother ; and again his wish prevailed and they sat down.

At midday the Sun stood still in the sky, and looked down and saw this beautiful woman, and by the power of his withdrawing rays quickly snatched her from them while they were sitting there talking, she carrying her little children.

The brothers looked around and said : " Where is our wife ? "

"Ah, there she is," cried the younger ; "I will shoot her."

"Shoot your wife !" cried the elder brother. "No, let her go ! Serves you right !"

"No," said the younger, "I will shoot her !" He looked up and drew his arrow, and as his aim was absolutely unerring, *swish* went the arrow directly to her, and she was killed. The power of life by which the Sun was drawing her up was gone, the thread was cut, and she fell over and over and struck the earth.

The two little children were so very small, and their bones so soft, that the fall did not hurt them much. They fell on the soft bank, and rolled and rolled down the hill, and the younger brother ran forward and caught them up in his arms, crying : "Oh, my little children !" and brought them to the elder brother, who said : " Now, what can be done with these little babies, with no mother, no food?"

"We will take them home to grandmother," said the younger brother.

"Your grandmother cannot take care of these babies," said the elder brother.

"Yes, she can, of course," said the younger brother. "Come on, come on! I did n't want to lose my wife and children, too; I thought I must still have the children; that is the reason why I shot her."

So one of them took one of the children, and the other one took the other, and they carried them up to the top of Thunder Mountain.

"Now, then," said the elder brother, "we went off to marry; we come home with no wife and two little children and with nothing to feed them."

"Oh, grandmother!" called out the younger brother.

The old woman had n't heard them for many a day, for many a month, even for years. She looked out and said: "My grandchildren are coming," and she called to them: "I am so glad you have come!"

"Here, see what we have," said the younger brother. "Here are your grandchildren. Come and take them!"

"Oh, you miserable boy, you are always doing something foolish; where is your wife?" asked the grandmother.

"Oh, I shot her!" was the response.

"Why did you do that?"

"I did n't want my father, the Sun, to take them

9

away with my wife. I knew you would not care anything about my wife, but I knew you would be very fond of the grandchildren. Here they are."

But she would n't look at all. So the younger brother drew his face down, and taking the poor little children in his arms said: "You unnatural grandmother, you! Here are two nice little grandchildren for you!"

She said: "How shall I feed them? or what shall I do with them?"

He replied: "Oh, take care of them, take care of them!"

She took a good look at them, and became a true grandmother. She ran and clasped the little ones, crying out: "Let me take you away from these miserable children of mine!" She made some beds of sand for them, as Zuñi mothers do today, got some soft skins for them to lie on, and fed them with a kind of milk made of corn toasted and ground and mixed with water; so that they gradually enlarged and grew up to be nice children.

Thus it was in the days of the ancients, and has been told to us in these days, that even the most cruel and heartless of the gods do these things. Even they took these helpless children to their grandmother, and she succored them and brought them up to the time of reason. Therefore it is the duty of those who find helpless babies or children, inasmuch as they are not so cruel and terrible as were the Gods of War,—not nearly,—surely it is their duty to take those children and succor and bring them up to the time of reason, when they can care for themselves.   That is why our people, when children have been abandoned, provide and care for them as if they were their own.

Thus long is my story.

THE FOSTER-CHILD OF THE DEER

ONCE, long, long ago, at Háwikuh, there lived a maiden most beautiful. In her earlier years her father, who was a great priest, had devoted her to sacred things, and therefore he kept her always in the house secure from the gaze of all men, and thus she grew.

She was so beautiful that when the Sun looked down along one of the straight beams of his own light, if one of those beams chanced to pass through a chink in the roof, the sky-hole, or the windows of the upper part of the maiden's room, he beheld her and wondered at her rare beauty, unable to compare it with anything he saw in his great journeys round about the worlds. Thus, as the maiden grew apace and became a young woman, the Sun loved her exceedingly, and as time went on he became so enamored of her that he descended to earth and entered on one of his own beams of light into her apartment, so that suddenly, while she was sitting one noon-day weaving pretty baskets, there stood before her a glorious youth, gloriously dressed. It was the Sun-father. He looked upon her gently and lovingly; she looked upon him not fearfully: and so it came about that she loved him and he loved her, and he won her to be his wife. And many were the days in which he visited her and dwelt with her for a space at noon-time; but as she was alone mostly, or as she kept sitting weaving her trays when any one of the family entered her apartment, no one suspected this.

Now, as she knew that she had been devoted to sacred things, and that if she explained how it was that she was a mother she would not be believed, she was greatly exercised in mind and heart. She therefore decided that when her child was born she would put it away from her.

When the time came, the child one night was born. She carefully wrapped the little baby boy in some soft cotton-wool, and in the middle of the night stole out softly over the roof-tops, and, silently descending, laid the child on the sheltered side of a heap of refuse near the little stream that flows by Háwikuh, in the valley below. Then, mourning as a mother will mourn for her offspring, she returned to her room and lay herself down, poor thing, to rest.

As daylight was breaking in the east, and the hills and the valleys were coming forth one after another from the shadows of night, a Deer with her two little brightly-speckled fawns descended from the hills to the south across the valley, with ears and eyes alert, and stopped at the stream to drink. While drinking they were startled by an infant's cry, and, looking up, they saw dust and cotton-wool and other things flying about in the air, almost as if a little whirlwind were blowing on the site of the refuse-heap where the child had been laid. It was the child, who, waking and finding itself alone, hungry, and cold, was crying and throwing its little hands about.

"Bless my delight!" cried the Deer to her fawns.
"I have this day found a waif, a child, and though
it be human it shall be mine; for, see, my children, I love you so much that surely I could love
another."

Thereupon she approached the little infant, and
breathed her warm breath upon it and caressed it
until it became quiet, and then after wrapping
about it the cotton-wool, she gently lifted it on her
broad horns, and, turning, carried it steadily away
toward the south, followed on either side by her
children, who kept crying out "Neh! neh!" in
their delight.

The home of this old Deer and her little ones,
where all her children had been born for years,
was south of Háwikuh, in the valley that turns off
among the ledges of rocks near the little spring
called Póshaan. There, in the shelter of a clump
of piñon and cedar trees, was a soft and warm
retreat, winter and summer, and this was the lair
of the Deer and her young.

The Deer was no less delighted than surprised
next morning to find that the infant had grown
apace, for she had suckled it with her own milk,
and that before the declining of the sun it was already creeping about. And greater was her surprise and delight, as day succeeded day, to find
that the child grew even more swiftly than grow
the children of the Deer. Behold! on the evening
of the fourth day it was running about and playing
with its foster brother and sister. Nor was it slow
of foot, even as compared with those little Deer.

Behold! yet greater cause for wonder, on the eighth day it was a youth fair to look upon—looking upon itself and seeing that it had no clothing, and wondering why it was not clothed, like its brother and sister, in soft warm hair with pretty spots upon it.

As time went on, this little foster-child of the Deer (it must always be remembered that it was the offspring of the Sun-father himself), in playing with his brother and sister, and in his runnings about, grew wondrously strong, and even swifter of foot than the Deer themselves, and learned the language of the Deer and all their ways.

When he had become perfected in all that a Deer should know, the Deer-mother led him forth into the wilds and made him acquainted with the great herd to which she belonged. They were exceedingly happy with this addition to their number; much they loved him, and so sagacious was the youth that he soon became the leader of the Deer of the Háwikuh country.

When these Deer and the Antelopes were out on the mesas ranging to and fro, there at their head ran the swift youth. The soles of his feet became as hard as the hoofs of the Deer, the skin of his person strong and dark, the hair of his head long and waving and as soft as the hair on the sides of the Deer themselves.

It chanced one morning, late that summer, that the uncle of the maiden who had cast away her child went out hunting, and he took his way southward past Póshaan, the lair of the Deer-mother and her foster-child. As he traversed the borders of the great mesas that lie beyond, he saw a vast herd of Deer gathered, as people gather in council. They were quiet and seemed to be listening intently to some one in their midst. The hunter stole along carefully on hands and knees, twisting himself among the bushes until he came nearer; and what was his wonder when he beheld, in the midst of the Deer, a splendid youth, broad of shoulder, tall and strong of limb, sitting nude and graceful on the ground, and the old Deer and the young seemed to be paying attention to what he was saying. The hunter rubbed his eyes and looked again; and again he looked, shading his eyes with his hands. Then he elevated himself to peer yet more closely, and the sharp eyes of the youth discovered him. With a shout he lifted himself to his feet and sped away like the wind, followed by the whole herd, their hoofs thundering, and soon they were all out of sight.

The hunter dropped his bow and stood there musing; then picking it up, he turned himself about and ran toward Háwikuh as fast as he could. When he arrived he related to the father of the girl what he had seen. The old priest summoned his hunters and warriors and bade the uncle repeat the story. Many there were who said: "You have seen an apparition, and of evil omen to your family, alas! alas!"

"No," said he, "I looked, and again I looked, and yet again, and again, and I avow to you that what I saw was as plain and as mortal as the Deer themselves."

Convinced at last, the council decided to form a grand hunt, and word was given from the house-tops that on the fourth day from that day a hunt should be undertaken—that the southern mesa should be surrounded, and that the people should gather in from all sides and encompass the herd there, in order that this wonderful youth should not escape being seen, or possibly captured.

Now, when the Deer had gone to a safe distance they slackened their pace and called to their leader not to fear. And the old foster-mother of the youth for the first time related to him, as she had related to them long ago, that he was the child of mortals, telling how she had found him.

The youth sat with his head bowed, thinking of these things. Then he raised his head proudly, and said: "What though I be the child of mortals, they have not loved me: they have cast me from their midst, therefore will I be faithful to thee alone."

But the old Deer-mother said to him: "Hush, my child! Thou art but a mortal, and though thou might'st live on the roots of the trees and the bushes and plants that mature in autumn, yet surely in the winter time thou could'st not live, for my supply of milk will be withholden, and the fruits and the nuts will all be gone."

And the older members of that large herd gathered round and repeated what she had been saying. And they said: "We are aware that we shall be hunted now, as is the invariable custom when our herd has been discovered, on the fourth day from the day on which we were first seen. Amongst the people who come there will be, no doubt, those who will seek you; and you must not endeavor to escape. Even we ourselves are accustomed to give up our lives to the brave hunters among this people, for many of them are sacred of thought, sacred of heart, and make due sacrifices unto us, that our lives in other form may be spared unceasingly."

A splendid Deer rose from the midst of the herd, and, coming forward, laid his cheek on the cheek of the boy, and said: "Yet we love you, but we must now part from you. And, in order that you may be like unto other mortals, only exceeding them, accompany me to the Land of the Souls of Men, where sit in council the Gods of the Sacred Dance and Drama, the Gods of the Spirit World."

To all this the youth, being convinced, agreed. And on that same day the Deer who had spoken set forward, the swift youth running by his side, toward the Lake of the Dead. On and on they sped, and as night was falling they came to the borders of that lake, and the lights were shining over its middle and the Gardens of the Sacred Dance. And the old Drama-woman and the old Drama-man were walking on its shores, back and forth, calling across to each other.

As the Deer neared the shore of the lake, he turned and said to his companion: "Step in boldly with me. Ladders of rushes will rise to receive you, and down underneath the waters into the great Halls of the Dead and of the Sacred Dance we will be borne gently and swiftly."

Then they stepped into the lake. Brighter and lighter it grew. Great ladders of rushes and flags lifted themselves from the water, and upon them the Deer and his companion were borne downward into halls of splendor, lighted by many lights and fires. And in the largest chamber the gods were sitting in council silently. Páutiwa, the Sun-priest of the Sacred Drama (*Káká*), Shúlawitsi (the God of Fire), with his torch of ever-living flame, and many others were there; and when the strangers arrived they greeted and were greeted, and were given a place in the light of the central fire. And in through the doors of the west and the north and the east and the south filed long rows of sacred dancers, those who had passed through the Lake of the Dead, clad in cotton mantles, white as the daylight, finely embroidered, decked with many a treasure shell and turquoise stone. These performed their sacred rites, to the delight of the gods and the wonder of the Deer and his foster-brother.

And when the dancers had retired, Páutiwa, the Sun-priest of the Sacred Dance, arose, and said: " What would'st thou ?"—though he knew full well beforehand. " What would'st thou, oh, Deer of the forest mesas, with thy companion, thy foster-brother; for not thinking of nothing would one visit the home of the *Káká*."

Then the Deer lifted his head and told his story.

" It is well," said the gods.

"Appear, my faithful one," said Páutiwa **to**

Shúlawitsi. And Shúlawitsi appeared and waved his flame around the youth, so that he became convinced of his mortal origin and of his dependence upon food prepared by fire. Then the gods who speak the speech of men gathered around and breathed upon the youth, and touched to his lips moisture from their own mouths, and touched the portals of his ears with oil from their own ears, and thus was the youth made acquainted with both the speech and the understanding of the speech of mortal man. Then the gods called out, and there were brought before them fine garments of white cotton embroidered in many colors, rare necklaces of sacred shell with many turquoises and coral-like stones and shells strung in their midst, and all that the most beautifully clad of our ancients could have glorified their appearance with. Such things they brought forth, and, making them into a bundle, laid them at the feet of the youth. Then they said: "Oh, youth, oh, brother and father, since thou art the child of the Sun, who is the father of us all, go forth with thy foster-brother to thy last meeting-place with him and with his people; and when on the day after the morrow hunters shall gather from around thy country, some of ye, oh, Deer," said he, turning to the Deer, "yield thyselves up that ye may die as must thy kind ever continue to die, for the sake of this thy brother."

"I will lead them," simply replied the Deer. "Thanks."

And Páutiwa continued: "Here full soon wilt thou be gathered in our midst, or with the winds and the mists of the air at night-time wilt sport, ever-living. Go ye forth, then, carrying this bundle, and, as ye best know how, prepare this our father and child for his reception among men. And, O son and father," continued the priest-god, turning to the youth, " Fear not ! Happy wilt thou be in the days to come, and treasured among men. Hence thy birth. Return with the Deer and do as thou art told to do. Thy uncle, leading his priest-youths, will be foremost in the hunt. He will pursue thee and thy foster-mother. Lead him far away ; and when thou hast so led him, cease running and turn and wait, and peacefully go home whither he guides thee."

The sounds of the Sacred Dance came in from the outer apartments, and the youth and the Deer, taking their bundle, departed. More quickly than they had come they sped away ; and on the morning when the hunters of Háwikuh were setting forth, the Deer gathered themselves in a vast herd on the southern mesa, and they circled about the youth and instructed him how to unloose the bundle he had brought. Then closer and closer came the Deer to the youth and bade him stand in his nakedness, and they ran swiftly about him, breathing fierce, moist breaths until hot steam enveloped him and bathed him from head to foot, so that he was purified, and his skin was softened, and his hair hung down in a smooth yet waving mass at the back of his head. Then the youth put on the costume, one article after another, he having seen them worn by the Gods of the Sacred Dance, and by the dancers; and into his hair at the back, under the band which he placed round his temples, he thrust the glowing feathers of the macaw which had been given him. Then, seeing that there was still one article left,—a little string of conical shells,—he asked what that was for; and the Deer told him to tie it about his knee.

The Deer gathered around him once more, and the old chief said: "Who among ye are willing to die?" And, as if it were a festive occasion to which they were going, many a fine Deer bounded forth, striving for the place of those who were to die, until a large number were gathered, fearless and ready. Then the Deer began to move.

Soon there was an alarm. In the north and the west and the south and the east there was cause for alarm. And the Deer began to scatter, and then to assemble and scatter again. At last the hunters with drawn bows came running in, and soon their arrows were flying in the midst of those who were devoted, and Deer after Deer fell, pierced to the heart or other vital part.

At last but few were left,—amongst them the kind old Deer-mother and her two children; and, taking the lead, the glorious youth, although encumbered by his new dress, sped forth with them. They ran and ran, the fleetest of the tribe of Háwikuh pursuing them; but all save the uncle and his brave sons were soon left far behind. The youth's foster-brother was soon slain, and the youth, growing angry, turned about; then bethinking himself of the words of the gods, he sped away again. So his foster-sister, too, was killed ; but he kept on, his old mother alone running behind him. At last the uncle and his sons overtook the old mother, and they merely caught her and turned her away, saying : "Faithful to the last she has been to this youth." Then they renewed the chase for the youth ; and he at last, pretending weariness, faced about and stood like a stag at bay. As soon as they approached, he dropped his arms and lowered his head. Then he said : "Oh, my uncle" (for the gods had told who would find him)—"Oh, my uncle, what wouldst thou ? Thou hast killed my brothers and sisters ; what wouldst thou with me ? "

The old man stopped and gazed at the youth in wonder and admiration of his fine appearance and beautiful apparel. Then he said : " Why dost thou call me uncle ? "

" Because, verily," replied the youth, "thou art my uncle, and thy niece, my maiden-mother, gave birth to me and cast me away upon a dust-heap ; and then my noble Deer found me and nourished me and cherished me."

The uncle and his sons gazed still with wonder. Then they thought they saw in the youth's clear eyes and his soft, oval face a likeness to the mother, and they said : " Verily, this which he says is true." Then they turned about and took him by the hands gently and led him toward Háwikuh, while one of them sped forward to test the truth of his utterances.

When the messenger arrived at Háwikuh he took

his way straight to the house of the priest, and told him what he had heard. The priest in anger summoned the maiden.

"Oh, my child," said he, "hast thou done this thing which we are told thou hast done?" And he related what he had been told.

"Nay, no such thing have I done," said she.

"Yea, but thou hast, oh, unnatural mother! And who was the father?" demanded the old priest with great severity.

Then the maiden, thinking of her Sun-lover, bowed her head in her lap and rocked herself to and fro, and cried sorely. And then she said: "Yea, it is true; so true that I feared thy wrath, oh, my father! I feared thy shame, oh, my mother! and what could I do?" Then she told of her lover, the Sun,—with tears she told it, and she cried out: "Bring back my child that I may nurse him and love but him alone, and see him the father of children!"

By this time the hunters arrived, some bringing game, but others bringing in their midst this wondrous youth, on whom each man and maiden in Háwikuh gazed with delight and admiration.

They took him to the home of his priest-grandfather; and as though he knew the way he entered the apartment of his mother, and she, rising and opening wide her arms, threw herself on his breast and cried and cried. And he laid his hand on her head, and said: "Oh, mother, weep not, for I have come to thee, and I will cherish thee.

So was the foster-child of the Deer restored to his mother and his people.

Wondrously wise in the ways of the Deer and their language was he—so much so that, seeing them, he understood them. This youth made little ado of hunting, for he knew that he could pay those rites and attentions to the Deer that were most acceptable, and made them glad of death at the hand of the hunter. And ere long, so great was his knowledge and success, and his preciousness in the eyes of the Master of Life, that by his will and his arm alone the tribe of Háwikuh was fed and was clad in buckskins.

A rare and beautiful maiden he married, and most happy was he with her.

It was his custom to go forth early in the morning, when the Deer came down to drink or stretch themselves and walk abroad and crop the grass; and, taking his bow and quiver of arrows, he would go to a distant mesa, and, calling the Deer around him, and following them as swiftly as they ran, he would strike them down in great numbers, and, returning, say to his people: "Go and bring in my game, giving me only parts of what I have slain and taking the rest yourselves."

So you can readily see how he and his people became the greatest people of Háwikuh. Nor is it marvellous that the sorcerers of that tribe should have grown envious of his prosperity, and sought to diminish it in many ways, wherein they failed.

At last one night the Master of Sorcerers in secret places raised his voice and cried:

10

"*Weh-h-h-h! Weh-h-h-h-h-h!*" And round about him presently gathered all the sorcerers of the place, and they entered into a deep cavern, large and lighted by green, glowing fires, and there, staring at each other, they devised means to destroy this splendid youth, the child of the Sun.

One of their number stood forth and said: "I will destroy him in his own vocation. He is a hunter, and the Coyote loves well to follow the hunter." His words were received with acclamation, and the youth who had offered himself sped forth in the night to prepare, by incantation and with his infernal appliances, a disguise for himself.

On the next morning, when the youth went forth to hunt, an old Coyote sneaked behind him after he reached the mesas, and, following stealthily, waited his throwing down of the Deer; and when the youth had called and killed a number of Deer and sat down to rest on a fallen tree, the Coyote sneaked into sight. The youth, looking at him, merely thought: "He seeks the blood of my slain Deer," and he went on with his prayers and sacrifices to the dead of the Deer. But soon, stiffening his limbs, the Coyote swiftly scudded across the open, and, with a puff from his mouth and nostrils like a sneeze toward the youth, threw himself against him and arose a man,—the same man who had offered his services in the council of the wizards—while the poor youth, falling over, ran away, a human being still in heart and mind, but in form a coyote.

Off to the southward he wandered, his tail drag-

ging in the dust; and growing hungry he had
naught to eat; and cold on the sides of the mesas
he passed the night, and on the following morning
wandered still, until at last, very hungry, he was
fain even to nip the blades of grass and eat the
berries of the juniper.   Thus he became ill and
worn; and one night as he was seeking a warm
place to lay him down and die, he saw a little red
light glowing from the top of a hillock.   Toward
this light he took his way, and when he came near
he saw that it was shining up through the sky-hole
of someone's house.   He peered over the edge
and saw an old Badger with his grizzly wife, sitting before a fire, not in the form of a badger but
in the form of a little man, his badger-skin hanging
beside him.

Then the youth said to himself: " I will cast
myself down into their house, thus showing them
my miserable condition."   And as he tried to step
down the ladder, he fell, *teng*, on the floor before
them.

The Badgers were disgusted.   They grabbed
the Coyote, and hauling him up the ladder, threw
him into the plain, where, *toonoo*, he fell far away
and swooned from loss of breath.   When he recovered his thoughts he again turned toward the
glowing sky-hole, and, crawling feebly back, threw
himself down into the room again.   Again he
was thrown out, but this time the Badger said:
" It is marvellously strange that this Coyote, the
miserable fellow, should insist on coming back,
and coming back."

"I have heard," said the little old Badger-woman, "that our glorious beloved youth of Há-wikuh was changed some time ago into a Coyote. It may be he. Let us see when he comes again if it be he. For the love of mercy, let us see!"

Ere long the youth again tried to clamber down the ladder, and fell with a thud on the floor before them. A long time he lay there senseless, but at last opened his eyes and looked about. The Badgers eagerly asked if he were the same who had been changed into a Coyote, or condemned to inhabit the form of one. The youth could only move his head in acquiescence.

Then the Badgers hastily gathered an emetic and set it to boil, and when ready they poured the fluid down the throat of the seeming Coyote, and tenderly held him and pitied him. Then they laid him before the fire to warm him. Then the old Badger, looking about in some of his burrows, found a sacred rock crystal, and heating it to glowing heat in the fire, he seared the palms of the youth's hands, the soles of his feet, and the crown of his head, repeating incantations as he performed this last operation, whereupon the skin burst and fell off, and the youth, haggard and lean, lay before them. They nourished him as best they could, and, when well recovered, sent him home to join his people again and render them happy. Clad in his own fine garments, happy of counte-nance and handsome as before, and, according to his regular custom, bearing a Deer on his back, returned the youth to his people, and there he lived most happily.

As I have said, this was in the days of the ancients, and it is because this youth lived so long with the Deer and became acquainted with their every way and their every word, and taught all that he knew to his children and to others whom he took into his friendship, that we have today a class of men— the Sacred Hunters of our tribe,—who surpassingly understand the ways and the language of the Deer.

Thus shortens my story.

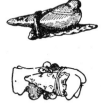

THE BOY HUNTER WHO NEVER
SACRIFICED TO THE DEER
HE HAD SLAIN:

OR THE ORIGIN OF THE SOCIETY OF RATTLESNAKES

IN very ancient times, there lived at Tâ'ia,[1] below
the Zuñi Mountains, an old *shíwani* or priest-
chief, who had a young son named Héasailuhtiwa
("Metal-hand"), famed throughout the land of the
Zuñis for his success in hunting.

When very young, this lad had said to his
parents: "My old ones, let me go away from the
home of my fathers and dwell by myself."

"Why do you, a young boy, wish to go and
dwell by yourself, my son? Know you not that
you would fare but badly, for you are careless and
forgetful? No, no! remain with us, that we may
care for you."

But the boy answered: "Why should I fare
badly? Can I not hunt my own game and roast
the meat over the fire? It is because you never
care to have me go forth alone that I wish to live
by myself, for I long to travel far and hunt deer in
the mountains of many countries: yet whenever I
start forth you call me back, and it is painful to
my longing thoughts thus to be held back when I
would go forward."

It was not until the lad had spoken thus again

---

[1] The native name of the Zuñi town of Las Nutrias.

and again, and once more, that the parents sadly yielded to his wish. They insisted, however, much to the boy's displeasure, that his younger sister, Waíasialuhtitsa, should go with him, only to look after his house, and to remind him here and there, at times, of his forgetfulness. So the brother and sister chose the lofty rooms of a high house in the upper part of the pueblo and lived there.

The boy each day went out hunting and failed not each time to bring in slain animals, while the sister cooked for him and looked after the house. Yet, although the boy was a great hunter, he never sacrificed to the Deer he had slain, nor to the Gods of Prey who delight in aiding the hunter who renews them ; for the lad was forgetful and careless of all things.

One day he went forth over the mountain toward the north, until he came to the Waters of the Bear.[1] There he started up a huge Buck, and, finding the trail, followed it far toward the northward. Yet, although swift of foot, the youth could not overtake the running Deer, and thus it happened that he went on and on, past mesas, valleys, and mountains, until he came to the brink of a great river which flows westwardly from the north.[2] On the banks of this great river grew forests of cottonwood, and into the thickets of these forests led the trail, straight toward the river bank. Just as the young man was about to follow the track to the

---

[1] Aínshik'yanakwin, or Bear Spring, where Fort Wingate now stands.

[2] Probably Green River, or some important tributary of the Colorado Grande.

bank, he thought he saw under a large tree in the midst of the thickets the form of the Deer, so, bending very low, he ran around close to the bank, and came up between the river and the thicket.

As he guardedly approached the tree, his eyes now following the track, now glancing up, he discovered a richly dressed, handsome young man, who called out to him : " How art thou these days, and whither art thou going ? "

The young man straightened up, and quickly drawing his breath, replied : " I am hunting a Deer whose tracks I have followed all the way from the Waters of the Bear."

" Indeed ! " exclaimed the stranger, " and where has thy Deer gone ? "

" I know not," replied the youth, " for here are his tracks." Then he observed that they led to the place where the stranger was sitting, and the latter at the same time remarked :

" I am the Deer, and it was as I would have it that I enticed thee hither."

" *Hai-i !* " exclaimed the young man.

" Aye," continued the stranger. " Alas ! alas ! thou forgetful one ! Thou hast day after day chased my children over the plains and slain them ; thou hast made thyself happy of their flesh, and of their flesh added unto thine own meat and that of thy kindred ; but, alas ! thou hast been forgetful and careless, and not once hast thou given unto their souls the comfort of that which they yearn for and need. Yet hast thou had good fortune in the chase. At last the Sun·

father has listened to the supplications of my children and commanded that I bring thee here, and here have I brought thee. Listen! The Sun-father commands that thou shalt visit him in his house at the western end of the world, and these are his instructions."

"Indeed! Well, I suppose it must be, and it is well!" exclaimed the young man.

"And," continued the Deer-being, "thou must hasten home and call thy father. Tell him to summon his *Pithlan Shiwani* (Priest of the Bow, or Warrior) and command him that he shall instruct his children to repair to the rooms of sacred things and prepare plumed prayer-sticks for the Sun-father, the Moon-mother, and the Great Ocean, and red plumes of sacrifice for the Beings of Prey; that fully they must prepare everything, for thou, their child and father, shalt visit the home of the Sun-father, and in payment for thy forgetfulness and carelessness shalt render him, and the Moon-mother, and the Beings of the Great Ocean, plumes of sacrifice. Hasten home, and tell thy father these things. Then tell thy sister to prepare sweetened meal of parched corn to serve as the food of thy journey, and pollen of the flowers of corn; and ask thy mother to prepare great quantities of new cotton, and, making all these things into bundles, thou must summon some of thy relatives, and come to this tree on the fourth day from this day. Make haste, for thou art swift of foot, and tell all these things to thy father; he will understand thee, for is he not a priest-chief? Hast thou knives of flint?"

"Yes," said the young man, "my father has many."

"Select from them two," said the Deer-being— "a large one and a smaller one; and when thou hast returned to this place, cut down with the larger knife yonder great tree, and with the smaller knife hollow it out. Leave the large end entire, and for the smaller end thou must make a round door, and around the inside of the smaller end cut a notch that shall be like a terrace toward the outside, but shall slope from within that thou mayest close it from the inside with the round door; then pad the inside with cotton, and make in the bottom a padding thicker than the rest; but leave space that thou mayest lie thy length, or sit up and eat. And in the top cut a hole larger inside than out, that thou mayest close it from the inside with a plug of wood. Then when thou hast placed the sweetened meal of parched corn inside, and the plumed prayer-sticks and the sacred pollen of corn-flowers, then enter thyself and close the door in the end and the hole in the top that thy people may roll thee into the river. Thou wilt meet strange beings on thy way. Choose from amongst them whom thou shalt have as a companion, and proceed, as thy companion shall direct, to the great mountain where the Sun enters. Haste and tell thy father these things." And ere the youth could say, "Be it well," and, "I will," the Deer-being had vanished, and he lifted up his face and started swiftly for the home of his fathers.

At sunset the sister looked forth from her high house-top, but nowhere could she see her brother coming. She turned at last to enter, thinking and saying to her breast: "Alas! what did we not think and guess of his carelessness." But just as the country was growing dim in the darkness, the young man ran breathlessly in, and, greeting his sister, sat down in the doorway.

The sister wondered that he had no deer or other game, but placed a meal before him, and, when he had done, herself ate. But the young man remained silent until she had finished, then he said: "Younger sister, I am weary and would sit here; do you go and call father, for I would speak to him of many things."

So the sister cleared away the food and ran to summon the father. Soon she returned with the old man, who, sighing, "*Ha hua!*" from the effort of climbing, greeted his son and sat down, looking all about the room for the fresh deer-meat; but, seeing none, he asked: "What and wherefore hast thou summoned me, my son?"

"It is this," replied the son, and he related all that had been told him by the Deer-being, describing the magnificent dress, the turquoise and shell ear-rings, necklaces, and wristlets of the handsome stranger.

"Certainly," replied the father. "It is well; for as the Sun-father hath directed the Deer-being, thus must it be done."

Then he forthwith went away and commanded his Priest of the Bow, who, mounting to the topmost house, directed the elders and priests of the tribe, saying:

"Ye, our children, listen!
Ye I will this day inform,
Our child, our father,
He of the strong hand,
He who so hunts the Deer,
Goes unto the Sunset world,
Goes, our Sun-father to greet;
Gather at the sacred houses,
Bring thy prayer-sticks, twines, and feathers,
And prepare for him,—
For the Sun-father,
For the Moon-mother,
For the Great Ocean,
For the Prey-beings, plumes and treasures.
Hasten, hasten, ye our children, in the morning!"

So the people gathered in the *kiwetsiwe* and sacred houses next morning and began to make prayer-plumes, while the sister of the young man and her relatives made sweet parched cornmeal and gathered pollen. Toward evening all was completed. The young man summoned his relatives, and chose his four uncles to accompany him. Then he spread enough cotton-wool out to cover the floor, and, gathering it up, made it into a small bundle. The sweet meal filled a large sack of buckskin, and he took also a little sack of sacred red paint and the black warrior paint with little shining particles in it. Then he bade farewell to his lamenting people and rested for the evening journey.

Next morning, escorted by priests, the young man, arrayed in garments of embroidered white cotton and carrying his plumes in his arms, started out of the town, and, accompanied only by his four uncles, set out over the mountains. On the third day they reached the forest on the bank of the great river and encamped.

Then the young man left the camp of his uncles and went alone into the forest, and, choosing the greatest tree he could find, hacked midway through it with his great flint knife. The next day he cut the other half and felled it, when he found it partly hollow. So with his little knife he began to cut it as he had been directed, and made the round door for it and the hole through the top. With his bundle of cotton he padded it everywhere inside until it was thickly coated and soft, and he made a bed on the bottom as thick as himself.

When all was ready and he had placed his food and plumes inside, he called his uncles and showed them the hollow log. "In this," said he, "I am to journey to the western home of our Sun-father. When I have entered and closed the round door tightly and put the plug into the upper hole securely, do ye, never thinking of me, roll the log over and over to the high brink of the river, and, never regarding consequences, push it into the water."

Then it was that the uncles all lamented and tried to dissuade him; but he persisted, and they bade him "Go," as forever, "for," said they, "could one think of journeying even to the end of the earth and across the waters that embrace the world without perishing?"

Then, hastily embracing each of them, the young man entered his log, and, securely fastening the door from the inside, and the plug, called out (they heard but faintly), "*Kesi!*" which means "All is ready."

Sorrowfully and gently they rolled the log over and over to the high river bank, and, hesitating a moment, pushed it off with anxious eyes and closed mouths into the river. Eagerly they watched it as it tumbled end-over-end and down into the water with a great splash, and disappeared under the waves, which rolled one after another across to the opposite banks of the river. But for a long time they saw nothing of it. After a while, far off, speeding on toward the Western Waters of the World, they saw the log rocking along on the rushing waters until it passed out of sight, and they sadly turned toward their homes under the Mountains of the South.

When the log had ceased rocking and plunging, the young man cautiously drew out the plug, and, finding that no water flowed in, peered out. A ray of sunlight slanted in, and by that he knew it was not yet midday, and he could see a round piece of sky and clouds through the hole. By-and-by the ray of sunlight came straight down, and then after a while slanted the other way, and finally toward evening it ceased to shine in, and then the youth took out some of his meal and ate his supper. When after a while he could see the stars, and later the Hanging Lines [the sword-belt of Orion], he knew it was time to rest, so he lay down to sleep.

Thus, day after day, he travelled until he knew he was out on the Great Waters of the World, for no longer did his log strike against anything or whirl around, nor could he see, through the chink, leaves of overhanging trees, nor rocks and banks of earth. On the tenth morning, when he looked up through the hole, he saw that the clouds did not move, and wondering at this, kicked at his log, but it would not move. Then he peered out as far as he could and saw rocks and trees. When he tried to rock his log, it remained firm, so he determined to open the door at the end.

Now, in reality, his log had been cast high up on the shore of a great mountain that rose out of the waters; and this mountain was the home of the Rattlesnakes. A Rattlesnake maiden was roaming along the shore just as the young man was about to open the door of his log. She espied the curious vessel, and said to herself in thought: "What may this be? Ah, yes, and who? Ah, yes, the mortal who was to come; it must be he!" Whereupon she hastened to the shore and tapped on the log.

"Art thou come?" she asked.

"Aye," replied the youth. "Who may you be, and where am I?"

"You are landed on the Island of the Rattlesnakes, and I am one of them. The other side of the mountain here is where our village is. Come out and go with me, for my old ones have expected you long."

"Is it dry, surely?" asked the young man.

"Why, yes! Here you are high above the waters."

Thereupon the young man opened from the inside his door, and peered out. Surely enough, there he was high among the rocks and sands. Then he looked at the Rattlesnake maiden, and scarcely believed she was what she called herself, for she was a most beautiful young woman, and like a daughter of men. Yet around her waist—she was dressed in cotton mantles—was girt a rattlesnake-skin which was open at the breast and on the crown of the head.

"Come with me," said the maiden; and she led the way over the mountain and across to a deep valley, where terrible Serpents writhed and gleamed in the sunlight so thickly that they seemed, with their hissing and rattling, like a dry mat shaken by the wind. The youth drew back in horror, but the maiden said: "Fear not; they will neither harm you nor·frighten you more, for they are my people." Whereupon she commanded them to fall back and make a pathway for the young man and herself; and they tamely obeyed her commands. Through the opening thus made they passed down to a cavern, on entering which they found a great room. There were great numbers of Rattlesnake people, old and young, gathered in council, for they knew of the coming of the young man. Around the walls of their houses were many pegs and racks with serpent skins hanging on them—skins like the one the young girl wore as a girdle. The elders arose and greeted the youth, saying: "Our child and our father, comest thou, comest thou happily these many days ? "

" Aye, happily," replied the youth.

And after a feast of strange food had been placed before the young man, and he had eaten a little, the elders said to him : " Knowest thou whither thou goest, that the way is long and fearful, and to mortals unknown, and that it will be but to meet with poverty that thou journeyest alone ? Therefore have we assembled to await thy coming and in order that thou shouldst journey preciously, we have decided to ask thee to choose from amongst us whom thou shalt have for a companion."

" It is well, my fathers," said the young man, and, casting his eyes about the council to find which face should be kindest to him, he chose the maiden, and said : " Let it be this one, for she found me and loved me in that she gently and without fear brought me into your presence."

And the girl said : " It is well, and I will go."

Instantly the grave and dignified elders, the happy-faced youths and maidens, the kind-eyed matrons, all reached up for their serpent skins, and, passing them over their persons,—lo ! in the time of the telling of it, the whole place was filled with writhing and hissing Serpents and the din of their rattles. In horror the young man stood against the wall like a hollow stalk, and the Serpent maiden, going to each of the members of the council, extracted from each a single fang, which she wrapped together in a piece of fabric, until she had a great bundle. Then she passed her hand over her person, and lo! she became a beautiful human maiden again, holding in her hand a rattle-snake skin. Then taking up the bundle of fangs, she said to the young man : "Come, for I know the way and will guide you,"—and the young man followed her to the shore where his log lay.

"Now," said she, "wait while I fix this log anew, that it may be well," and she bored many little holes all over the log, and into these holes she inserted the crooked fangs, so that they all stood slanting toward the rear, like the spines on the back of a porcupine.

When she had done this, she said : "First I will enter, for there may not be room for two, and in order that I may make myself like the space I enter, I will lay on my dress again. Do you, when I have entered, enter also, and with your feet kick the log down to the shore waters, when you must quickly close the door and the waters will take us abroad upon themselves."

In an instant she had passed into her serpent form again and crawled into the log. The young man did as he was bidden, and as he closed the door a wave bore them gently out upon the waters. Then, as the young man turned to look upon his companion coiled so near him, he drew back in horror.

"Why do you fear ?" asked the Rattlesnake.

"I know not, but I fear you ; perhaps, though you speak gently, you will, when I sleep, bite me and devour my flesh, and it is with thoughts of this that I have fear."

"Ah, no!" replied the maiden, "but, that you may not fear, I will change myself." And so saying, she took off her skin, and, opening the upper part of the door, hung the skin on the fangs outside.

Finally, toward noon-time, the youth prepared his meal food, and placing some before the maiden, asked her to eat.

"Ah, no! alas, I know not the food of mortals. Have you not with you the yellow dust of the corn-flower?"

"Aye, that I have," said the young man, and producing a bag, opened it and asked the girl: "How shall I feed it to you?"

"Scatter it upon the cotton, and by my knowledge I will gather it."

Then the young man scattered a great quantity on the cotton, wondering how the girl would gather it up. But the maiden opened the door, and taking down the skin changed herself to a serpent, and passing to and fro over the pollen, received it all within her scales. Then she resumed her human form again and hung the skin up as before.

Thus they floated until they came to the great forks of the Mighty Waters of the World, and their floating log was guided into the southern branch. And on they floated toward the westward for four months from the time when the uncles had thrown him into the river.

One day the maiden said to the youth: "We are nearing our journey's end, and, as I know the way, I will guide you. Hold yourself hard and ready, for the waters will cast our house high upon the shores of the mountain wherein the Sun enters, and these shores are inaccessible because so smooth."

Then the log was cast high above the slippery bank, and when the waters receded there it remained, for the fangs grappled it fast.

Then said the maiden : " Let us now go out. Fear not for your craft, for the fangs will hold it fast ; it matters little how high the waves may roll, or how steep and slippery the bank."

Then, taking in his arms the sacred plumes which his people had prepared for him, he followed the girl far up to the doorway in the Mountain of the Sea. Out of it grew a great ladder of giant rushes, by the side of which stood an enormous basket-tray. Very fast approached the Sun, and soon the Sun-father descended the ladder, and the two voyagers followed down. They were gently greeted by a kind old woman, the grand-mother of the Sun, and were given seats at one side of a great and wonderfully beautiful room.

Then the Sun-father approached some pegs in the wall and from them suspended his bow and quiver, and his bright sun-shield, and his wonderful travelling dress Behold ! there stood, kindly smiling before the youth and maiden, the most magnificent and gentle of beings in the world—the Sun-father.

Then the Sun-father greeted them, and, turning to a great package which he had brought in, opened it and disclosed thousands of shell beads, red and white, and thousands more of brilliant turquoises. These he poured into the great tray at the door-side, and gave them to the grandmother, who forthwith began to sort them with great rapidity. But, ere she had done, the Sun-father took them from her; part of them he took out with unerring judgment and cast them abroad into the great waters as we cast sacred prayer-meal. The others he brought below and gave them to the grand-mother for safe-keeping.

Then he turned once more to the youth and the maiden, and said to the former: "So thou hast come, my child, even as I commanded. It is well, and I am thankful." Then, in a stern and louder voice, which yet sounded like the voice of a father, he asked: "Hast thou brought with thee that whereby we are made happy with our children?"

And the young man said: "Aye, I have."

"It is well; and if it be well, then shalt thou precious be; for knowest thou not that I recognize the really good from the evil,—even of the thoughts of men,—and that I know the prayer and sacrifice that is meant, from the words and treasures of those who do but lie in addressing them to me, and speak and act as children in a joke? Behold the treasure which I brought with me from the cities of mankind today! Some of them I cherished preciously, for they are the gifts to me of good hearts and I treasure them that I may return them in good fortune and blessing to those who gave them. But some thou sawest I cast abroad into the great waters that they may again be gathered up and presented to me; for they were the gifts of double and foolish hearts, and as such cannot be treasured by me nor returned unto those who gave them. Bring forth, my child, the plumes and gifts thou hast brought. Thy mother dwelleth in the next room, and when she appeareth in this, thou shalt with thine own hand present to her thy sacrifice."

So the youth, bowing his head, unwrapped his bundle and laid before the Sun-father the plumes he had brought. And the Sun-father took them and breathed upon them and upon the youth, and said: "Thanks, this day. Thou hast straightened thy crooked thoughts."

And when the beautiful Mother of Men, the Moon-mother — the wife of the Sun-father — appeared, the boy placed before her the plumes he had brought, and she, too, breathed upon them, and said: "Thanks, this day," even as the Sun-father had.

Then the Sun-father turned to the youth and said: "Thou shalt join me in my journey round the world, that thou mayest see the towns and nations of mankind—my children; that thou mayest realize how many are my children. Four days shalt thou join me in my journeyings, and then shalt thou return to the home of thy fathers."

And the young man said: "It is well!" but he turned his eyes to the maiden.

"Fear not, my child," added the Father, "she shall sit preciously in my house until we have returned."

And after they had feasted, the Sun-father again enrobed himself, and the youth he dressed in appearance as he himself was dressed. Then, taking the sun-dress from the wall, he led the way down through the four great apartments of the world, and came out into the Lower Country of the Earth.

Behold! as they entered that great world, it was filled with snow and cold below, and the tracks of men led out over great white plains, and as they passed the cities of these nether countries people strange to see were clearing away the snow from their housetops and doorways.

And so they journeyed to the other House of the Sun, and, passing up through the four great rooms, entered the home of the aunts of the Sun-father; and here, too, the young man presented plumes of prayer and sacrifice to the inmates, and received their thanks and blessings.

Again they started together on their journey; and behold! as they came out into the World of Daylight, the skies below them were filled with the rain of summer-time.

Across the great world they journeyed, and they saw city after city of men, and many tribes of strange peoples. Here they were engaged in wars and in wasting the lives of one another; there they were dying of famine and disease; and more of misery and poverty than of happiness saw the young man among the nations of men. "For," said the Sun-father, "these be, alas! my children, who waste their lives in foolishness, or slay one another in useless anger; yet they are brothers to one another, and I am the father of all."

Thus journeyed they four days; and each evening when they returned to the home where the Sun-father enters, he gave to his grandmother the great package of treasure which his children among men had sacrificed to him, and each day he cast the treasures of the bad and double-hearted into the great waters.

On the fourth day, when they had entered the western home of the Sun-father, said the latter to the youth : " Thy task is meted out and finished ; thou shalt now return unto the home of thy fathers —my children below the mountains of Shíwina. How many days, thinkest thou, shalt thou journey ? "

" Many days more than ten," replied the youth with a sigh.

"Ah ! no, my child," said the Sun-father. " Listen ; thou shalt in one day reach the banks of the river whence thou camest. Listen ! Thou shalt take this, my shaft of strong lightning ; thou shalt grasp its neck with firm hands, and as thou extendest it, it will stretch out far to thy front and draw thee more swiftly than the arrow's flight through the water. Take with thee this quiver of unerring arrows, and this strong bow, that by their will thou mayest seek life ; but forget not thy sacrifices nor that they are to be made with true word and a faithful heart. Take also with thee thy guide and companion, the Rattlesnake maiden. When thou hast arrived at the shore of the country of her people, let go the lightning, and it will land thee high. On the morrow I will journey slowly, that ere I be done rising thou mayest reach the home of the maiden. There thou must stop but briefly, for thy fathers, the Rattle-tailed Serpents, will instruct thee, and to their counsel thou must pay strict heed, for thus only will it be well. Thou shalt present to them the plumes of the Prey-beings thou bringest, and when thou hast presented these, thou must continue thy journey. Rest thou until the morrow, and early as the light speed hence toward the home of thy fathers. May all days find ye, children, happy." With this, the Sun-father, scarce listening to the prayers and thanks of the youth and maiden, vanished below.

Thus, when morning approached, the youth and the maiden entered the hollow house and closed it. Scarce did the youth grasp the lightning when, drawn by the bright shaft, the log shot far out into the great waters and was skimming, too fast to be seen, toward the home of the Rattle-tailed Serpents.

And the Sun had but just climbed above the mountains of this world of daylight when the little tube was thrown high above the banks of the great island whither they were journeying.

Then the youth and the maiden again entered the council of the Rattlesnakes, and when they saw the shining black paint on his face they asked that they too might paint their faces like his own; but they painted their cheeks awkwardly, as to this day may be seen; for all rattlesnakes are painted unevenly in the face. Then the young man presented to each the plumes he had brought, and told the elders that he would return with their maiden to the home of his father.

"Be it well, that it may be well," they replied; and they thanked him with delight for the treasure-plumes he had bestowed upon them.

"Go ye happily all days," said the elders. "Listen, child, and father, to our words of advice. But a little while, and thou wilt reach the bank whence thou started. Let go the shaft of lightning, and, behold, the tube thou hast journeyed with will plunge far down into the river. Then shalt thou journey with this our maiden three days. Care not to embrace her, for if thou doest this, it will not be well. Journey ye preciously, our children, and may ye be happy one with the other."

So again they entered their hollow log, and, before entering, the maiden placed her rattlesnake skin as before on the fangs. With incredible swiftness the lightning drew them up the great surging river to the banks where the cottonwood forests grow, and when the lad pressed the shaft it landed them high among the forest trees above the steep bank. Then the youth pressed the lightning-shaft with all his might, and the log was dashed into the great river. While yet he gazed at the bounding log, behold! the fangs which the maiden had fixed into it turned to living serpents; hence today, throughout the whole great world, from the Land of Summer to the Waters of Sunset, are found the Rattlesnakes and their children.

Then the young man journeyed with the maiden southward; and on the way, with the bow and arrows the Sun-father had given him, he killed game, that they might have meat to eat. Nor did he forget the commandments of his Sun-father. At night he built a fire in a forest of piñons, and made a bower for the maiden near to it; but she could not sit there, for she feared the fire, and its light pained her eyes. Nor could she eat at first of the food he cooked for her, but only tasted a few mouthfuls of it. Then the young man made a bed for her under the trees, and told her to rest peacefully, for he would guard her through the night.

And thus they journeyed and rested until the fourth day, when at evening they entered the town under the mountains of Shíwina and were happily welcomed by the father, sister, and relatives of the young man. Blessed by the old priest-chief, the youth and the maiden dwelt with the younger sister Waíasialuhtitsa, in the high house of the upper part of the town. And the boy was as before a mighty hunter, and the maiden at last grew used to the food and ways of mortals.

After they had thus lived together for a long time, there were born of the maiden two children, twins.

Wonderful to relate, these children grew to the power of wandering, in a single day and night; and hence, when they appeared suddenly on the housetops and in the plazas, people said to one another:

"Who are these strange people, and whence came they?"—and talked much after the manner of our foolish people. And the other little children in the town beat them and quarrelled with them, as strange children are apt to do with strange children. And when the twins ran in to their mother, crying and complaining, the poor young woman was saddened ; so she said to the father when he returned from hunting in the evening :

" Ah ! 'their father,' it is not well that we remain longer here. No, alas ! I must return to the country of my fathers, and take with me these little ones," and, although the father prayed her not, she said only : " It must be," and he was forced to consent.

Then for four days the Rattlesnake woman instructed him in the prayers and chants of her people, and she took him forth and showed him the medicines whereby the bite of her fathers might be assuaged, and how to prepare them. Again and again the young man urged her not to leave him, saying : " The way is long and filled with dangers. How, alas ! will you reach it in safety ? "

" Fear not," said she ; " go with me only to the shore of the great river, and my fathers will come to meet me and take me home."

Sadly, on the last morning, the father accompanied his wife and children to the forests of the great river. There she said he must not follow ; but as he embraced them he cried out :

" Ah, alas ! my beautiful wife, my beloved children, flesh of my flesh, how shall I not follow ye ? "

Then his wife answered : " Fear not, nor trouble thyself with sad thoughts. Whither we go thou

canst not follow, for thou eatest cooked food—
(thou art a mortal) ; but soon thy fathers and mine
will come for thee, and thou wilt follow us, never
to return." Then she turned from him with the
little children and was seen no more, and the young
man silently returned to his home below the mountains of Shíwina.

It happened here and there in time that young
men of his tribe were bitten by rattlesnakes ; but
the young man had only to suck their wounds, and
apply his medicines, and sing his incantations
and prayers, to cure them. Whenever this happened, he breathed the sacred breath upon them,
and enjoined them to secrecy of the rituals and
chants he taught them, save only to such as they
should choose and teach the practice of their
prayers.

Thus he had cured and taught eight, when one
day he ascended the mountains for wood. There,
alone in the forest, he was met and bitten by his
fathers. Although he slowly and painfully crawled
home, long ere he reached his town he was so
swollen that the eight whom he had instructed
tried in vain to cure him, and, bidding them cherish
as a precious gift the knowledge of his beloved
wife, he died.

Immediately his fathers met his breath and being
and took them to the home of the Maiden of the
Rattlesnakes and of his lost children. Need we
ask why he was not cured by his disciples ?

Thus it was in the days of the ancients, and
hence today we have fathers amongst us to whom

the dread bite of the rattlesnake need cause no sad thoughts,—the *Tchi Kialikwe* (Society of the Rattlesnakes).

Thus much and thus shortened is my story.

HOW ÁHAIYÚTA AND MÁTSAILÉMA STOLE THE THUNDER-STONE AND THE LIGHTNING-SHAFT

ÁHAIYÚTA and Mátsailéma, with their grand-mother, lived where now stands the ancient Middle Place of Sacrifice on Thunder Mountain.

One day they went out hunting prairie-dogs, and while they were running about from one prairie-dog village to another, it began to rain, which made the trail slippery and the ground muddy, so that the boys became a little wrathful. Then they sat down and cursed the rain for a brief space. Off in the south it thundered until the earth trembled, and the lightning-shafts flew about the red-bordered clouds until the two brothers were nearly blinded with the beholding of it. Presently the younger brother smoothed his brow, and jumped up with an exclamation somewhat profane, and cried out: " Elder brother, let us go to the Land of Ever-lasting Summer and steal from the gods in council their thunder and lightning. I think it would be fine fun to do that sort of thing we have just been looking at and listening to."

The elder brother was somewhat more cautious; still, on the whole, he liked the idea. So he said : " Let us take our prairie-dogs home to the grand-mother, that she shall have something to eat mean-while, and we will think about going tomorrow morning."

The next morning, bright and early, they started out. In vain the old grandmother called rather crossly after them : "Where are you going now?" She could get no satisfaction, for she knew they lied when they called back : "Oh, we are only going to hunt more prairie-dogs." It is true that they skulked round in the plains about Thunder Mountain a little while, as if looking for prairie-dogs. Then, picking up their wondrously swift heels, they sped away toward that beautiful country of the corals, the Land of Everlasting Summer.

At last,—it may be in the mountains of that country, which are said to glow like shells of the sea or the clouds of the sunset,—they came to the House of the Beloved Gods themselves. And that red house was a wondrous terrace, rising wall after wall, and step after step, like a high mountain, grand and stately ; and the walls were so smooth and high that the skill and power of the little War-gods availed them nothing ; they could not get in.

"What shall we do?" asked the younger brother.

"Go home," said the elder, "and mind our own affairs."

"Oh, no," urged the younger ; " I have it, elder brother. Let us hunt up our grandfather, the Centipede."

"Good!" replied the elder. "A happy thought is that of yours, my brother younger."

Forthwith they laid down their bows and quivers of mountain-lion skin, their shields, and other things, and set about turning over all the flat stones they could find. Presently, lifting one with their united strength, they found under it the very old fellow they sought. He doubled himself, and covered his eyes from the sharpness of the daylight. He did not much like being thus disturbed, even by his grandchildren, the War-gods, in the middle of his noonday nap, and was by no means polite to them. But they prodded him a little in the side, and said : " Now, grandfather, look here ! We are in difficulty, and there is no one in the wide world who can help us out as you will."

The old Centipede was naturally flattered. He unrolled himself and viewed them with a look which he intended to be extremely reproachful and belittling. " Ah, my grandchildren," said he, " what are you up to now ? Are you trying to get your-selves into trouble, as usual ? No doubt of it ! I will help you all I can ; but the consequences be on your own heads !"

" That's right, grandfather, that's right ! No one in the world could help us as you can," said one of them. " The fact is, we want to get hold of the thunder-stone and the lightning-shaft which the Rain-gods up there in the tremendous house keep and guard so carefully, we understand. Now, in the first place, we cannot get up the wall ; in the second place, if we did, we would probably have a fuss with them in trying to steal these things. Therefore, we want you to help us, if you will."

" With all my heart, my boys ! But I should advise you to run along home to your grand-mother, and let these things alone."

12

"Oh, pshaw, nonsense! We are only going to play a little while with the thunder and lightning."

"All right," replied the old Worm; "sit here and wait for me." He wriggled himself and stirred about, and his countless legs were more countless than ever with rapid motions as he ran toward the walls of that stately terrace. A vine could not have run up more closely, nor a bird more rapidly; for if one foot slipped, another held on; so the old Centipede wriggled himself up the sides and over the roof, down into the great sky-hole; and, scorning the ladder, which he feared might creak, he went along, head-downward, on the ceiling to the end of the room over the altar, ran down the side, and approached that most forbidden of places, the altar of the gods themselves. The beloved gods, in silent majesty, were sitting there with their heads bowed in meditation so deep that they heard not the faint scuffle of the Centipede's feet as he wound himself down into the altar and stole the thunder-stone. He took it in his mouth—which was larger than the mouths of Centipedes are now—and carried it silently, weighty as it was, up the way he had come, over the roof, down the wall, and back to the flat stone where he made his home, and where, hardly able to contain themselves with impatience, the two youthful gods were awaiting him.

"Here he comes!" cried the younger brother, "and he's got it! By my war-bonnet, he's got it!"

The old grandfather threw the stone down. It began to sound, but Áhaiyúta grabbed it, and, as it were, throttled its world-stirring speech. "Good! good!" he cried to the grandfather; "thank you, old grandfather, thank you!"

"Hold on!" cried the younger brother; "you did n't bring both. What can we do with the one without the other?"

"Shut up!" cried the old Worm. "I know what I am about!" And before they could say any more he was off again. Ere long he returned, carrying the shaft of lightning, with its blue, shimmering point, in his mouth.

"Good!" cried the War-gods. And the younger brother caught up the lightning, and almost forgot his weapons, which, however, he did stop to take up, and started on a full run for Thunder Mountain, followed by his more deliberate, but equally interested elder brother, who brought along the thunder-stone, which he found a somewhat heavier burden than he had supposed.

It was not long, you may well imagine, so powerful were these Gods of War, ere they reached the home of their grandmother on the top of Thunder Mountain. They had carefully concealed the thunder-stone and the shaft of lightning meanwhile, and had taken care to provide themselves with a few prairie-dogs by way of deception.

Still, in majestic revery, unmoved, and apparently unwitting of what had taken place, sat the Rain-gods in their home in the mountains of Summerland.

Not long after they arrived, the young gods began to grow curious and anxious to try their new playthings. They poked one another considerably, and whispered a great deal, so that their grandmother began to suspect they were about to play some rash joke or other, and presently she espied the point of lightning gleaming under Mátsailéma's dirty jacket.

"Demons and corpses!" she cried. "By the moon! You have stolen the thunder-stone and lightning-shaft from the Gods of Rain themselves! Go this instant and return them, and never do such a thing again!" she cried, with the utmost severity; and, making a quick step for the fireplace, she picked up a poker with which to belabor their backs, when they whisked out of the room and into another. They slammed the door in their grandmother's face and braced it, and, clearing away a lot of rubbish that was lying around the rear room, they established themselves in one end, and, nodding and winking at one another, cried out: "Now, then!" The younger let go the lightning-shaft; the elder rolled the thunder-stone. The lightning hissed through the air, and far out into the sky, and returned. The thunder-stone rolled and rumbled until it shook the foundations of the mountain. "Glorious fun!" cried the boys, rubbing their thighs in ecstasy of delight. "Do it again!" And again they sent forth the lightning and rolled the thunder-stone.

And now the gods in Summerland arose in their majesty and breathed upon the skies; and the winds rose, and the rains fell like rivers from the clouds, centering their violence upon the roof of

the poor old grandmother's house. Heedlessly
those reckless wretches kept on playing the thunder-
stone and lightning-shaft without the slightest
regard to the tremendous commotion they were
raising all through the skies and all over Thunder
Mountain ; but nowhere else as above the house
where their poor old grandmother lived fell the
torrent of the rain, and there alone, of course, burst
the lightning and rolled the thunder.

Soon the water poured through the roof of the
house ; but, move the things as the old grandmother
would, she could not keep them dry ; scold the boys
as she would, she could not make them desist.
No, they would only go on with their play more
violently than ever, exclaiming : " What has she
to say, anyway ? It won't hurt her to get a good
ducking, and this is fun ! " By-and-by the waters
rose so high that they extinguished the fire. Soon
they rose still higher, so that the War-gods had
to paddle around half submerged. Still they kept
rolling the thunder-stone and shooting the lightning.
The old grandmother scolded harder and harder,
but after awhile desisted and climbed to the top
of the fireplace, whence, after recovering from her
exertion, she began again. But the boys heeded
her not, only saying : " Let her yell ! Let her scold !
This is fun ! " At last they began to take the old
grandmother's scolding as a matter of course, and
allowed nothing but the water to interrupt their
pastime. It rose so high, finally, that they were
near drowning. Then they climbed to the roof,
but still they kept on.

" By the bones of the dead! why did we not think to come here before? 'T is ten times as fine up here. See him shoot!" cried one to the other, as the lightning sped through the sky, ever returning.

" Hear it mutter and roll!" cried the other, as the thunder bellowed and grumbled.

But no sooner had the Two begun their sport on the roof, than the rain fell in one vast sheet all about them; and it was not long ere the house was so full that the old grandmother—locked in as she was—bobbed her poor pate on the rafters in trying to keep it above the water. She gulped water, and gasped, coughed, strangled, and shrieked to no purpose.

" What a fuss our old grandmother is making, to be sure!" cried the boys. And they kept on, until, forsooth, the water had completely filled the room, and the grandmother's cries gurgled away and ceased. Finally, the thunder-stone grew so terrific, and the lightning so hot and unmanageable, that the boys, drawing a long breath and thinking with immense satisfaction of the fun they had had, possibly also influenced as to the safety of the house, which was beginning to totter, flung the thunder-stone and the lightning-shaft into the sky, where, rattling and flashing away, they finally disappeared over the mountains in the south.

Then the clouds rolled away and the sun shone out, and the boys, wet to the skin, tired in good earnest, and hungry as well, looked around. " Goodness! the water is running out of the windows of our house! This is a pretty mess we are in! Grandmother! Grandmother!" they shouted. "Open the door, and let us in!" But the old grandmother had piped her last, and never a sound came except that of flowing water. They sat themselves down on the roof, and waited for the water to get lower. Then they climbed down, and pounded open the door, and the water came out with a rush, and out with a rush, too, their poor old grandmother,—her eyes staring, her hair all mopped and muddied, and her fingers and legs as stiff as cedar sticks.

"Oh, ye gods! ye gods!" the two boys exclaimed; "we have killed our own grandmother— poor old grandmother, who scolded us so hard and loved us so much! Let us bury her here in front of the door, as soon as the water has run away."

So, as soon as it became dry enough, there they buried her; and in less than four days a strange plant grew up on that spot, and on its little branches, amid its bright green leaves, hung long, pointed pods of fruit, as red as the fire on the breast of the red-bird.

"It is well," said the boys, as they stood one day looking at this plant. "Let us scatter the seeds abroad, that men may find and plant them. It seems it was not without good cause that in the abandonment to our sport we killed our old grandmother, for out of her heart there sprung a plant into the fruits of which, as it were, has flowed the color as well as the fire of her scolding tongue; and, if we have lost our grandmother, whom we loved much, but who loved us more, men have gained a new food, which, though it burn them, shall please them more than did the heat of her discourse please us. Poor old grandmother! Men will little dream when they eat peppers that the seed of them first arose from the fiery heart of the grandmother of Áhaiyúta and Mátsailéma."

Thereupon the two seized the pods and crushed them between their hands, with an exclamation of pleasure at the brisk odor they gave forth. They cast the seeds abroad, which seeds here and there took root; and the plants which sprang from them being found by men, were esteemed good and were cultivated, as they are to this day in the pepper gardens of Zuñi.

Ever since this time you hear that mountain wherein lived the gods with their grandmother called Thunder Mountain; and often, indeed, to this day, the lightning flashes and the thunder plays over its brows and the rain falls there most frequently.

It is said by some that the two boys, when asked how they stole the lightning-shaft and the thunder-stone, told on their poor old grandfather, the Centipede. The beloved Gods of the Rain gave him the lightning-shaft to handle in another way, and it so burned and shrivelled him that he became small, as you can see by looking at any of his numerous descendants, who are not only small but appear like a well-toasted bit of buckskin, fringed at the edges.

So shortens my story.

THE WARRIOR SUITOR OF MOKI

WE take up a story. Of the times of the ancients, a story. Listen, ye young ones and youths, and from what I say draw inference. For behold! the youth of our nation in these recent generations have become less sturdy than of old; else what I relate had not happened.

To our shame be it told that not many generations ago there lived in Moki a poor, ill-favored outcast of a young man, a not-to-be-thought-of-as-hero youth, yet nevertheless the hero of my story; for this youth, the last-mentioned in the numbering of the men of Moki in those days, alone brought great grief on the nation of Zuñi.

And it happened that in Walpi, on the first mesa of the Mokis, there lived an amiable, charming, and surpassingly beautiful girl, whose face was shining, eyes bright, cheeks red like the frost-bite on the datila[1]; whose hair was abundant and soft, black and waving, and done up in large whorls above her ears,—larger than those of the other maidens of her town or nation,—and whose beautiful possessions were as many as were the charms of her person.

What wonder, then, that the youths of the Moki towns should be enamored of her, and seek constantly, with much urgent bespeaking, for the favor

---

[1] Fruit of the yucca, or soap-weed plant.

of her affections? Yet she would none of them.
She would shake her head with a saucy smile, and
reply to every one, as well as to every recommenda-
tion of one from her elders : " A hero for me or no
one ! Any one of these young men may win my
affections if he will, for who knows until the time
comes whether a man be a hero or not ? "

So she made a proposition. She said to all the
youths who came suing for her hand : " Behold !
our nation is at enmity with the Zuñis, far off to
the eastward, over the mountains. If any of you be
so stout of limb and strong of heart and brave of
will, let him go to Zuñi, slay the men of that nation,
our enemies, and bring home, not only as proofs of
his valor, but as presentations to the warrior socie-
ties of our people, scalps in goodly number. Him
will I admire to the tips of my eyelashes ; him will
I cherish to the extent of my powers ; him will I
make my husband, and in such a husband will I
glory ! "

But most of the young and handsome suitors who
worried her with their importunities would depart
forthwith, crestfallen, loving the girl as they did,
forsooth, much less than they feared the warriors of
Zuñi,—so degenerate they had become, for shame !
Months passed by. Not one of those who went to
the maiden's house full of love came away from it
with as much love as want of valor.

At last this outcast youth I have mentioned—
who was spoken to by none, who lived not even in
the houses of his people, but, all filth and rags,
made himself comfortable as best he could with the

dogs and eagles and other creatures captive of the people, eating like them the castaway and unwholesome scraps of ordinary meals—heard these jilted lovers conversing from time to time, exclaiming one to another : " A valuable maiden, indeed, for whom one would risk one's life single handed against a nation whose ancients ever prevailed over all men ! No ! though she be the loveliest of women, I care not for her on those conditions."   " Nor I ! "   " Nor I ! " others would exclaim.

Overhearing this talk, the youth formed a most presumptuous resolution—no other, in fact, than this : that he himself would woo the maiden.

All dirty and ragged as he was, with hair unkempt, finger-nails long, and person calloused by much exposure, lean and wiry like an abused but hardened cur, he took himself one night to the home of the maiden's father.

" *She-e !* " he exclaimed at the entrance of the house, on the top.

And the people within called out : " *Kwátchi !* "

" Are ye in ? " inquired the youth, in such an affable and finished tone and manner of speaking that the people expected to see some magnificent youth enter, and to listen to his proposal of marriage with their maiden.

When they called out " Come in ! " and he came stepping down the ladder into the lighted room, they were, therefore, greatly surprised to see this vagabond in the place of what they expected ; nevertheless, the old father greeted him pleasantly and politely and showed him a seat before the fireplace, and bade the women set food before him. And the youth, although he had not for many a day tasted good food or consumed a full meal even, ate quite sparingly; and, having finished, joined, by the old man's invitation, in the smoking and conversation of the evening.

At last the old man asked him what he came thinking of; and the youth stated that, although it might seem presumptuous, he had heard of the conditions which the maiden of this house had made for those who would win her, and it had occurred to him that he would be glad to try,—so little were his merits, yet so great his love.

The old man listened, with an inward smile; and the maiden, though she conceived no dislike for the youth (there was something about him, strange to say, now that his voice had been heard, which changed her opinion of him), nevertheless was quite merry, all to herself, over this unheard-of proposal. So, when she was asked what she thought of the matter, merely to test the seriousness of the young vagabond's motives, she made the conditions for him even harder than she had for the others, saying: "Look you, stranger! If you will slay single-handed some of the warriors of the valiant Zuñis and bring back to our town, to the joy of our warriors and people, a goodly number of their scalps, I will indeed wed you, as I have said I would the others."

This satisfied the youth, and, bidding them all pass a happy night, he went forth into the dark.

Not quite so poor and helpless as he seemed, was

this youth ; but one of those wonderful beings of this earth in reality, for, behold ! as he had lived all his days since childhood with the dogs and eagles and other captive animals of the towns of Moki-land, so, from long association with them, he had learned their ways and language and had gained their friendship and allegiance as no other mortal ever did.   No family had he ; no one to advise him, save this great family of dogs and other animals with which he lived.

What do you suppose he did ?   He went to each hole, sheltered nook, and oven in the town and called on the Dogs to join him in council, not long before morning of that same night.   Every Dog in the town answered the summons ; and, below the mesa on which Walpi stands, on one of those sloping banks lighted by the moon, they gathered and made a tremendous clamor with their yelpings and barkings and other noises such as you are accustomed to hear from Dogs at night-time.   The proposition which the youth made to this council of Dogs was as follows :

" My friends and brothers, I am about to go forth on the path of war to the cities of the Zuñis toward the sunrise.   If I succeed, my reward will be great.   Now, as I well know from having lived amongst you and been one of you so long, there are two things which are more prized in a Dog's life than anything else.   An occasional good feast is one of them ; being let alone is another.   I think I can bring about both of these rewards for you all if you will, four days hence, after I have prepared a sufficiency of food for the party, join me in my warlike expedition against the Zuñis."

The Dogs greeted this proposition with vociferous acclamation, and the council dispersed.

On the following day, toward evening, the youth again presented himself at the home of the maiden. "My friends," said he to the family; "I am, as you know, or can easily perceive, extremely poor. I have no home nor source of food; yet, as I anticipate that I shall be long on this journey, and as I neither possess nor know how to use a bow and arrow, I come to humbly beseech your assistance. I will undertake this thing which has been proposed to me; but, in order that I may be enabled the more easily to do so, I desire that you will present to me a sufficiency of food for my journey; or, if you will lend it to me, I shall be satisfied."

Now, the maiden's people were among the first in the nation, and well-to-do in all ways. They most willingly consented to give the young man not only a sufficiency of food for days, but for months; and when he went away that night he had all that he could carry of meal, coarse and fine, *piki* or Moki wafer-rolls, tortillas, and abundant grease-cakes, which he well knew would be most tempting to Dogs.

On the fourth day thereafter,—for he had been making his weapons: some flint knives and a good hard war-club,—at evening, he again called at each of the holes and places the Dogs of the town inhabited, and he said to all of them: "I shall leave forthwith on my journey, having provided myself

with a sufficiency of food for much feasting on the
way.   Like yourselves, I have become inured to
hardship and am swift of foot, and by midnight I
shall be half-way to Zuñi.   As soon as the people
are asleep, that they may not pelt you with stones
and drive you back, follow on the trail to Zuñi as
fast as you can.   I will await you by the side of
the Black Mountains, near the Spring of the Night-
hawks, and there I will cook the provisions, that
we may have a jolly feast and the more strongly
proceed on our journey the day following."

The Dogs gave him repeated assurances of their
willingness to follow ; and, heavily laden with his
provisions, the youth, just at dusk, climbed unob-
served down the nether side of the mesa and set
out through the plains of sagebrush, over the hills
far east of Moki, and so on along the plateaus and
valleys leading to this our town of Zuñi.   At the
place he had appointed as a rendezvous he arrived
not long before midnight, lighted a fire, unstrapped
his provisions, and began to cook mush in great
quantities.

Now, after the lights in the windows of Moki
began to go out—shutting up their red eyes, as it
were, as the maidens of Moki shut up their bright
eyes — there was tremendous activity observed
among the Dogs.   But they made not much noise
about it until every last Dog in town—as motley a
crowd of curs and mongrels as ever were seen, unless one might see all the Dogs of Moki today—
descended the mesa, and one by one gathered in a
great pack, and started, baying, barking, and

howling louder and louder as they went along over the eastern hills on the trail which the youth had taken.

By-and-by he heard them coming; *te-ne-e-e-e* they sounded as they ran; *wo-wo-o-o-o* they came, baying and barking in all sorts of voices, nearer and nearer. So the youth prepared his provisions, and as the nearest of them came into the light of the fire, cried out: " Ho, my friends, ye come! I am glad to see ye come! Sit ye round my camp-fire. Let us feast and be merry and lighten the load of my provisions. Methinks we will all carry some of them when we start out tomorrow."

Thereupon he liberally distributed mush, tortillas, and paper bread,—inviting the hot, tired Dogs to drink their fill from the spring and eat their fill from the feast. The Dogs, being very hungry, as Dogs always are—and the more so from the memory of many a long fast—fell to with avidity (and you know what that means with Dogs); and the Short-legs and Beagles would not have fared very well had the youth not considered them and held back a good supply of provisions against their tardy appearance.

Finally, when all were assembled and had eaten, if not to their satisfaction — that was impossible—yet to their temporary gratification, a merry, noisy, much-wriggling crowd they became. Some lay down and rested, others were impatient for the journey; so that even before daylight the youth, making up his bundle of provisions, again set forth at a swift trot, followed by this pack of Dogs which ran along either side of him and strung out on the trail the length of a race-course behind him.

Before night, see this valiant youth quietly hiding himself away in one of the deep arroyos around the western end of Grand Mountain, and the foot-hills of Twin Mountain, near which, as you know, the trail from Moki leads to our town. He is giving directions to the Dogs in a quiet manner, and feeding them again, rather more sparingly than at first that they may be anxious for their work.

He says to them : " My friends and brothers, lay yourselves about here, each one according to his color in places most suited for concealment,—some near the gray sage-bushes ; and you fellows with fine marks on your backs keep out of sight, pray, in these deep holes, and come in as our reserve force when we want you. Now, lie here patiently, for you will have enough work to do, and can afford to rest. Tomorrow morning, not long after sunrise, I shall doubtless come, with more precipitation than willingness, toward your ambuscade, with a pack of Dogs less worthy the name than yourselves at my heels. Be ready to help me ; they are well-nurtured Dogs, and doubtless, if you like, you will be wise enough to make much of this fact."

The Dogs were well pleased with his proposition, and, in louder voices than was prudent, attested their readiness to follow his suggestion, going so far as to assure him that he need have no fear whatsoever, that they alone would vanquish the Zuñi

13

nation—which, they had heard from other Dogs, was becoming rather lazy and indifferent in manly matters, Dogs and all.

The night wore on; the youth had refreshed himself with sleep, and somewhat after the herald-stars of the morning-star had appeared, he stealthily picked his way across our broad plain, toward the hill of Zuñi; and out west there, only a short space from the sunset front of our town, he crouched down on a little terrace to wait.

Not long after the morning-star had risen, a fine old Zuñi came out of his house, shook his blanket, wrapped it round him, and came stealing down in the daylight to the river side. After he had presented his morning sacrifice toward the rising sun, he returned and sat down a moment. He had no sooner seated himself than the wily, sinewy youth with a quick motion sprang up, pulled the poor man over, and with his war-club knocked his brains out, after which he leisurely took off the scalp of the one he had slain. He had barely finished this operation when he heard a ladder creak in one of the upper terraces of the town. He quickly tucked the scalp in his belt, pulled himself together, and thrusting the body of the dead man into the bottom of a hole, which was very near, crouched over it and waited. The footsteps of the man who was coming sounded nearer and nearer. Presently he also came to this place; but no sooner had he reached the terrace than the Moki youth leaped up and dealt him such a blow on the head that, without uttering a sound, he instantly expired. This one he like-

wise scalped, and then another and another he
served in the same way, until, there being four slain
men in the pit, he had to drag some out of the way
and throw them behind the dust-heap. Just as he
returned another man sauntered down to the place.
The youth murdered him like the rest, and was
busy skinning his scalp, when another who had followed him somewhat closely appeared at the hole,
and discovering what was going on, ran toward the
town for his weapons, shouting the war-cry of alarm
as he went. Picking up the scalps and snatching
from the bodies of the slain their ornaments of
greatest value, the Moki youth sped off over the
plain.

In less time than it takes to tell it, the people of
Zuñi were in arms; dogs barked, children cried,
women screamed,—for no one knew how many the
enemy might be,—and the Priests of the Bow, in
half-secured armor of buckskin, and with weapons
in hand, came thundering down the hill and across
the plains in pursuit of the fleeing youth and in
readiness to oppose his band. Long before this
crowd of warriors, now fully awake and wild with
rage, had reached the spot, the youth plunged into
the arroyo and called out to his Dogs: " Now for it,
my friends! They will be here in a minute! Do
you hear them coming?"

"Oh, ho!" softly barked the Dogs; and they
stiffened their claws and crouched themselves to
spring when the time should come.

Presently on came the crowd of warriors, now
feeling that they had but a small force, if indeed

more than one man to oppose. And they came with such precipitation that they took the gray and dun and yellow-shaded Dogs for so many rocks and heaps of sand, and were fairly in the midst of those brutes before they became aware of them at all. Death and ashes! what a time there was of it! The youth fell in with his war-club, the Dogs around, behind, and in front of them howling, snarling, biting, tearing, and shaking the Zuñis on every hand, until every one of the band was torn to pieces or so mangled that a few taps of the club of the youth dispatched them. Those who had followed behind, not knowing what to think of it all, frantically ran back to their people,—the shame-begrimed cowards!—while the youth, with abundant leisure, went on skinning scalps, until, perceiving much activity in the distant town, concluded it would be wise to abandon some few he had not finished. So, catching up his pack of provisions and his bloody string of scalps (which was so long and thick he could hardly carry it, and which dragged on the ground behind him), he trotted over the hills, followed by some of the Dogs—the others remaining behind, feeling more secure of swiftness—to take advantage of the ample feast spread before them.

When the youth and the Dogs who followed him, or afterward joined him, had again reached the great spring by the Black Mountains, leaving those who pursued far behind, they stopped; and, building a fire of brush and pine-knots, the youth cooked all the provisions he had. " Thanks this day, my friends and brothers!" he cried to the

Dogs. " Ye have nobly served me. I will feast ye of the best." Whereupon he produced the grease-cakes and the more delicate articles of food which he had reserved as a reward for the Dogs. They ate and ate, and loud were their demonstrations of satisfaction. Then the youth, taking up the string of scalps again, attached them to a long pole, which, to keep the lower ones from dragging on the ground, he elevated over his shoulder, and, striking up a song of victory, he wound his way along the trail toward Moki.

The Dogs, crazy with victory and much glutted, could not contain themselves, but they bow-wowed with delight and yelped and scurried about, cutting circles dusty and wide around their father, the conquering youth. They hurried on so fast that by-and-by it was noticeable that the Beagle Dogs fell in the rear. " By the music of marrowbones !" exclaimed some of the swifter of foot ; "we will have to slacken our pace, father." Said they, addressing the youth : " Our poor brothers, the Short-legs, are evidently getting tired ; they are falling far in the rear, and it is not valorous, however great your victory and however strong your desire to proclaim it at home, to leave a worn-out brother lagging behind. The enemy might come unawares and cut off his return and his daylight." Most reluctantly, therefore, they slackened their pace, and with shouts and yelps encouraged as much as possible the stump-legged Dogs following behind.

Now, on that day in Moki there had been much surprise expressed at the absence of the Dogs, except those which were so young or so old that they could not travel; and the people began to think that some devil or all the wizards in Mokidom had been conjuring their Dogs away from them, when toward evening they heard a distant sound, which was the approaching victors' demonstration of rejoicing, and clear above all was the song of victory shouted by the lusty youth as he came bringing his scalps along. "Woo, woo, woo!" the Dogs sounded as they came across the valley and approached the foot of the mesa; and when the people looked down and saw the blood and dirt with which every Dog was covered, they knew not what to make of it,—whether their Dogs had been enticed away and foully beaten, or whether they had taken after a herd of antelope, perhaps, and vanquished them. But presently they espied in the midst of the motley crowd of Curs the tall lank form of the vagabond youth and heard his lusty song. The youths who had been jilted by the maiden at once had their own ideas. Some of them sneaked away; others ground their teeth and covered their eyes, filled with rage and shame; while the elder-men of the nation, seeing what feats of valor this neglected youth had accomplished, glorified him with answering songs of victory and gathered in solemn council, as if for a most honored and precious guest, to receive him.

So, victorious and successful in all ways, the outcast dog of a youth who went to Zuñi and returned the hero of the Moki nation right willingly was accepted by this beauteous maiden as her husband after the ceremonies of initiation and purification had been performed over him.

Ah, well! that was very fine; but all this praise of one who had been despised and abused by themselves, and, more than all, the possession of such a beautiful wife, wrought fierce jealousy in the breasts of the many jilted lovers; making those who had looked askance at one another before, true friends and firm brothers in a single cause—the undoing of this lucky vagabond youth.   Nor were they alone in this desire, for behold! copying their lucky sister, all the pretty maidens in Moki declared that they would marry no one who did not show himself at least in some degree heroic, like the youth of the dog-holes who had married their pretty sister.   It therefore came about that the whole tribe of Moki, so far as the young men were concerned, became a company of jilted lovers, and all the maidens became confirmed in their resolutions of virgin maidenhood.

The jilted lovers got together one night in a cautious sort of way (for they were all afraid of this hero) and held a council.   But the fools did n't think of the Dogs lying around outside, who heard what they said.   They concluded the best way to get even with this youth was to kill him; but how to kill him was the problem, for they were cowards. "We will get up a hunt," said one; "and make friends with him and ask him to go, paying him all sorts of attention, and ask him to instruct us in the arts of war, the wretch!   He will readily join us in our hunting excursion, and some of us will sling a throwing-stick at him and finish the conceited fellow's days!"

Now, the Dogs scrambled off immediately and informed their friend and brother what was going on.

He said: "All right! I will accept their advances and go with them on the hunt."

He went off that night to a cave, where he had often sought shelter from the wind when driven out of the town of Walpi, and thus had made acquaintance with those most unerring travellers in crooked places—the Cave-swallows. He went to one of them, an elderly, wise bird, and, addressing him as "Grandfather," told him what was going on.

"Very well," said the old bird; "I will help you." And he made a boomerang for the youth which had the power to fly around bushes and down into gullies; and if well thrown, of course, it could not be dodged by any rabbit, however swift of foot or sly in hiding. Having finished this boomerang, he told the youth to take it and use it freely in hunting. The youth thanked him, and returning to his town passed a peaceful night.

When he appeared the next morning, the others greeted him pleasantly—those who happened to see him—to which greetings he replied with equal cordiality. They were so importunate with the priest-chiefs to be allowed to undertake a grand rabbit-hunt that these fathers of the people, always desirous of contributing to the happiness of their children, ordered a grand hunt for the very next day. So everybody was busy forthwith in making throwing-sticks and boomerangs.

The next day all the able-bodied youth of the town, selecting the hero of whom we have told as their leader, took their way to the great plain south of Moki, and there, spreading out into an enormous circle, they drove hundreds of rabbits closer and closer together among the sagebrush in the center of the valley. Some of them succeeded in striking down one—some of them three or four —but ere long every one observed that each time the youth threw his stick he struck a rabbit and secured it, until he had so many that he was forced to call some boys who had followed along to carry them for him.

Already inflamed by their jealousies to great anger, what was the chagrin of this crowd of dandies, now that this youth whom they so heartily despised actually surpassed them even in hunting rabbits! They gnashed their teeth with rage, and one of them in a moment of excitement, when two or three rabbits were trying to escape, took deliberate aim at the youth and threw his boomerang at him. The youth, who was wily, sprang into the air so high, pretending meanwhile to throw his boomerang, that the missile missed his vital parts, but struck his leg and apparently broke it, so that he fell down senseless in the midst of the crowd; and the people set up a great shout—some of lamentation, some of exultation.

"Let him lie there and rot!" said the angry suitors, catching up their own rabbits and making off for the pueblo. But some of the old men, who deplored this seeming accident of the youth, ran as fast as they could toward the town—fearing to raise him lest they should make his hurt worse—for medicine.

When the youth had been left alone, he opened his eyes and smiled. Then, taking from his pouch a medicine unfailing in its effects, applied it to the bruised spot and quickly became relieved of pain, if not even of injury. Rising, he looked about and found the rabbits where, panic-stricken, the boys had dropped them and fled away. He made up a huge bundle, and not long before sunset, behold! singing merrily, he came marching, though limping somewhat, through the plain before the foot-hills of Moki, bearing an enormous burden of rabbits. He climbed the mesa, greeted every one pleasantly as though nothing had occurred, took his way to his home, and became admired of all the women of Moki, young and old, as a paragon of valor and manhood.

It became absolutely necessary after that, of course,—for these faint-hearted dandies tried no more tricks with the youth,—for anyone who would marry a Moki maiden to show himself a man in some way or other; and, as the ugliest and most neglected of children generally turn out sharpest because they have to look out for themselves, so it happens that to this day the husbands of Moki are generally very ugly; but one thing is certain—they are men.

Reflect on these things, ye young ones and youths.

Thus shortens my story.

HOW THE COYOTE JOINED THE DANCE
OF THE BURROWING-OWLS

YOU may know the country that lies south of the valley in which our town stands. You travel along the trail which winds round the hill our ancients called *Ishana-tak'yapon,*—which means the Hill of Grease, for the rocks sometimes shine in the light of the sun at evening, and it is said that strange things occurred there in the days of the ancients, which makes them thus to shine, while rocks of the kind in other places do not,—you travel on up this trail, crossing over the arroyos and foot-hills of the great mesa called Middle Mountain, until you come to the foot of the cliffs. Then you climb up back and forth, winding round and round, until you reach the top of the mountain, which is as flat as the floor of a house, merely being here and there traversed by small valleys covered with piñon and cedar, and threaded by trails made not only by the feet of our people but by deer and other animals. And so you go on and on, until, hardly knowing it, you have descended from the top of Middle Mountain, and found yourself in a wide plain covered with grass, and here and there clumps of trees. Beyond this valley is an elevated sandy plain, rather sunken in the middle, so that when it rains the water filters down into the soil of the depressed portion (which is wide enough to be a country in itself) and nourishes tne grasses there; so that most of the year they grow green and sweet.

Now, a long, long time ago, in this valley or basin there lived a village of Prairie-dogs, on fairly peaceable terms with Rattlesnakes, Adders, Chameleons, Horned-toads, and Burrowing-owls. With the Owls they were especially friendly, looking at them as creatures of great gravity and sanctity. For this reason these Prairie-dogs and their companions never disturbed the councils or ceremonies of the Burrowing-owls, but treated them most respectfully, keeping at a distance from them when their dances were going on.

It chanced one day that the Burrowing-owls were having a great dance all to themselves, rather early in the morning. The dance they were engaged in was one peculiarly prized by them, requiring no little dexterity in its execution. Each dancer, young man or maiden, carried upon his or her head a bowl of foam, and though their legs were crooked and their motions disjointed, they danced to the whistling of some and the clapping beaks of others, in perfect unison, and with such dexterity that they never spilled a speck of the foam on their sleek mantles of dun-black feather-work.

It chanced this morning of the Foam-dance that a Coyote was nosing about for Grasshoppers and Prairie-dogs. So quite naturally he was prowling around the by-streets in the borders of the Prairie-dog town. His house where he lived with his old grandmother stood back to the westward, just over the elevations that bounded Sunken Country, among the rocks. He heard the click-clack of the musicians and their shrill, funny little song:

> "I yami hota utchu tchapikya,
> Tokos! tokos! tokos! tokos!"

So he pricked up his ears, and lifting his tail, trotted forward toward the level place between the hillocks and doorways of the village, where the Owls were dancing in a row. He looked at them with great curiosity, squatting on his haunches, the more composedly to observe them. Indeed, he became so much interested and amused by their shambling motions and clever evolutions, that he could no longer contain his curiosity. So he stepped forward, with a smirk and a nod toward the old master of ceremonies, and said: "My father, how are you and your children these many days?"

"Contented and happy," replied the old Owl, turning his attention to the dancing again.

"Yes, but I observe you are dancing," said the Coyote. "A very fine dance, upon my word! Charming! Charming! And why should you be dancing if you were not contented and happy, to be sure?"

"We are dancing," responded the Owl, "both for our pleasure and for the good of the town."

"True, true," replied the Coyote; "but what's that which looks like foam these dancers are carrying on their heads, and why do they dance in so limping a fashion?"

"You see, my friend," said the Owl, turning toward the Coyote, "we hold this to be a very sacred performance—very sacred indeed. Being such, these my children are initiated and so trained in the mysteries of the sacred society of which this is a custom that they can do very strange things in the observance of our ceremonies. You ask what it is that looks like foam they are balancing on their heads. Look more closely, friend. Do you not observe that it is their own grandmothers' heads they have on, the feathers turned white with age?"

"By my eyes!" exclaimed the Coyote, blinking and twitching his whiskers; "it seems so."

"And you ask also why they limp as they dance," said the Owl. "Now, this limp is essential to the proper performance of our dance—so essential, in fact, that in order to attain to it these my children go through the pain of having their legs broken. Instead of losing by this, they gain in a great many ways. Good luck always follows them. They are quite as spry as they were before, and enjoy, moreover, the distinction of performing a dance which no other people or creatures in the world are capable of!"

"Dust and devils!" ejaculated the Coyote. "This is passing strange. A most admirable dance, upon my word! Why, every bristle on my body keeps time to the music and their steps! Look here, my friend, don't you think that I could learn that dance?"

"Well," replied the old Owl; "it is rather hard to learn, and you have n't been initiated, you know; but, still, if you are determined that you would like to join the dance—by the way, have you a grandmother?"

"Yes, and a fine old woman she is," said he, twitching his mouth in the direction of his house. "She lives there with me. I dare say she is looking after my breakfast now."

"Very well," continued the old Owl, "if you care to join in our dance, fulfill the conditions, and I think we can receive you into our order." And he added, aside: "The silly fool; the sneaking, impertinent wretch! I will teach him to be sticking that sharp nose of his into other people's affairs!"

"All right! All right!" cried the Coyote, excitedly. "Will it last long?"

"Until the sun is so bright that it hurts our eyes," said the Owl; "a long time yet."

"All right! All right! I'll be back in a little while," said the Coyote; and, switching his tail into the air, away he ran toward his home. When he came to the house, he saw his old grandmother on the roof, which was a rock beside his hole, gathering fur from some skins which he had brought home, to make up a bed for the Coyote's family.

"Ha, my blessed grandmother!" said the Coyote, "by means of your aid, what a fine thing I shall be able to do!"

The old woman was singing to herself when the Coyote dashed up to the roof where she was sitting, and, catching up a convenient leg-bone, whacked her over the pate and sawed her head off with the teeth of a deer. All bloody and soft as it was, he clapped it on his own head and raised himself on his hind-legs, bracing his tail against the ground, and letting his paws drop with the toes outspread, to imitate as nearly as possible the drooping wings of the dancing Owls. He found that it worked very well; so, descending with the head in one paw and a stone in the other, he found a convenient sharp-edged rock, and, laying his legs across it, hit them a tremendous crack with the stone, which broke them, to be sure, into splinters.

"Beloved Powers! Oh!" howled the Coyote. "Oh-o-o-o-o! the dance may be a fine thing, but the initiation is anything else!"

However, with his faith unabated, he shook himself together and got up to walk. But he could walk only with his paws; his hind-legs dragged helplessly behind him. Nevertheless, with great pain, and getting weaker and weaker every step of the way, he made what haste he could back to the Prairie-dog town, his poor old grandmother's head slung over his shoulders.

When he approached the dancers,—for they were still dancing,—they pretended to be greatly delighted with their proselyte, and greeted him, notwithstanding his rueful countenance, with many congratulatory epithets, mingled with very proper and warm expressions of welcome. The Coyote looked sick and groaned occasionally and kept looking around at his feet, as though he would like to lick them. But the old Owl extended his wing and cautioned him not to interfere with the working power of faith in this essential observance, and invited him (with a *hem* that very much resembled a suppressed giggle), to join in their dance. The Coyote smirked and bowed and tried to stand up gracefully on his stumps, but fell over, his grandmother's head rolling around in the dirt. He picked up the grisly head, clapped it on his crown again and raised himself, and with many a howl, which he tried in vain to check, began to prance around; but ere long tumbled over again. The Burrowing-owls were filled with such merriment at his discomfiture that they laughed until they spilled the foam all down their backs and bosoms; and, with a parting fling at the Coyote which gave him to understand that he had made a fine fool of himself, and would know better than to pry into other people's business next time, skipped away to a safe distance from him.

Then, seeing how he had been tricked, the Coyote fell to howling and clapping his thighs; and, catching sight of his poor grandmother's head, all bloody and begrimed with dirt, he cried out in grief and anger: "Alas! alas! that it should have come to this! You little devils! I'll be even with you! I'll smoke you out of your holes."

"What will you smoke us out with?" tauntingly asked the Burrowing-owls.

"Ha! you'll find out. With yucca!"

"O! O! ha! ha!" laughed the Owls. "That is our succotash!"

"Ah, well! I'll smoke you out!" yelled the Coyote, stung by their taunts.

"What with?" cried the Owls.

"Grease-weed."

"He, ha! ho, ho! We make our mush-stew of that!"

"Ha! but I 'll smoke you out, nevertheless, you little beasts!"

"What with? What with?" shouted the Owls.

"Yellow-top weeds," said he.

"Ha, ha! All right; smoke away! We make our sweet gruel with that, you fool!"

"I 'll fix you! I 'll smoke you out! I 'll suffocate the very last one of you!"

"What with? What with?" shouted the Owls, skipping around on their crooked feet.

"Pitch-pine," snarled the Coyote.

This frightened the Owls, for pitch-pine, even to this day, is sickening to them. Away they plunged into their holes, pell-mell.

Then the Coyote looked at his poor old grandmother's begrimed and bloody head, and cried out —just as Coyotes do now at sunset, I suppose— "Oh, my poor, poor grandmother! So this is what they have caused me to do to you!" And, tormented both by his grief and his pain, he took up the head of his grandmother and crawled back as best he could to his house.

When he arrived there he managed to climb up to the roof, where her body lay stiff. He chafed her legs and sides, and washed the blood and dirt from her head, and got a bit of sinew, and sewed her head to her body as carefully as he could and as hastily. Then he opened her mouth, and, putting his muzzle to it, blew into her throat, in the hope of resuscitating her; but the wind only leaked out from the holes in her neck, and she gave no signs of animation. Then the Coyote mixed some pap of fine toasted meal and water and poured it down her throat, addressing her with vehement expressions of regret at what he had done, and apology and solicitation that she should not mind, as he did n't mean it, and imploring her to revive. But the pap only trickled out between the stitches in her neck, and she grew colder and stiffer all the while; so that at last the Coyote gave it up, and, moaning, he betook himself to a near clump of piñon trees, intent upon vengeance and designing to gather pitch with which to smoke the Owls to death. But, weakened by his injuries, and filled with grief and shame and mortification, when he got there he could only lie down.

He was so engrossed in howling and thinking of his woes and pains that a Horned-toad, who saw him, and who hated him because of the insults he had frequently suffered from him and his kind, crawled into the throat of the beast without his noticing it. Presently the little creature struck up a song:

> " Tsakina muuu-ki
> Iyami Kushina tsoiyakya
> Aisiwaiki muki, muki,
> Muuu ka! "

"Ah-a-a-a-a-a," the Coyote was groaning. But when he heard this song, apparently far off, and yet so near, he felt very strangely inside, so he thought and no doubt wondered if it were the song of some musician. At any rate, he lifted his head and looked all around, but hearing nothing, lay down again and bemoaned his fate.

Then the Horned-toad sang again. This time the Coyote called out immediately, and the Horned-toad answered: "Here I am." But look as he would, the Coyote could not find the Toad. So he listened for the song again, and heard it, and asked who it was that was singing. The Horned-toad replied that it was he. But still the Coyote could not find him. A fourth time the Horned-toad sang, and the Coyote began to suspect that it was under him. So he lifted himself to see; and one of the spines on the Horned-toad's neck pricked him, and at the same time the little fellow called out: "Here I am, you idiot, inside of you! I came upon you here, and being a medicine-man of some prominence, I thought I would explore your vitals and see what was the matter."

"By the souls of my ancestors!" exclaimed the Coyote, "be careful what you do in there!"

The Horned-toad replied by laying his hand on the Coyote's liver, and exclaiming: "What is this I feel?"

"Where?" said the Coyote.

"Down here."

"Merciful daylight! it is my liver, without which no one can have solidity of any kind, or a proper vitality. Be very careful not to injure that; if you do, I shall die at once, and what will become of my poor wife and children?"

Then the Horned-toad climbed up to the stomach

of the Coyote. "What is this, my friend?" said he, feeling the sides of the Coyote's food-bag.

"What is it like?" asked the Coyote.

"Wrinkled," said the Horned-toad, "and filled with a fearful mess of stuff!"

"Oh! mercy! mercy! good daylight! My precious friend, be very careful! That is the very source of my being—my stomach itself!"

"Very well," said the Horned-toad. Then he moved on somewhat farther and touched the heart of the Coyote, which startled him fearfully. "What is this?" cried the Horned-toad.

"Mercy, mercy! what are you doing?" exclaimed the Coyote.

"Nothing—feeling of your vitals," was the reply. "What is it?"

"Oh, what is it like?" said the Coyote.

"Shaped like a pine-nut," said the Horned-toad, "as nearly as I can make out; it keeps leaping so."

"Leaping, is it?" howled the Coyote. "Mercy! my friend, get away from there! That is the very heart of my being, the thread that ties my existence, the home of my emotions, and my knowledge of daylight. Go away from there, do, I pray you! If you should scratch it ever so little, it would be the death of me, and what would my wife and children do?"

"Hey!" said the Horned-toad, "you would n't be apt to insult me and my people any more if I touched you up there a little, would you?" And he hooked one of his horns into the Coyote's heart.

The Coyote gave one gasp, straightened out his limbs, and expired.

"Ha, ha! you villain! Thus would you have done to me, had you found the chance; thus unto you"—saying which he found his way out and sought the nearest water-pocket he could find.

So you see from this, which took place in the days of the ancients, it may be inferred that the instinct of meddling with everything that did not concern him, and making a universal nuisance of himself, and desiring to imitate everything that he sees, ready to jump into any trap that is laid for him, is a confirmed instinct with the Coyote, for those are precisely his characteristics today.

Furthermore, Coyotes never insult Horned-toads nowadays, and they keep clear of Burrowing-owls. And ever since then the Burrowing-owls have been speckled with gray and white all over their backs and bosoms, because their ancestors spilled foam over themselves in laughing at the silliness of the Coyote.

Thus shortens my story.

THE COYOTE WHO KILLED THE
DEMON SÍUIUKI:

OR WHY COYOTES RUN THEIR NOSES INTO DEADFALLS

IT was very long ago, in the days of the ancients. There stood a village in the cañon south of Thunder Mountain where the Gods of Prey all lived with their sisters and mothers: the Mountain Lion, the great Black Bear, the Wildcat, the Gray Wolf, the Eagle, and even the Mole—all the Gods of Prey lived there together with their mothers and sisters. Day after day they went out hunting, for hunting was their business of life, and they were great hunters.

Now, right up on the edge of Thunder Mountain there lived a spotted Demon, named Síuiuki, and whenever the people of the towns round about went hunting, he lay in wait for them and ate them up.

After a long while the Gods of Prey grew discontented, and they said to one another: "What in the world can we do? None of the children of men ever make sacrifices to us, for, whenever our children among men go out hunting, this Demon who lives on the top of Thunder Mountain destroys them and eats them up. What in the world can be done?"

"It would be a good thing if we could kill him," said some of them.

Now, just down below the house of the Demon,

in Wolf Cañon, lived a Coyote, and he had found out where the Gods of Prey lived, and whenever he wanted a feast of sinew and gristle, he went below their houses and gnawed at the bones that they had thrown away, and thus it happened that when the gods were talking together in this way he was near their doorway gnawing a bone, and he heard all they said.

"Yes," said one or two of the others, "and if anybody will go and kill Síuiuki, we will give him our sister to marry."

"Aha!" said the Coyote to himself. "Ha, ha!" —and he dropped the bone he was gnawing and cut off for home as fast as ever he could.

Next morning, bright and early, he began to dig into the side of the cañon below the Demon's home, and after he had dug a great hollow in the side of the arroyo, he rolled a heavy stone into it, and found another, which he placed beside it. Then he brought a great many leg-bones of deer and antelope. Then he found a large bowl and put a lot of yellow medicine-fluid in it, and placed it beside the rock. He then sat down and began to crack the leg-bones with the two stones he had brought there.

The old Demon was not in the habit of rising very early, but when he arose that morning he came out and sat down on the edge of the cliff; there the Coyote was, battering away at the bones and pretending to bathe his own lips with the medicine-fluid.

"I wonder what in the world that little sneak is

doing down there," said the old Demon. So he put on his war-badge and took his bow and arrows, as though he were going out to hunt, and started down to where the Coyote was.

"Hello!" said the Coyote, "how did you pass the night?"

"What in the world are you doing here?" asked the Demon.

"Why, don't you know?" replied the Coyote. "This is the way I train myself for running, so as to catch the deer; I can run faster than any deer in the country. With my medicine, here, I take the swiftness out of these bones."

"Is it possible?" said the old Demon.

"Of course it is," said the Coyote. "There is no deer that can run away from me."

"Will you show me?" said the Demon, eagerly.

"Why, yes, of course I will; and then we will go hunting together."

"Good, good!" said the old Demon. "I have a hard time catching deer and antelope."

"Well, now, you sit down right over there and watch me," said the Coyote, "and I will show you all about it."

So he laid his left leg over the rock, and then slily took an antelope bone and laid it by the side of it. Then he picked up a large stone and struck it as hard as ever he could against the bone. Whack! went the stone, and it split the bone into splinters; and the Coyote pretended that it was the bone of his own leg.

"Aye! Ah! Oh!" exclaimed he. "But then it

will get well!" Still crying "Oh! Ah!" he splashed the leg with the medicine-water and rubbed it. "Did n't I tell you?" said he, "it is all right now." And then away he went and ran like lightning round and round on the plain below, and rushed back again. "Did n't I tell you so?" said he.

"Fury! what a runner it makes out of you," said the old Demon, and his eyes stuck out more than ever. "Let me try it now."

"Hold on, hold on," said the Coyote; "I have not half finished yet."

So he repeated the experiment with his other leg, and made great ado, as if it hurt him more than ever. But, pretending to cure himself with the medicine-water, he ran round and round on the plain below so fast that he fairly left a streak of dust behind him.

"Why, indeed, you are one of the fastest runners I ever saw!" said the Demon, rubbing his eyes.

Then the Coyote repeated the experiment first with his left paw and then with his right; and the last time he ran more swiftly than before.

"Why, do you mean to say that if I do that I can run as fast as you do?" said the Demon.

"Certainly," replied the Coyote. "But it will hurt you."

"Ho! who cares for a little hurt?" said the Demon.

"Oh! but it hurts terribly," said the Coyote, "and I am afraid you won't have the pluck to go through with it."

"Do you think I am a baby?" said the old Demon, getting up,—"or a woman, that I should be afraid to pound my legs and arms?"

"Well, I only thought I'd tell you how much it hurts," said the Coyote; "but if you want to try it yourself, why, go ahead. There's one thing certain: when you make yourself as swift as I am, there's no deer in all the country that can get away from us two."

"What shall I do?" said the Demon.

"You just sit right down there, and I'll show you how," said the Coyote. So the Demon sat down by the rock.

"There, now, you just lay your leg right over that stone and take the other rock and strike your leg just as hard as you can; and as soon as you have done, bathe it in the medicine-water. Then do just the same way to the other."

"All right," said the Demon. So he laid his leg over the rock, and picking up the other stone, brought it down with might and main across his thigh—so hard, indeed, that he crushed the bone into splinters.

"Oh, my! Oh, my! what shall I do?" shouted the Demon.

"Be patient, be patient; it will get well," said the Coyote, and he splashed it with the medicine-fluid.

Then, picking up the stone again, the Demon hit the other thigh even harder, from pain.

"It will get well, my friend; it will get well," shouted the Coyote; and he splashed more of the medicine-water on the two wounded legs.

Then the Demon picked up the stone once more, and, laying his left arm across the other stone, pounded that also until it was broken.

"Hold on; let me bathe it for you," said the Coyote. "Does it hurt? Oh, well, it will get well. Just wait until you have doctored the other arm, and then in a few minutes you will be all right."

"Oh, dear! Oh, dear!" groaned the Demon. "How in the world can I doctor the other arm, for my left arm is broken?"

"Lay it across the rock, my friend," said the Coyote, "and I'll doctor it for you."

So the Demon did as he was bidden, and the Coyote brought the stone down with might and main against his arm. "Have patience, my friend, have patience," said he, as he bathed the injured limb with more of the medicine-water. But the Demon only groaned and howled, and rolled over and over in the dust with pain.

"Ha, ha!" laughed the Coyote, as he keeled a somersault over the rocks and ran off over the plain. "How do you feel now, old man?"

"But it hurts! It hurts!" cried the Demon. "I shall never get well; it will kill me!"

"Of course it will," laughed the Coyote. "That's just what I wanted it to do, you old fool!"

So the old Demon lay down and died from sheer pain.

Then the Coyote took the Demon's knife from him, and, cutting open his breast, tore out his heart, wind-pipe, and all. Then, stealing the war-badge that the Demon had worn, he cut away as fast as ever he could for the home of the Prey-gods. Before noon he neared their house, and, just as he ran up into the plaza in front of it, the youngest sister of the Prey-gods came out to hang up some meat to dry.   Now, her brothers had all gone hunting; not one of them was at home.

"I say, wife," said the Coyote.   "Wife! Wife!"

"Humph!" said the girl.   "Impertinent scoundrel!   I wonder where he is and who he is that has the impudence to call me his wife, when he knows that I have never been married!"

"Wife! Wife!" shouted the Coyote again.

"Away with you, you shameless rascal!" cried the girl, in indignation.   Then she looked around and spied the Coyote sitting there on the ash-heap, with his nose in the air, as though he were the biggest fellow in the world.

"Clear out, you wretch!" cried the girl.

"Softly, softly," replied the Coyote.   "Do you remember what your brothers said last night?"

"What was that?" said the girl.

"Why, whoever would kill the speckled Demon, they declared, should have you for his wife."

"Well, what of that?" said the girl.

"Oh, nothing," replied the Coyote, "only I 've killed him!"   And, holding up the Demon's heart and war-badge, he stuck his nose in the air again.

So the poor girl said not a word, but sat there until the Coyote called out: "I say, wife, come down and take me up; I can't climb the ladders."

So the poor girl went down the ladder, took her

foul-smelling husband in her arms, and climbed up with him.

"Now, take me in with you," said the Coyote. So she did as she was bidden. Then she was about to mix some dough, but the Coyote kept getting in her way.

"Get out of the way a minute, won't you?" said the girl, "until I cook something for you."

"I want you to come and sit down with me," said the Coyote, "and let me kiss you, for you know you are my wife, now." So the poor girl had to submit to the ill-smelling creature's embraces.

Presently along came her brother, the Gray Wolf, but he was a very good-natured sort of fellow; so he received the Coyote pleasantly. Then along came the Bear, with a big antelope over his shoulder; but he did n't say anything, for he was a lazy, good-natured fellow. Then presently the other brothers came in, one by one; but the Mountain Lion was so late in returning that they began to look anxiously out for him. When they saw him coming from the north with more meat and more game than all the others together had brought, he was evidently not in good humor, for as he approached the house he exclaimed, with a howl: "*Hu-hu-ya!*"

"There he goes again," said the brothers and sisters, all in a chorus. "Always out of temper with something."

"*Hu-hu-ya!*" exclaimed the Mountain Lion again, louder than before. And, as he mounted the ladder, he exclaimed for a third time: "*Hu-hu-ya!*" and, throwing his meat down, entered swear-

THE YOUTH AND HIS EAGLE

ZUÑI FROM THE SOUTH

WAÍHUSIWA

A BURRO TRAIN IN A ZUÑI STREET

Photo by Hillers

THUNDER MOUNTAIN FROM ZUÑI

Photo by A. C. Vroman

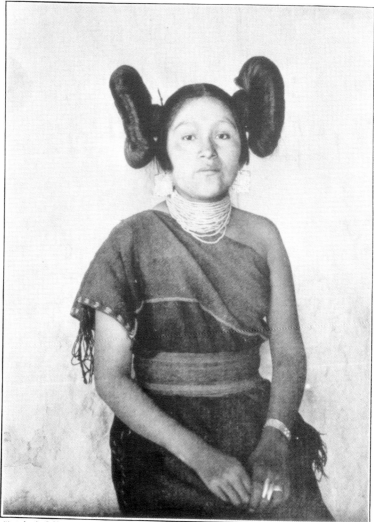

Photo by A. C. Vroman

A HOPI (MOKI) MAIDEN

A DANCE OF THE KÂKÂ

Photo by A. C. Vroman

Photo by A. C. Vroman

ACROSS THE TERRACES OF ZUÑI

Photo by A. C. Vroman

THE PINNACLES OF THUNDER MOUNTAIN

Photo by A. C. Vroman

PÁLOWAHTIWA

ZUÑI WOMEN CARRYING WATER

Photo by A. C. Vroman

ing and growling until his brothers were ashamed of him, and told him he had better behave himself.

"Come and eat," said the sister, as she brought a bowl of meat and put it on the floor.

"*Hu-hu-ya !*" again exclaimed the Mountain Lion, as he came nearer and sat down to eat. "What in the world is the matter with you, sister? You smell just like a Coyote. *Hu-hu-ya !*"

"Have you no more decency than to come home and scold your sister in that way?" exclaimed the Wolf. "I'm disgusted with you."

"*Hu-hu-ya !*" reiterated the Mountain Lion.

Now, when the Coyote had heard the Mountain Lion coming, he had sneaked off into a corner; but he stuck his sharp nose out, and the Mountain Lion espied it. "*Hu-hu-ya !*" said he. "Sling that bad-smelling beast out of the house! Kick him out!" cried the old man, with a growl. So the sister, fearing that her brother would eat her husband up, took the Coyote in her arms and carried him into another room.

"Now, stay there and keep still, for brother is very cross; but then he is always cross if things don't go right," she said.

So when evening came her brothers began to discuss where they would go hunting the next day; and the Coyote, who was listening at the door, heard them. So he called out: "Wife! Wife!"

"*Shom-me !*" remarked old Long Tail. "Shut up, you dirty whelp." And as the sister arose to go to see what her husband wanted, the Mountain

Lion remarked: "You had better sling that foul-smelling cub of yours over the roof."

No sooner had the girl entered than the Coyote began to brag what a runner he was, and to cut around at a great rate.

"*Shom-me!*" exclaimed the Mountain Lion again. "A Coyote always will make a Coyote of himself, foul-smelling wretch! *Hu-hu-ya!*"

"Shut up, and behave yourself!" cried the Wolf. "Don't you know any better than to talk about your brother-in-law in that way?" But neither the Coyote nor the girl could sleep that night for the growlings and roarings of their big brother, the Long Tail.

When the brothers began to prepare for the hunt the next morning, out came the Coyote all ready to accompany them. "You, you?" said the Mountain Lion. "You going to hunt with us? You conceited sneak!"

"Let him go if he wants to," said the Wolf.

"*Hu-hu-ya!* Fine company!" remarked the Mountain Lion. "If you fellows want to walk with him, you may. There's one thing certain, I'll not be seen in his company," and away strode the old fellow, lashing his tail and growling as he went. So the Coyote, taking a luncheon of dried meat that his wife put up for him, sneaked along behind with his tail dragging in the dust. Finally they all reached the mountain where they intended to hunt, and soon the Mountain Lion and the Bear started out to drive in a herd of antelope that they had scented in the distance. Presently along rushed the leaders of the herd,

" Now, then, I 'll show your cross old brother whether I can hunt or not," cried the Coyote, and away he rushed right into the herd of antelope and deer before anyone could restrain him.   Of course he made a Coyote of himself, and away went the deer in all directions.   Nevertheless, the brothers, who were great hunters, succeeded in catching a few of them ; and, just as they sat down to lunch, the Mountain Lion returned with a big elk on his shoulders.

" Where is our sweet-scented brother-in-law ? " he asked.

" Nobody knows," replied they.   " He rushed off after the deer and antelope, and that was the last of him."

" Of course the beast will make a Coyote of himself.   But he can go till he can go no longer, for all I care," added the Mountain Lion, as he sat down to eat.

Presently along came the Coyote.

" Where 's your game, my fine hunter ? " asked the Mountain Lion.

" They all got away from me," whined the Coyote.

" Of course they did, you fool ! " sneered the Mountain Lion.   " The best thing that you can do is to go home and see your wife.   Here, take this meat to sister," said he, slinging him a haunch of venison.

" Where 's the road ? " asked the Coyote.

" Well," said the Wolf, " follow that path right over there until you come to where it forks ; then be sure to take the right-hand trail, for if you

15

follow the left-hand trail it will lead you away from home and into trouble."

"Which trail did you say?" cried the Coyote.

"*Shom-me!*" again exclaimed the Mountain Lion.

"Oh, yes," hastily added the Coyote; "the right-hand trail. No, the left-hand trail."

"Just what you might expect," growled the Mountain Lion. "Already the fool has forgotten what you told him. Well, as for me, he can go on the left-hand trail if he wants to, and the farther he goes the better."

"Now, be sure and take the right-hand trail," called the Wolf, as the Coyote started.

"I know, I know," cried the Coyote; and away he went with his heavy haunch of venison slung over his shoulder. After a while he came to the fork in the trail. "Let me see," said he, "it's the left-hand trail, it seems to me. No, the right-hand trail. Well, I declare, I've forgotten! Perhaps it is the right-hand trail, and maybe it is the left-hand trail. Yes, it is the left-hand trail. Now I'm certain." And, picking up his haunch of venison, away he trotted along the left-hand trail. Presently he came to a steep cliff and began to climb it. But he had no sooner reached the middle than a lot of Chimney-swallows began to fly around his head and pick at his eyes, and slap him on the nose with their wings.

"Oh, dear! oh, dear!" exclaimed the Coyote. "Aye! aye!" and he bobbed his head from side to side to dodge the Swallows, until he missed his footing, and down he tumbled, heels over head,—

meat, Coyote, and all,—until he struck a great pile of rocks below, and was dashed to pieces.

That was the end of the Coyote ; but not of my story.

Now, the brothers went on hunting again. Then, one by one, they returned home. As before, the Mountain Lion came in last of all. He smelt all about the room. "Whew!" exclaimed he. "It still smells here as if twenty Coyotes had been around. But it seems to me that our fine brother-in-law is n't anywhere about."

"No," responded the rest, with troubled looks on their faces. "Nobody has seen anything of him yet."

"*Shom—m-m!*" remarked the Mountain Lion again. "Did n't I tell you, brothers, that he was a fool and would forget your directions? I say I told you that before he started. Well, for my part, I hope the beast has gone so far that he will never return," and with that he ate his supper.

When supper was over, the sister said : "Come, brothers, let 's go and hunt for my husband."

At first the Mountain Lion growled and swore a great deal ; but at last he consented to go. When they came to where the trails forked, there were the tracks of the Coyote on the left-hand trail.

"The idiot!" exclaimed the Mountain Lion. "I hope he has fallen off the cliff and broken every bone in his body !"

When at last the party reached the mountain, sure enough, there lay the body of the Coyote, with not a whole bone in him except his head.

"Good enough for you," growled the Mountain Lion, as he picked up a great stone and, *tu-um !* threw it down with all his strength upon the head of the Coyote.

That's what happened a great while ago. And for that reason whenever a Coyote sees a bait of meat inside of a stone deadfall he is sure to stick his nose in and get his head mashed for his pains.

Thus shortens my story.

HOW THE COYOTES TRIED TO STEAL THE CHILDREN OF THE SACRED DANCE

IN the times of the ancients, when our people lived in various places about the valley of Zuñi where ruins now stand, it is said that an old Coyote lived in Cedar Cañon with his family, which included a fine litter of pups. It is also said that at this time there lived on the crest of Thunder Mountain, back of the broad rock column or pinnacle which guards its western portion, one of the gods of the Sacred Drama Dance (*Káká*)[1], named K'yámakwe, with his children, many in number and altogether like himself.

[1] The *Káká*, or Sacred Drama Dance, is represented by a great variety of masks and costumes worn by Zuñi dancers during the performance of this remarkable dramatic ceremony. Undoubtedly many of the traditional characters of the Sacred Drama thus represented are conventionalizations of the mythic conceptions or personifications of animal attributes. Therefore many of these characters partake at once of the characteristics, in appearance as well as in other ways, of animals and men. The example in point is a good illustration of this. The K'yámakwe are supposed to have been a most wonderful and powerful tribe of demi-gods, inhabiting a great valley and range of mesas some forty miles south of Zuñi. Their powers over the atmospheric phenomena of nature and over all the herbivorous animals are supposed to have been absolute. Their attitude toward man was at times inimical, at times friendly or beneficent. Such a relationship, controlled simply by either laudatory or propitiatory worship, was supposed to hold spiritually, still, between these and other beings represented in the Sacred Drama and men. It is believed that through the power of breath communicated by these ancient gods to men, from one man to another man, and thus from generation to generation, an actual connection has been kept up between initiated members of the *Káká* drama and these original demigod characters which it represents ; so that when a member is properly dressed in the costume of any one of these characters, a ceremony (the

One day the old Coyote of Cedar Cañon went out hunting, and as he was prowling around among the sage-bushes below Thunder Mountain, he heard the clang and rattle and the shrill cries of the K'yámakwe. He pricked up his ears, stuck his nose into the air, sniffed about and looked all around, and presently discovered the K'yámakwe children running rapidly back and forth on the very edge of the mountain.

"Delight of my senses, what pretty creatures they are! Good for me!" he piped, in a jovial

description of which is too long for insertion here) accompanying the putting on of the mask is supposed not only to place him *en rapport* spiritually with the character he represents, but even to possess him with the spirit of that character or demi-god. He is, therefore, so long as he remains disguised as one of these demi-gods, treated as if he were actually that being which he personates. One of the K'yámakwe is represented by means of a mask, round and smooth-headed, with little black eyes turned up at the corners so as to represent a segment of a diminishing spiral ; the color of the face is green, and it is separated from the rest of the head by a line composed of alternate blocks of black and yellow ; the crown and back of the head are snow-white ; and the ears are pendent and conical in shape, being composed of husks or other paper-like material ; the mouth is round, and furnished with a four-pointed beak of husks, which extends two or three inches outward and spreads at the end like the petals of a half-closed lily ; round the neck is a collar of fox fur, and covering the body are flowing robes of sacred embroidered mantles, which (notwithstanding the gay ornaments and other appurtenances of the costume) have, in connection with the expression of the mask, a spectral effect ; the feet are encased in brilliantly painted moccasins, of archaic form, and the wrists laden with shell bracelets and bowguards. When the long file of these strange figures making up the K'yámakwe Drama Dance comes in from the southward to the dance plazas of the pueblo, each member of it bears on his back freshly slain deer, antelope, rabbits, and other game animals or portions of them in abundance, made up in packages, highly decorated with tufts of evergreen, and painted toys for presentation to the children. In one hand are carried bows and arrows, and in the other a peculiar rattle or clanger made of the shoulder-blades of deer. The wonder expressed by the coyote as the story goes on, and his excessive admiration of the children of the K'yámakwe may therefore be understood.

voice. "I am the finder of children. I must capture the little fellows tomorrow, and bring them up as Coyotes ought to be brought up. Are n't they handsome, though?"

All this he said to himself, in a fit of conceit, with his nose in the air (presumptuous cur!), planning to steal the children of a god! He hunted no more that day, but ran home as fast as he could, and, arriving there, he said: "Wife! Wife! O wife! I have discovered a number of the prettiest waifs one ever saw. They are children of the *Káká*, but what matters that? They are there, running back and forth and clanging their rattles along the very edge of Thunder Mountain. I mean to steal them tomorrow, every one of them, and bring them here!"

"Mercy on us!" exclaimed the old Coyote's wife. "There are children enough and to spare already. What in the world can we do with all of them, you fool?"

"But they are pretty," said the Coyote. "Immensely fine! Every Coyote in the country would envy us the possession of them!"

"But you say they are many," continued the wife.

"Well, yes, a good many," said the Coyote.

"Well, why not divide them among our associated clans?" suggested the old woman. "You never can capture them alone; it is rare enough that you capture *anything* alone, leave out the children of the K'yámakwe. Get your relatives to help you, and divide the children amongst them."

"Well, now, come to think of it, it is a good plan," said the Coyote, with his nose on his neck. "If I get up this expedition I 'll be a big chief, won't I? Hurrah! Here's for it!" he shouted; and, switching his tail in the face of his wife, he shot out of the hole and ran away to a high rock, where, squatting down with a most important air and his nose lifted high, he cried out:

> "*Au hii lâ-â-â-â!*
>> *Su Homaya-kwe!*
>> *Su Kemaya-kwe!*
>> *Su Ayalla-kwe!*
>> *Su Kutsuku-kwe!*

> [Listen ye all!
>> Coyotes of the Cedar-cañon tribe!
>> Coyotes of the Sunflower-stalk-plain tribe!
>> Coyotes of the Lifted-stone-mountain tribe!
>> Coyotes of the Place-of-rock-gullies tribe!]

I have instructions for you this day. I have found waif children many—of the K'yámakwe, the young. I would steal the waif-children many, of the K'yámakwe, the young. I would steal them tomorrow, that they may be adopted of us. I would have your aid in the stealing of the K'yáma-kwe young. Listen ye all, and tomorrow gather in council. Thus much I instruct ye:

> "Coyotes of the Cedar-cañon tribe!
>> Coyotes of the Sunflower-stalk-plain tribe!
>> Coyotes of the Lifted-stone-mountain tribe!
>> Coyotes of the Place-of-rock-gullies tribe!"

It was growing dark, and immediately from all quarters, in dark places under the cañons and arroyos, issued answering howls and howls. You should have seen that crowd of Coyotes the next morning, large and small, old and young,—all four tribes gathered together in the plain below Thunder Mountain!

When they had all assembled, the Coyote who had made the discovery mounted an ant-hill, sat down, and, lifting his paw, was about to give directions with the air of a chief when an ant bit him. He lost his dignity, but resumed it again on the top of a neighboring rock. Again he stuck his nose into the air and his paw out, and with ridiculous assumption informed the Coyotes that he was chief of them all and that they would do well to pay attention to his directions. He then showed himself much more· skilful than you might have expected. As you know, the cliff of Thunder Mountain is very steep, especially that part back of the two standing rocks. Well, this was the direction of the Coyote:

"One of you shall place himself at the base of the mountain; another shall climb over him, and the first one shall grasp his tail; and another over them, and his tail shall be grasped by the second, and so on until the top is reached. Hang tight, my friends, every one of you, and every one fall in line. Eructate thoroughly before you do so. If you do not, we may be in a pretty mess; for, supposing that any one along the line should hiccough, he would lose his hold, and down we would all fall!"

So the Coyotes all at once began to curve their necks and swell themselves up and strain and wriggle and belch wind as much as possible. Then all fell into a line and grabbed each other's tails, and thus they extended themselves in a long string up the very face of Thunder Mountain. A ridiculous little pup was at one end and a good, strong, grizzled old fellow—no other than the chief of the party—at the other.

" Souls of my ancestors! Hang tight, my friends! Hang tight! Hang tight!" said he, when, suddenly, one near the top, in the agitation of the moment, began to sneeze, lost his hold, and down the whole string, hundreds of them, fell, and were completely flattened out among the rocks.

The warrior of the *Káká*—he of the Long Horn, with frightful, staring eyes, and visage blue with rage,—bow and war-club in hand, was hastening from the sacred lake in the west to rescue the children of the K'yámakwe. When he arrived they had been rescued already, so, after storming around a little and mauling such of the Coyotes as were not quite dead, he set to skin them all.

And ever since then you will observe that the dancers of the Long Horn have blue faces, and whenever they arrive in our pueblo wear collars of coyote-skin about their necks. That is the way they got them. Before that they had no collars. It is presumable that that is the reason why they bellow so and have such hoarse voices, having previously taken cold, every one of them, for the want of fur collars.

Thus shortens my story.

THE COYOTE AND THE BEETLE

IN remote times, after our ancients were settled at Middle Ant Hill, a little thing occurred which will explain a great deal.

My children, you have doubtless seen Tip-beetles. They run around on smooth, hard patches of ground in spring time and early summer, kicking their heels into the air and thrusting their heads into any crack or hole they find.

Well, in ancient times, on the pathway leading around to Fat Mountain, there was one of these Beetles running about in all directions in the sunshine, when a Coyote came trotting along. He pricked up his ears, lowered his nose, arched his neck, and stuck out his paw toward the Beetle. "Ha!" said he, "I shall bite you!"

The Beetle immediately stuck his head down close to the ground, and, lifting one of his antennæ deprecatingly, exclaimed: "Hold on! Hold on, friend! Wait a bit, for the love of mercy! I hear something very strange down below here!"

"Humph!" replied the Coyote. "What do you hear?"

"Hush! hush!" cried the Beetle, with his head still to the ground. "Listen!"

So the Coyote drew back and listened most attentively. By-and-by the Beetle lifted himself with a long sigh of relief.

"*Okwe!*" exclaimed the Coyote. "What was going on?"

"The Good Soul save us!" exclaimed the Beetle, with a shake of his head. "I heard them saying down there that tomorrow they would chase away and thoroughly chastise everybody who defiled the public trails of this country, and they are making ready as fast as they can!"

"Souls of my ancestors!" cried the Coyote. "I have been loitering along this trail this very morning, and have defiled it repeatedly. I'll cut!" And away he ran as fast as he could go.

The Beetle, in pure exuberance of spirits, turned somersaults and stuck his head in the sand until it was quite turned.

Thus did the Beetle in the days of the ancients save himself from being bitten. Consequently the Tip-beetle has that strange habit of kicking his heels into the air and sticking his head in the sand.

Thus shortens my story.

HOW THE COYOTE DANCED WITH
THE BLACKBIRDS

ONE late autumn day in the times of the ancients, a large council of Blackbirds were
gathered, fluttering and chattering, on the smooth,
rocky slopes of Gorge Mountain, northwest of
Zuñi. Like ourselves, these birds, as you are well
aware, congregate together in autumn time, when
the harvests are ripe, to indulge in their festivities
before going into winter quarters; only we do not
move away, while they, on strong wings and swift, retreat for a time to the Land of Everlasting Summer.

Well, on this particular morning they were
making a great noise and having a grand dance,
and this was the way of it: They would gather in
one vast flock, somewhat orderly in its disposition,
on the sloping face of Gorge Mountain,—the older
birds in front, the younger ones behind,—and down
the slope, chirping and fluttering, they would hop,
hop, hop, singing:

> " *Ketchu, Ketchu, oñtilã, oñtilã,*
> *Ketchu, Ketchu, oñtilã, oñtilã!*
> *Ãshokta a yd-à-laa Ke-e-tchu,*
> *Oñtilã,*
> *Oñtilã!* "—

Blackbirds, Blackbirds, dance away, O, dance away, O!
Blackbirds, Blackbirds, dance away, O, dance away, O!
Down the Mountain of the Gorges, Blackbirds,
Dance away, O!
Dance away, O!—

and, spreading their wings, with many a flutter, flurry, and scurry, *keh keh,—keh keh,—keh keh,— keh keh,*—they would fly away into the air, swirling off in a dense, black flock, circling far upward and onward; then, wheeling about and darting down, they would dip themselves in the broad spring which flows out at the foot of the mountain, and return to their dancing place on the rocky slopes.

A Coyote was out hunting (as if he could catch anything, the beast!) and saw them, and was enraptured.

"You beautiful creatures!" he exclaimed. "You graceful dancers! Delight of my senses! How do you do that, anyway? Could n't I join in your dance—the first part of it, at least?"

"Why, certainly; yes," said the Blackbirds. "We are quite willing," the masters of the ceremony said.

"Well," said the Coyote, "I can get on the slope of the rocks and I can sing the song with you; but I suppose that when you leap off into the air I shall have to sit there patting the rock with my paw and my tail and singing while you have the fun of it."

"It may be," said an old Blackbird, "that we can fit you out so that you can fly with us."

"Is it possible!" cried the Coyote, "Then by all means do so. By the Blessed Immortals! Now, if I am only able to circle off into the air like you fellows, I 'll be the biggest Coyote in the world!"

"I think it will be easy," resumed the old Blackbird. "My children," said he, "you are many, and many are your wing-feathers. Contribute each one of you a feather to our friend." Thereupon the Blackbirds, each one of them, plucked a feather from his wing. Unfortunately they all plucked feathers from the wings on the same side.

"Are you sure, my friend," continued the old Blackbird, "that you are willing to go through the operation of having these feathers planted in your skin? If so, I think we can fit you out."

"Willing?—why, of course I am willing." And the Coyote held up one of his arms, and, sitting down, steadied himself with his tail. Then the Blackbirds thrust in the feathers all along the rear of his forelegs and down the sides of his back, where wings ought to be. It hurt, and the Coyote twitched his mustache considerably; but he said nothing. When it was done, he asked: "Am I ready now?"

"Yes," said the Blackbirds; "we think you 'll do."

So they formed themselves again on the upper part of the slope, sang their songs, and hopped along down with many a flutter, flurry, and scurry, — *Keh keh, keh keh, keh keh,*— and away they flew off into the air.

The Coyote, somewhat startled, got out of time, but followed bravely, making heavy flops; but, as I have said before, the wings he was supplied with were composed of feathers all plucked from one side, and therefore he flew slanting and spirally and brought up with a whack, which nearly knocked the breath out of him, against the side of the mountain. He picked himself up, and shook himself, and cried out: "Hold! Hold! Hold on, hold on, there!" to the fast-disappearing Blackbirds. "You've left me behind!"

When the birds returned they explained: "Your wings are not quite thick enough, friend; and, besides, even a young Blackbird, when he is first learning to fly, does just this sort of thing that you have been doing—makes bad work of it."

"Sit down again," said the old Blackbird. And he called out to the rest: "Get feathers from your other sides also, and be careful to select a few strong feathers from the tips of the wings, for by means of these we cleave the air, guide our movements, and sustain our flight."

So the Blackbirds all did as they were bidden, and after the new feathers were planted, each one plucked out a tail-feather, and the most skilful of the Blackbirds inserted these feathers into the tip of the Coyote's tail. It made him wince and "yip" occasionally; but he stood it bravely and reared his head proudly, thinking all the while: "What a splendid Coyote I shall be! Did ever anyone hear of a Coyote flying?"

The procession formed again. Down the slope they went, hopity-hop, hopity-hop, singing their song, and away they flew into the air, the Coyote in their midst. Far off and high they circled and circled, the Coyote cutting more eager pranks than any of the rest. Finally they returned, dipped themselves again into the spring, and settled on the slopes of the rocks.

"There, now," cried out the Coyote, with a flutter of his feathery tail, "I can fly as well as the rest of you."

"Indeed, you do well!" exclaimed the Blackbirds. "Shall we try it again?"

"Oh, yes! Oh, yes! I'm a little winded," cried the Coyote, "but this is the best fun I ever had."

The Blackbirds, however, were not satisfied with their companion. They found him less sedate than a dancer ought to be, and, moreover, his irregular cuttings-up in the air were not to their taste. So the old ones whispered to one another: "This fellow is a fool, and we must pluck him when he gets into the air. We'll fly so far this time that he will get a little tired out and cry to us for assistance."

The procession formed, and hopity-hop, hopity-hop, down the mountain slope they went, and with many a flutter and flurry flew off into the air. The Coyote, unable to restrain himself, even took the lead. On and on and on they flew, the Blackbirds and the Coyote, and up and up and up, and they circled round and round, until the Coyote found himself missing a wing stroke occasionally and falling out of line; and he cried out: "Help! help, friends, help!"

"All right!" cried the Blackbirds. "Catch hold of his wings; hold him up!" cried the old ones. And the Blackbirds flew at him; and every time they caught hold of him (the old fool all the time thinking they were helping) they plucked out a feather, until at last the feathers had become so thin that he began to fall, and he fell and fell and

16

fell,—flop, flop, flop, he went through the air,—the few feathers left in his forelegs and sides and the tip of his tail just saving him from being utterly crushed as he fell with a thud to the ground. He lost his senses completely, and lay there as if dead for a long time. When he awoke, he shook his head sadly, and, with a crestfallen countenance and tail dragging between his legs, betook himself to his home over the mountains.

The agony of that fall had been so great and the heat of his exertions so excessive, that the feathers left in his forelegs and tail-tip were all shrivelled up into little ugly black fringes of hair. His descendants were many.

Therefore you will often meet coyotes to this day who have little black fringes along the rear of their forelegs, and the tips of their tails are often black. Thus it was in the days of the ancients.

Thus shortens my story.

HOW THE TURTLE OUT HUNTING
DUPED THE COYOTE

IN the times of the ancients, long, long ago, near
the Highflowing River on the Zuñi Mountains,
there lived an old Turtle.   He went out hunting,
one day, and by means of his ingenuity killed a
large, fine deer.   When he had thrown the deer to
the ground, he had no means of skinning it.   He
sat down and reflected, scratching the lid of his eye
with the nail of his hind foot.   He concluded he
would have to go hunting for a flint-knife ; therefore he set forth.   He came after a while to a place
where old buildings had stood.   Then he began to
hum an old magic song, such as, it is said, the
ancients sung when they hunted for the flint of
which to make knives.   He sang in this way:

> " *Apatsinan tse wash,*
> *Apatsinan tse wash,*
>   *Tsepa !   Tsepa !* "

which may be translated, not perhaps correctly,
but well enough :

> Fire-striking flint-stone, oh, make yourself known !
> Fire-striking flint-stone, oh, make yourself known !
>   Magically ! Magically !

As he was thus crawling about and singing, a
Coyote running through the woods overheard him.
He exclaimed: " Uh ! I wonder who is singing
and what he is saying.   Ah, he is hunting for a

flint-knife, is he?—evidently somebody who has killed a deer!" He turned back, and ran over to where the old Turtle was. As he neared him, he cried out: "Halloo, friend! Did n't I hear you singing?"

"Yes," was the reply of the Turtle.

"What were you singing?"

"Nothing in particular."

"Yes, you were, too. What were you saying?"

"Nothing in particular, I tell you; at least, nothing that concerns you."

"Yes, you were saying something, and this is what you said." And so the Coyote, who could not sing the song, deliberately repeated the words he had heard.

"Well, suppose I did say so; what of that?" said the Turtle.

"Why, you were hunting for a flint-knife; that is why you said what you did," replied the Coyote.

"Well, what of that?"

"What did you want the flint-knife for?"

"Nothing in particular," replied the Turtle.

"Yes, you did; you wanted it for something. What was it?"

"Nothing in particular, I say," replied the Turtle. "At least, nothing that concerns you."

"Yes, you did want it for something," said the Coyote, "and I know what it was, too."

"Well, what?" asked the Turtle, who was waxing rather angry.

"You wanted it to skin a deer with; that 's what you wanted it for. Where is the deer now, come? You have killed a deer and I know it. Tell, where is it."

"Well, it lies over yonder," replied the Turtle.

"Where? Come, let us go; I'll help you skin it."

"I can get along very well without you," replied the Turtle.

"What if I do help you a little? I am very hungry this morning, and would like to lap up the blood."

"Well, then, come along, torment!" replied the Turtle. So, finding a knife, they proceeded to where the deer was lying.

"Let me hold him for you," cried the Coyote. Whereupon he jumped over the deer, spread out its hind legs, and placed a paw on each of them, holding the body open; and thus they began to skin the deer. When they had finished this work, the Coyote turned to the Turtle and asked: "How much of him are you going to give me?"

"The usual parts that fall to anyone who comes along when the hunter is skinning a deer," replied the Turtle.

"What parts?" eagerly asked the Coyote.

"Stomach and liver," replied the Turtle, briefly.

"I won't take that," whined the Coyote. "I want you to give me half of the deer."

"I'll do no such thing," replied the Turtle. "I killed the deer; you only helped to skin him, and you ought to be satisfied with my liberality in giving you the stomach and liver alone. I'll throw in a little fat, to be sure, and some of the intestines; but I'll give you no more."

"Yes, you will, too," snarled the Coyote, showing his teeth.

"Oh, will I?" replied the Turtle, deliberately, hauling in one or two of his flippers.

"Yes, you will; or I'll simply murder you, that's all."

The Turtle immediately pulled his feet, head, and tail in, and cried: "I tell you, I'll give you nothing but the stomach and liver and some of the intestines of this deer!"

"Well, then, I will forthwith kill you!" snapped the Coyote, and he made a grab for the Turtle. *Kopo!* sounded his teeth as they struck on the hard shell of the Turtle; and, bite as he would, the Turtle simply slipped out of his mouth every time he grabbed him. He rolled the Turtle over and over to find a good place for biting, and held him between his paws as if he were a bone, and gnawed at him; but, do his best, *kopo, kopo!* his teeth kept slipping off the Turtle's hard shell. At last he exclaimed, rather hotly: "There's more than one way of killing a beast like you!" So he set the Turtle up on end, and, catching up a quantity of sand, stuffed it into the hole where the Turtle's head had disappeared and tapped it well down with a stick until he had completely filled the crevice. "There, now," he exclaimed, with a snicker of delight. "I think I have fixed you now, old Hardshell, and served you right, too, you old stingy-box!"—whereupon he whisked away to the meat.

The Turtle considered it best to die, as it were;

but he listened intently to what was going on. The
Coyote cut up the deer and made a package of him
in his own skin. Then he washed the stomach in
a neighboring brook and filled it with choppings of
the liver and kidneys, and fat stripped from the intestines, and clots of blood, dashing in a few sprigs
of herbs here and there. Then, according to the
custom of hunters in all times, he dug an oven in
the ground and buried the stomach, in order to
make a baked blood-pudding of it while he was
summoning his family and friends to help him take
the meat home.

The Turtle clawed a little of the sand away from
his neck and peered out just a trifle. He heard
the Coyote grunting as he tried to lift the meat in
order to hang it on a branch of a neighboring pine
tree. He was just exclaiming: "What a lucky
fellow I am to come on that lame, helpless old
wretch and get all this meat from him without the
trouble of hunting for it, to be sure! Ah, my
dear children, my fine old wife, what a feast we
will have this day!"—for you know the Coyote
had a large family over the way,—he was just
exclaiming this, I say, when the Turtle cried out,
faintly: "*Natipa!*"

"You hard-coated old scoundrel! You ugly,
crooked-legged beast! You stingy-box!" snarled
the Coyote. "So you are alive, are you?"
Dropping the meat, he leaped back to where the
Turtle was lying, his head hauled in again, and,
jamming every crevice full of sand, made it hard
and firm. Then, hitting the Turtle a clip with the

tip of his nose, he sent him rolling over and over like a flat, round stone down the slope.

"This is fine treatment to receive from the hands of such a sneaking cur as that," thought the Turtle. "I think I will keep quiet this time and let him do as he pleases. But through my ingenuity I killed the deer, and it may be that through ingenuity I can keep the deer."

So the Turtle kept perfectly dead, to all appearances, and the Coyote, leaving the meat hanging on a low branch of a tree and building a fire over the oven he had excavated, whisked away with his tail in the air to his house just the other side of the mountain.

When he arrived there he cried out: "Wife, wife! Children, children! Come, quick! Great news! Killed an enormous deer today. I have made a blood-pudding in his stomach and buried it. Let us go and have a feast; then you must help me bring the meat home."

Those Coyotes were perfectly wild. The cubs, half-grown, with their tails more like sticks than brushes, trembled from the ends of their toe-nails to the tips of their stick-like tails; and they all set off—the old ones ahead, the young ones following single file—as fast as they could toward the place where the blood-pudding was buried.

Now, as soon as the old Turtle was satisfied that the Coyote had left, he dug the sand out of his collar with his tough claws, and, proceeding to the place where the meat hung, first hauled it up, piece by piece, to the very top of the tree; for Turtles

have claws, you know, and can climb, especially if
the trunk of the tree leans over, as that one did.
Having hauled the meat to the very topmost
branches of the tree, and tied it there securely, he
descended and went over to where the blood-pudding was buried. He raked the embers away from
it and pulled it out; then he dragged it off to a
neighboring ant-hill where the red fire-ants were
congregated in great numbers. Immediately they
began to rush out, smelling the cooked meat, and
the Turtle, untying the end of the stomach, chucked
as many of the ants as he could into it. Then he
dragged the pudding back to the fire and replaced
it in the oven, taking care that the coals should not
get near it.

He had barely climbed the tree again and nestled
himself on his bundle of meat, when along came
those eager Coyotes. Everything stuck up all
over them with anxiety for the feast—their hair,
the tips of their ears, and the points of their tails;
and as they neared the place and smelt the blood
and the cooked meat, they began to sing and dance
as they came along, and this was what they sang:

> " *Na-ti tsa, na-ti tsa!*
> *Tui-ya si-si na-ti tsa!*
> *Tui-ya si-si na-ti tsa!*
> *Tui-ya si-si! Tui-ya si-si!*"

We will have to translate this—which is so old
that who can remember exactly what it means?—
thus:

> Meat of the deer, meat of the deer!
> Luscious fruit-like meat of the deer!

> Luscious fruit-like meat of the deer !
> Luscious fruit-like !   Luscious fruit-like !

No sooner had they neared the spot where they smelt the meat than, without looking around at all, they made a bound for it. But the old Coyote grabbed the hindmost of the young ones by the ear until he yelped, shook him, and called out to all the rest : "Look you here ! Eat in a decent manner or you will burn your chops off ! I stuffed the pudding full of grease, and the moment you puncture it, the grease, being hot, will fly out and burn you. Be careful and dignified, children. There is plenty of time, and you shall be satisfied. Don't gorge at the first helping !"

But the moment the little Coyotes were freed, they made a grand bounce for the tempting stomach, tearing it open, and grabbing huge mouthfuls. It may be surmised that the fire-ants were not comfortable. They ran all over the lips and cheeks of the voracious little gormands and bit them until they cried out, shaking their heads and rubbing them in the sand : "*A tu-tu-tu-tu-tu-tu !*"

"There, now, did n't I tell you, little fools, to be careful? It was the grease that burnt you. Now I hope you know enough to eat a little more moderately. There's plenty of time to satisfy yourselves, I say," cried the old Coyote, sitting down on his haunches.

Then the little cubs and the old woman attacked the delicacy again. "*A tu-tu-tu-tu-tu-tu-tu !*" they exclaimed, shaking their heads and flapping their ears ; and presently they all went away and sat down, observing this wonderful hot pudding.[1]

Then the Coyote looked around and observed that the meat was gone, and, following the grease and blood spots up the tree with his eye, saw in the top the pack of meat with the Turtle calmly reclining upon it and resting, his head stretched far out on his hand. The Turtle lifted his head and exclaimed: "*Pe-sa-las-ta-i-i-i-i!*"

"You tough-hided old beast!" yelled the Coyote, in an ecstasy of rage and disappointment. "Throw down some of that meat, now, will you? I killed that deer; you only helped me skin him; and here you have stolen all the meat. Wife! Children! Didn't I kill the deer?" he cried, turning to the rest.

"Certainly you did, and he's a sneaking old wretch to steal it from you!" they exclaimed in chorus, looking longingly at the pack of meat in the top of the tree.

"Who said I stole the meat from you?" cried out the Turtle. "I only hauled it up here to keep it from being stolen, you villain! Scatter yourselves out to catch some of it. I will throw as fine a pair of ribs down to you as ever you saw. There, now, spread yourselves out and get close together. Ready?" he called, as the Coyotes lay down on their backs side by side and stretched their paws as

---

[1] It may be well to explain here that there is no more intensely painful or fiery bite known than the bite of the fire-ant or red ant of the Southwest and the tropics, named, in Zuñi, *halo*. Large pimples and blisters are raised by the bite, which is so venomous, moreover, that for the time being it poisons the blood and fills every vein of the body with burning sensations.

high as they could eagerly and tremblingly toward the meat.

"Yes, yes!" cried the Coyotes, in one voice. "We are all ready! Now, then!"

The old Turtle took up the pair of ribs, and, catching them in his beak, crawled out to the end of the branch immediately over the Coyotes, and, giving them a good fling, dropped them as hard as he could. Over and over they fell, and then came down like a pair of stones across the bodies of the Coyotes, crushing the wind out of them, so that they had no breath left with which to cry out, and most of them were instantly killed. But the two little cubs at either side escaped with only a hurt or two, and, after yelling fearfully, one of them took his tail between his legs and ran away. The other one, still very hungry, ran off with his tail lowered and his nose to the ground, sidewise, until he had got to a safe distance, and then he sat down and looked up. Presently he thought he would return and eat some of the meat from the ribs.

"Wait!" cried the old Turtle, "don't go near that meat; leave it alone for your parents and brothers and sisters. Really, I am so old and stiff that it took me a long time to get out to the end of that limb, and I am afraid they went to sleep while I was getting there, for see how still they lie."

"By my ancestors!" exclaimed the Coyote, looking at them; "that is so."

"Why don't you come up here and have a feast with me," said the Turtle, "and leave that meat alone for your brothers and sisters and your old ones?"

"How can I get up there?" whined the Coyote, crawling nearer to the tree.

"Simply reach up until you get your paw over one of the branches, and then haul yourself up," replied the Turtle.

The little Coyote stretched and jumped, and, though he sometimes succeeded in getting his paw over the branch, he fell back, *flop!* every time. And then he would yelp and sing out as though every bone in his body was broken.

"Never mind! never mind!" cried the Turtle. "I'll come down and help you." So he crawled down the tree, and, reaching over, grabbed the little Coyote by the topknot, and by much struggling he was able to climb up. When they got to the top of the tree the Turtle said: "There, now, help yourself."

The little Coyote fell to and filled himself so full that he was as round as a plum and elastic as a cranberry. Then he looked about and licked his chops and tried to breathe, but could n't more than half, and said: "Oh, my! if I don't get some water I'll choke!"

"My friend," said the Turtle, "do you see that drop of water gleaming in the sun at the end of that branch of this pine tree?" (It was really pitch.) "Now, I have lived in the tops of trees so much that I know where to go. Trees have springs. Look at that."

The Coyote looked and was convinced.

"Walk out, now, to the end of the branch, or until you come to one of those drops of water, then take it in your mouth and suck, and all the water you want will flow out."

The little Coyote started. He trembled and was unsteady on his legs, but managed to get half way. "Is it here?" he called, turning round and looking back.

"No, a little farther," said the Turtle.

So he cautiously stepped a little farther. The branch was swaying dreadfully. He turned his head, and just as he was saying, "Is it here?" he lost his balance and fell plump to the ground, striking so hard on the tough earth that he was instantly killed.

"There, you wretched beast!" said the old Turtle with a sigh of relief and satisfaction. "Ingenuity enabled me to kill a deer. Ingenuity enabled me to retain the deer."

It must not be forgotten that one of the little Coyotes ran away. He had numerous descendants, and ever since that time they have been characterized by pimples all over their faces where the mustaches grow out, and little blotches inside of their lips, such as you see inside the lips of dogs.

Thus shortens my story.

THE COYOTE AND THE LOCUST

IN the days of the ancients, there lived south of Zuñi, beyond the headland of rocks, at a place called Suski-ashokton ("Rock Hollow of the Coyotes"), an old Coyote. And this side of the headland of rocks, in the bank of a steep arroyo, lived an old Locust, near where stood a piñon tree, crooked and so bereft of needles that it was sunny.

One day the Coyote went out hunting, leaving his large family of children and his old wife at home. It was a fine day and the sun was shining brightly, and the old Locust crawled out of his home in the loam of the arroyo and ascended to one of the bare branches of the piñon tree, where, hooking his feet firmly into the bark, he began to sing and play his flute. The Coyote in his wanderings came along just as he began to sing these words:

> " *Tchumali, tchumali, shohkoya,*
>   *Tchumali, tchumali, shohkoya !*
>   *Yaamii heeshoo taatani tchupatchinte,*
>   *Shohkoya,*
>   *Shohkoya !* "

> Locust, locust, playing a flute,
> Locust, locust, playing a flute !
>   Away up above on the pine-tree bough,
>   closely clinging,
>   Playing a flute,
>   Playing a flute !

"Delight of my senses!" called out the Coyote,

squatting down on his haunches, and looking up, with his ears pricked and his mouth grinning; " Delight of my senses, how finely you play your flute!"

" Do you think so?" said the Locust, continuing his song.

"Goodness, yes!" cried the Coyote, shifting nearer. "What a song it is! Pray, teach it to me, so that I can take it home and dance my children to it. I have a large family at home."

"All right," said the Locust. " Listen, then." And he sang his song again:

> " *Tchumali, tchumali, shohkoya,*
> *Tchumali, tchumali, shohkoya !*
> *Yaamii heeshoo taatani tchupatchinte,*
> *Shohkoya,*
> *Shohkoya!*"

" Delightful!" cried the Coyote. " Now, shall I try?"

"Yes, try."

Then in a very hoarse voice the Coyote half growled and half sang (making a mistake here and there, to be sure) what the Locust had sung, though there was very little music in his repetition of the performance.

> " *Tchu u-mali, tchumali—shohshoh koya,*
> *Tchu tchu mali, tchumali shohkoya,*
> *Yaa mami he he shoo ta ta tante tchup patchin te,*
> *Shohkoya,*
> *Shohkoya!*"

" Ha!" laughed he, as he finished; " I have got it, have n't I?"

" Well, yes," said the Locust, " fairly well."

" Now, then, let us sing it over together."

And while the Locust piped shrilly the Coyote sang gruffly, though much better than at first, the song.

" There, now," exclaimed he, with a whisk of his tail ; " did n't I tell you ? " and without waiting to say another word he whisked away toward his home beyond the headland of rocks. As he was running along the plain he kept repeating the song to himself, so that he would not forget it, casting his eyes into the air, after the manner of men in trying to remember or to say particularly fine things, so that he did not notice an old Gopher peering at him somewhat ahead on the trail ; and the old Gopher laid a trap for him in his hole.

The Coyote came trotting along, singing : "*Shohkoya, shohkoya,*" when suddenly he tumbled heels over head into the Gopher's hole. He sneezed, began to cough, and to rub the sand out of his eyes ; and then jumping out, cursed the Gopher heartily, and tried to recall his song, but found that he had utterly forgotten it, so startled had he been.

" The lubber-cheeked old Gopher ! I wish the pests were all in the Land of Demons !" cried he. " They dig their holes, and nobody can go anywhere in safety. And now I have forgotten my song. Well, I will run back and get the old Locust to sing it over again. If he can sit there singing to himself, why can 't he sing it to me ? No doubt in the world he is still out there on that piñon branch singing away." Saying which, he ran back

17

as fast as he could. When he arrived at the piñon tree, sure enough, there was the old Locust still sitting and singing.

"Now, how lucky this is, my friend!" cried the Coyote, long before he had reached the place. "The lubber-cheeked, fat-sided old Gopher dug a hole right in my path; and I went along singing your delightful song and was so busy with it that I fell headlong into the trap he had set for me, and I was so startled that, on my word, I forgot all about the song, and I have come back to ask you to sing it for me again."

"Very well," said the Locust. "Be more careful this time." So he sang the song over.

"Good! Surely I'll not forget it this time," cried the Coyote; so he whisked about, and away he sped toward his home beyond the headland of rocks. "Goodness!" said he to himself, as he went along; "what a fine thing this will be for my children! How they will be quieted by it when I dance them as I sing it! Let's see how it runs. Oh, yes!

" *Tchumali, tchumali, shohkoya,*
Tchumali, tchumali, shohko—"

Thli-i-i-i-p, piu-piu, piu-piu! fluttered a flock of Pigeons out of the bushes at his very feet, with such a whizzing and whistling that the Coyote nearly tumbled over with fright, and, recovering himself, cursed the Doves heartily, calling them "gray-backed, useless sage-vermin"; and, between his fright and his anger, was so much shaken up that he again forgot his song.

Now, the Locust wisely concluded that this would be the case, and as he did not like the Coyote very well, having been told that sometimes members of his tribe were by no means friendly to Locusts and other insects, he concluded to play him a trick and teach him a lesson in the minding of his own affairs. So, catching tight hold of the bark, he swelled himself up and strained until his back split open ; then he skinned himself out of his old skin, and, crawling down the tree, found a suitable quartz stone, which, being light-colored and clear, would not make his skin look unlike himself. He took the stone up the tree and carefully placed it in the empty skin. Then he cemented the back together with a little pitch and left his exact counterfeit sticking to the bark, after which he flew away to a neighboring tree.

No sooner had the Coyote recovered his equanimity to some extent than, discovering the loss of his song and again exclaiming "No doubt he is still there piping away; I'll go and get him to sing it over,"—he ran back as fast as he could.

"Ah wha !" he exclaimed, as he neared the tree. "I am quite fatigued with all this extra running about. But, no matter ; I see you are still there, my friend. A lot of miserable, gray-backed Ground-pigeons flew up right from under me as I was going along singing my song, and they startled me so that I forgot it ; but I tell you, I cursed them heartily ! Now, my friend, will you not be good enough to sing once more for me ?"

He paused for a reply. None came.

"Why, what's the matter? Don't you hear me?" yelled the Coyote, running nearer, looking closely, and scrutinizing the Locust. "I say, I have lost my song, and want you to sing for me again. Will you, or will you not?" Then he paused.

"Look here, are you going to sing for me or not?" continued the Coyote, getting angry.

No reply.

The Coyote stretched out his nose, wrinkled up his lips, and snarled: "Look here, do you see my teeth? Well, I'll ask you just four times more to sing for me, and if you don't sing then, I'll snap you up in a hurry, I tell you. Will—you—sing—for me? Once. Will you sing—for me? Twice. Two more times! Look out! Will you sing for me? Are you a fool? Do you see my teeth? Only once more! Will—you—sing—for me?"

No reply.

"Well, you are a fool!" yelled the Coyote, unable to restrain himself longer, and making a quick jump, he snapped the Locust skin off of the bough, and bit it so hard that it crushed and broke the teeth in the middle of his jaw, driving some of them so far down in his gums that you could hardly see them, and crowding the others out so that they were regular tusks. The Coyote dropped the stone, rolled in the sand, and howled and snarled and wriggled with pain. Then he got up and shook his head, and ran away with his tail between his legs. So excessive was his pain that at the first brook he came to he stooped down to lap up water in order to alleviate it, and he there beheld what you and I see in the mouths of every Coyote we ever catch,—that the teeth back of the canines are all driven down, so that you can see only the points of them, and look very much broken up.

In the days of the ancients the Coyote minded not his own business and restrained not his anger. So he bit a Locust that was only the skin of one with a stone inside. And all his descendants have inherited his broken teeth. And so also to this day, when Locusts venture out on a sunny morning to sing a song, it is not infrequently their custom to protect themselves from the consequences of attracting too much attention by skinning themselves and leaving their counterparts on the trees.

Thus shortens my story.

THE COYOTE AND THE RAVENS WHO
RACED THEIR EYES

LONG, long ago, in the days of the ancients, there lived in Hómaiakwin, or the Cañon of the Cedars, a Coyote,—doubtless the same one I have told you of as having made friends with the Woodpounder bird. As you know, this cañon in which he lived is below the high eastern cliff of Face Mountain.

This Coyote was out walking one day. On leaving his house he had said that he was going hunting; but,—miserable fellow!—who ever knew a Coyote to catch anything, unless it were a prairie-dog or a wood-rat or a locust or something of the kind? So you may depend upon it he was out walking; that is, wandering around to see what he could see.

He crossed over the valley northward, with his tail dragging along in an indifferent sort of a way, until he came to the place on Thunder Mountain called Shoton-pia ("Where the Shell Breastplate Hangs"). He climbed up the foot-hills, and along the terraces at the base of the cliff, and thus happened to get toward the southeastern corner of the mountain. There is a little column of rock with a round top to it standing there, as you know, to this day.

Now, on the top of this standing rock sat two old Ravens, racing their eyes. One of them would

settle himself down on the rock and point with his
beak straight off across the valley to some pinnacle
in the cliffs of the opposite mesa. Then he would
say to his companion, without turning his head at
all : " You see that rock yonder ? Well, ahem !
Standing rock yonder, round you, go ye my eyes
and come back." Then he would lower his head,
stiffen his neck, squeeze his eyelids, and "*Pop !*"
he would say as his eyes flew out of their sockets,
and sailed away toward the rock like two streaks of
lightning, reaching which they would go round it,
and come back toward the Raven ; and as they
were coming back, he would swell up his throat
and say " *Whu-u-u-u-u-u-u*,"—whereupon his eyes
would slide with a *k'othlo !* into their sockets
again. Then he would turn toward his companion,
and swelling up his throat still more, and ducking
his head just as if he were trying to vomit his own
neck, he would laugh inordinately ; and the other
would laugh with him, bristling up all the feathers
on his body.

Then the other one would settle himself, and
say : " Ah, I 'll better you ! You see that rock
away yonder ? " Then he would begin to squeeze
his eyelids, and *thlut !* his eyes would fly out of
their sockets and away across the mesa and round
the rock he had named ; and as they flew back, he
would lower himself, and say "*Whu-u-u-u-u-u-u*,"
when *k'othlo !* the eyes would slide into their
sockets again. Then, as much amused as ever, the
Ravens would laugh at one another again.

Now, the Coyote heard the Ravens humming

their eyes back into their sockets; and the sound they made, as well as the way they laughed so heartily, exceedingly pleased him, so that he stuck his tail up very straight and laughed merely from seeing them laugh. Presently he could contain himself no longer. "Friends," he cried, in a shrieky little voice, "I say, friends, how do you do, and what are you doing?"

The Ravens looked down, and when they saw the Coyote they laughed and punched one another with their wings and cried out to him: "Bless you! Glad to see you come!"

"What is it you are doing?" asked he. "By the daylight of the gods, it is funny, whatever it is!" And he whisked his tail and laughed, as he said this, drawing nearer to the Ravens.

"Why, we are racing our eyes," said the older of the two Ravens. "Did n't you ever see anyone race his eyes before?"

"Good demons, no!" exclaimed the Coyote. "Race your eyes! How in the world do you race your eyes?"

"Why, this way," said one of the Ravens. And he settled himself down. "Do you see that tall rock yonder? Ahem! Well, tall rock, yonder,— ye my eyes go round it and return to me!" *K'othlo! k'othlo!* the eyes slipped out of their sockets, and the Raven, holding his head perfectly still, waited, with his upper lids hanging wrinkled on his lower, for the return of the eyes; and as they neared him, he crouched down, swelled up his neck, and exclaimed "*Whu-u-u-u-u-u.*" *Tsoko!*

the eyes flew into their sockets again. Then the Raven turned around and showed his two black bright eyes as good as ever. "There, now! what did I tell you?"

"By the moon!" squeaked the Coyote, and came up nearer still. "How in the world do you do that? It is one of the most wonderful and funny things I ever saw!"

"Well, here, come up close to me," said the Raven, "and I will show you how it is done." Then the other Raven settled himself down; and *pop!* went his eyes out of their sockets, round a rock still farther away. And as they returned, he exclaimed "*Whu-u-u-u-u-u-u,*" when *tsoko!* in again they came. And he turned around laughing at the Coyote. "There, now!" said he, "did n't I tell you?"

"By the daylight of the gods! I wish I could do that," said the Coyote. "Suppose I try my eyes?"

"Why, yes, if you like, to be sure!" said the Ravens. "Well, now, do you want to try?"

"Humph! I should say I did," replied the Coyote.

"Well, then, settle down right here on this rock," said the Ravens, making way for him, "and hold your head out toward that rock and say: 'Yonder rock, these my eyes go round it and return to me.'"

"I know! I know! I know!" yelled the Coyote. And he settled himself down, and squeezed and groaned to force his eyes out of his sockets, but they would not go. "Goodness!" said the

Coyote, "how can I get my eyes to go out of their sockets?"

"Why, don't you know how?" said the Ravens. "Well, just keep still, and we'll help you; we'll take them out for you."

"All right! all right!" cried the Coyote, unable to repress his impatience. "Quick! quick! here I am, all ready!" And crouching down, he laid his tail straight out, swelled up his neck, and strained with every muscle to force his eyes out of his head. The Ravens picked them out with a dexterous twist of their beaks in no time, and sent them flying off over the valley. The Coyote yelped a little when they came out, but stood his ground manfully, and cringed down his neck and waited for his eyes to come back.

"Let the fool of a beast go without his eyes," said the Ravens. "He was so very anxious to get rid of them, and do something he had no business with; let him go without them!" Whereupon they flew off across the valley, and caught up his eyes and ate them, and flew on, laughing at the predicament in which they had left the Coyote.

Now, thus the Coyote sat there the proper length of time; then he opened his mouth, and said "*Whu-u-u-u-u-u-u!*" But he waited in vain for his eyes to come back. And "*Whu-u-u-u-u-u-u-u!*" he said again. No use. "Mercy!" exclaimed he, "what can have become of my eyes? Why don't they come back?" After he had waited and "*whu-u-u-u-u-d*" until he was tired, he concluded that his eyes had got lost, and laid his head on his breast, wofully thinking of his misfortune. "How in the world shall I hunt up my eyes?" he groaned, as he lifted himself cautiously (for it must be remembered that he stood on a narrow rock), and tried to look all around; but he could n't see. Then he began to feel with his paws, one after another, to find the way down; and he slipped and fell, so that nearly all the breath was knocked out of his body. When he had recovered, he picked himself up, and felt and felt along, slowly descending, until he got into the valley.

Now, it happened as he felt his way along with his toes that he came to a wet place in the valley, not far below where the spring of Shuntakaiya flows out from the cliffs above. In feeling his way, his foot happened to strike a yellow cranberry, ripe and soft, but very cold, of course. "Ha!" said he, "lucky fellow, I! Here is one of my eyes." So he picked it up and clapped it into one of his empty sockets; then he peered up to the sky, and the light struck through it. "Did n't I tell you so, old fellow? It is one of your eyes, by the souls of your ancestors!" Then he felt around until he found another cranberry. "Ha!" said he, "and this proves it! Here is the other!" And he clapped that into the other empty socket. He did n't seem to see quite as well as he had seen before, but still the cranberries answered the purpose of eyes exceedingly well, and the poor wretch of a Coyote never knew the difference; only it was observed when he returned to his companions in the Cañon of the Cedars that he had yellow eyes instead of black ones, which everybody knows Coyotes and all other creatures had at first.

Thus it was in the days of the ancients, and hence to this day coyotes have yellow eyes, and are not always quick to see things.

Thus shortens my story.

THE PRAIRIE–DOGS AND THEIR PRIEST, THE BURROWING-OWL

ONCE, long, long ago, there stood in Prairie-dog Land a large Prairie-dog village. Prairie-dog Land is south of Zuñi, beyond Grease Mountain; and in the middle of that country, which is one of our smaller meadows, stands a mountain, which is a little mound. All round about the base of this mountain were the sky-holes and door-mounds and pathways of the grandfathers of the Prairie-dogs. In the very top of the mount was the house of an old Burrowing-owl and his wife.

One summer it rained and it rained and it rained, so that the fine fields of *mitäliko* (wild portulaca) were kept constantly fresh, and the Prairie-dogs had unfailing supplies of this, their favorite food. They became fat and happy, and gloried in the rain-storms that had produced such an abundant harvest for them. But still it kept raining, until by-and-by, when they descended to their fields of *mitäliko*, they found their feet were wet, which they did not like any more than Prairie-dogs like it today.

Now, you know that in some parts of the meadow of Prairie-dog Land are little hollows, in which the water collects when it rains hard. Just in these places were the fields of *mitäliko*. And still it rained and rained, until finally only the tops of the plants appeared above the waters.

Then the Prairie-dogs began to curse the rain and to fall off in flesh, for they could no longer go to the fields to collect food, and the stores in their granaries were running low. At last they grew very hungry and lean and could hardly get about, for it rained and rained day after day, so that they dare not go away from their holes, and their stores were all gone.

The old ones among the Prairie-dogs, the grandfathers, called a great council; three or four of them came out of their houses, stood up on the mounds in front of their sky-holes, and called out "*Wek wek,—wek wek,—wek wek,—wek wek!*" in shrill, squeaky voices, so that the women and children in the holes round about exclaimed: "Goodness, gracious! the old ones are calling a council!" And everybody trooped to the council, which was gathered round the base of the Burrowing-owl's mountain.

"Now," said the chief spokesman or counsellor, "you see those wretched rainers keep dropping water until our fields of *mitàliko* are flooded. They ought to know that we are short of leg, and that we can't go into the lakes to gather food, and here we are starving. Our women are dying, our children are crying, and we can scarcely go from door to door. Now, what is to be done? How can we stop the rain?—that is the question."

They talked and talked; they devised many plans, which were considered futile, most of them having been tried already. At last a wise old gray-cheeked fellow suggested that it would be well to apply to their grandfather, the Burrowing-owl, who lived in the top of the mountain.

"Hear! hear!" cried the council in one voice,—whereupon the old man who had spoken was chosen as messenger to the Burrowing-owl.

He climbed to the top of the mountain, with many a rest, and at last got near the doorway, and sitting down at a respectful distance, raised himself on his haunches, folded his hands across his breast, then cried out: "*Wek wek,—wek wek!*"

The old grandfather Burrowing-owl, not in very good humor, stepped out, blinking his eyes and asked what was the matter. He said: "It is n't your custom to come up to my house and make such a racket, though true enough it is that I hear your rackets down below. It cannot be for nothing that you come; therefore, what is your message?"

"My grandfather," said the Prairie-dog, "in council we have considered how to stop the irrepressible rainers; but all of our efforts and devices are quite futile, so that we are forced to apply to you."

"Ah, indeed," said the old Owl, scratching the corner of his eye with his claw. "Go down home, and I will see what I can do tomorrow morning. As you all know very well, I am a priest. I will set aside four days for fasting and meditation and sacred labors. Please await the result."

The old Prairie-dog humbly bade him farewell and departed for his village below.

Next morning the Burrowing-owl said to his

wife: "Put on a large quantity of beans, my old one, and cook them well,—small beans, of the kind that smell not pleasantly." He then bade her "Good morning," and left. He went about for a long time, hunting at the roots of bushes. At last he found one of those ill-smelling Beetles, with its head stuck way down in the midst of the roots. He grabbed him up, notwithstanding the poor creature's remonstrances, and took him home.

When he arrived there, said he: "My friend, it seems to me you are making a great fuss about this thing, but I am not going to hurt you, except in one way,—by the presentation to you of all the food you can eat."

"Bless me!" said the Tip-beetle, bobbing his head down into the ground and rearing himself into the air. Then he sat down quite relieved and contented.

"Old woman," said the Burrowing-owl, "lay out a dish of the beans on the floor." The wife complied. "My friend," said the Burrowing-owl to the Tip-beetle, "fall to and satisfy yourself."

The Tip-beetle, with another tip, sat down before the bowl of beans. He ate, and swallowed, and gulped until he had entirely emptied the dish, and began to grow rather full of girth.

"Not yet satisfied?" asked the Owl. "Old woman, lay out another bowl."

Another large bowl of the bean soup was placed before the Tip-beetle, who likewise gulped and gulped at this, and at last diminished it to nothing. Now, the Tip-beetle by this time looked like a well-blown-up paunch. Still, when the old Owl remarked " Is there left of your capacity ? " he replied : " Somewhat ; by the favor of a little more, I think I shall be satisfied."

" Old woman," said the Owl, " a little more."

The old woman placed another bowl before the Tip-beetle ; and he ate and ate, and swallowed and swallowed, and gulped and sputtered ; but with all the standing up and wiggling of his head that he could do he could not finish the bowl ; and at last, wiping the perspiration from his brow, he exclaimed : " Thanks, thanks, I am satisfied."

" Ha, indeed ! " said the Owl. Both the old woman and the Tip-beetle had noticed, while the feast was going on, that the Owl had cut out a good-sized round piece of buckskin, and he was running a thread round about the edge of it, leaving two strings at either side, like the strings with which one draws together a pouch. Just as the Tip-beetle returned his thanks the old Owl had finished his work.

" My friend," said he, turning to the Tip-beetle, " you have feasted to satisfaction, and it appears to me by your motions that you are exceedingly uncomfortable, being larger of girth than is safe and well for a Tip-beetle. Perhaps you are not aware that one who eats freely of bean soup is likely to grow still larger. I would advise you, therefore, when I lay this pouch on the floor, with the mouth of it toward you, to run your head into it and exhale as much wind as possible ; and to facilitate this I will squeeze you slightly."

8

The Tip-beetle was not very well pleased with the proposition; still he by no means refused to comply.

"You see," continued the Owl, "you are at once to be relieved of the serious consequences of your gluttony, while at the same time paying for your food."

"Now, this is an excellent idea, upon my word," replied the Tip-beetle, and forthwith he thrust himself into the bag. The old Owl embraced the Tip-beetle and gently squeezed him, increasing the pressure as time went on, until a large amount of his girth had been diminished; but behold! the girth of the bag was swelled until it was so full with struggling wind that it could hardly be tied up! Outside, the rain was rattling, rattling.

Said the old Owl to the Tip-beetle: "My friend, if you do not mind the rain, which I dare say you do not, you may now return to your home. Many thanks for your assistance."

The Tip-beetle, likewise with expression of thanks, took his departure.

When the morning of the fourth day came, and the rain still continued, in fact increased, the old Owl took the bag of wind out to the mount before his doorway.

Now, you know that if one goes near a Tip-beetle and disturbs him, that Tip-beetle will rear himself on his hands and head and disgorge breath of so pungent a nature that nobody can withstand it. Woe to the nose of that man who is in the neighborhood! It will be so seared with this over-powering odor that it cannot sneeze, though desiring never so much to do so.   You know, also, if you touch a Tip-beetle who is angry, all the good water in Zuñi River will not remove from your fingers the memory of that Beetle, whenever you chance to smell of them. And you know, also, how small stewed beans with thick skins affect one.   Conceive, then, the power of the medicine contained in that little bag.

The old Owl, taking up a stick, hit the bag one whack.   The clouds, before so thick, glaring with lightning, trembling and swirling with thunder, now began to thin out in the zenith and depart, and the sunlight sifted through.   The Owl hit the bag another stroke,—behold, afar off scudded the clouds as before a fierce blast.   Again the old Owl hit the bag.   The clouds were resting on the far away mountain-tops before he had lowered his stick. Then, with one mighty effort, he gave the bag a final whack, wholly emptying it of its contents, and the sky was as clear as it is on a summer's day in the noon-time of a drought.   So potent was this all-penetrating and irresistible odor, that even the Rain-gods themselves could not withstand it, and withdrew their forces and retired before it.

Out from their holes trooped the Prairie-dogs, and sitting up on their haunches all round about the mountain, they shouted at the tops of their shrill voices, "*Wek wek,—wek wek,—wek wek!*" in praise of their great priest, the Grandfather Bur-rowing-owl.

Behold, thus it was in the days of the ancients.

And for that reason prairie-dogs and burrowing-owls have always been great friends. And the burrowing-owls consider no place in the world quite so appropriate for the bringing forth, hatching, and rearing of their children as the holes of the prairie-dogs.

Thus shortens my story.

HOW THE GOPHER RACED WITH THE RUNNERS OF K'IÁKIME

THERE was a time in the days of the ancients when the runners of K'iákime were famed above those of all other cities in the Valley of Shí-wina for their strength, endurance, and swiftness of foot. In running the *tikwa,* or kicked-stick race, they overcame, one after another, the runners of Shíwina or Zuñi, of Mátsaki or the Salt City, of Pínawa or the Town of the Winds, and in fact all who dared to challenge them or to accept their challenges.

The people of Shíwina and Mátsaki did not give up easily. They ran again and again, only to be beaten and to lose the vast piles of goods and precious things which they had staked or bet; and at last they were wholly disheartened and bereft of everything which without shame a man might exhibit for betting.

So the people of the two towns called a council, and the old men and runners gathered and discussed what could be done that the runners of K'iákime might be overcome. They thought of all the wise men and wise beings they knew of; one after another of them was mentioned, and at last a few prevailed in contending that for both wisdom and cunning or craft the Gopher took precedence over all those who had been mentioned. Forthwith a young man was dispatched to find an old Gopher who lived on the side of the hill near which the race-course began.

He was out sunning himself, and finishing a cellar, when the young man approached him, and he called out : " Ha, grandson ! Don't bother me this morning ; I am busy digging my cellars."

The young man insisted that he came with an important message from his people. So the old Gopher ceased his work, and listened attentively while the young man related to him the difficulties they were in.

Said he : " Go back, my grandson, and tell your people to challenge the runners of K'iákime to run the race of the kicked stick with a runner whom they have chosen, a single one, the fourth day from this day ; and tell your people, moreover, that I will run the race for them, providing only that the runners of K'iákime will permit me to go my own way, on my own road, which as you know runs underground."

The youth thanked the old Gopher and was about to retire when the fat-sided, heavy-cheeked old fellow called to him to hold on a little. " Mind you," said he. " Tell your people also that they shall bet for me only two things—red paint and sacred yellow pollen. These shall, as it were, be the payment for my exertions, if I win, as I prize this sort of possession above all else."

The young man returned and reported what the Gopher had said. Thereupon the people of Shíwina and Mátsaki sent a challenge to the people of K'iákime for a race, saying : " We bet all that we

have against what you have won from us from time
to time that our runner, the Gopher, who lives beside
the beginning of our race-course, will beat you in
the race, which we propose shall be the fourth day
from this day. The only condition we name is,
that the Gopher shall be permitted to run in his
own way, on his own road, which is underground."

Right glad were the runners of K'iákime to run
against anyone proposed by those whom they had
so often beaten. They hesitated not a moment in
replying that they would run against the Gopher or
any other friend of the people of Mátsaki and Shíwina, stipulating only that the Gopher, if he ran
underground, should appear at the surface occasionally, that they might know where he was. So
it was arranged, and the acceptance of the challenge was reported to the Gopher, and the stipu-
lation also which was named by the runners of
K'iákime.

That night the old Gopher went to his younger
brother, old like himself, heavy-cheeked, gray-and-
brown-coated, and dusty with diggings of his cellars. " My younger brother," said the old Gopher,
"the fourth day from this day I am to run a race.
I shall start at the beginning of the race-course of
the people of K'iákime over here, which is near my
home, as you know. There I shall dig two holes ;
one at the beginning of the race-course, the other
a little farther on. Now, here at your home, near
the Place of the Scratching Bushes, do you dig a
hole, down below where the race-course passes
your place, off to one side of it, and another hole a

little beyond the first.   The means by which I shall be distinguished as a racer will be a red plume tied to my head.   Do you also procure a red plume and tie it to your head.   When you hear the thundering of the feet of the racers, run out and show yourself for a minute, and rush into the other hole as fast as you can."

" I understand what you would have of me, and right gladly will I do it.   It would please me exceedingly to take down the pride of those haughty runners of K'iákime, or at least to help in doing it," replied the younger brother.

The old Gopher went on to the Sitting Space of the Red Shell, where dwelt another of his younger brothers precisely like himself and the one he had already spoken to, near whose home the race-course also ran.   To him he communicated the same information, and gave the same directions.   Then he went on still farther to the place called K'ópak'yan, where dwelt another of his younger brothers.   To him also he gave the same directions ; and to still another younger brother, who dwelt beneath the base of the two broad pillars of Thunder Mountain, at the last turning-point of the race-course ; and to another brother, who dwelt at the Place of the Burnt Log ; and lastly to another brother quite as cunning and inventive as himself, who dwelt just below K'iákime where the race-course turned toward its end.   When all these arrangements had been made, the old Gopher went back and settled himself comfortably in his nest.

Bright and early on the fourth day preparations were made for the race. The runners of K'iákime had been fasting and training in the sacred houses, and they came forth stripped and begirt for the racing, carrying their stick. Then came the people of Mátsaki and Shíwina, who gathered on the plain, and there they waited. But they waited not long, for soon the old Gopher appeared close in their midst, popping out of the ground, and on his head was a little red plume. He placed the stick which had been prepared for him, on the ground, where he could grab it with his teeth easily, saying : " Of course, you will excuse me if I do not kick my stick, since my feet are so short that I could not do so. On the other hand," he said to the runners, " you do not have to dig your way as I do. Therefore, we are evenly matched."

The runners of K'iákime, contemptuously laughing, asked him why he did not ask for some privilege instead of talking about things which meant nothing to them.

At last the word was given. With a yell and a spring, off dashed the racers of K'iákime, gaily kicking their stick before them. Grabbing his stick in his teeth, into the ground plunged the old Gopher. Fearful lest their runner should be beaten, the people of Shíwina and Mátsaki ran to a neighboring hill, watching breathlessly for him to appear somewhere in the course of the race above the plain. Away over the plain in a cloud of dust swept the runners of K'iákime. They were already far off, when suddenly, some distance before them, out of the ground in the midst of the race-course, popped the old Gopher, to all appearance, the red plume dusty, but waving proudly on his forehead. After looking round at the runners, into the ground he plunged again. The people of Shíwina and Mátsaki yelled their applause. The runners of K'iákime, astounded that the Gopher should be ahead of them, redoubled their efforts. When they came near the Place of the Red Shell, behold! somewhat muddy round the eyes and nose, out popped the old Gopher again, to all appearance. Of course it was his brother, the red plume somewhat heavy with dirt, but still waving on his forehead.

On rushed the runners, and they had no sooner neared K'ópak'yan than again they saw the Gopher in advance of them, now apparently covered with sweat,—for this cunning brother had provided himself with a little water which he rubbed over his fur and made it all muddy, as though he were perspiring and had already begun to grow tired. He came out of his hole and popped into the other less quickly than the others had done; and the runners, who were not far behind him, raised a great shout and pushed ahead. When they thought they had gained on him, behold! in their pathway, all bedraggled with mud, apparently the same old Gopher appeared, moving with some difficulty, and then disappeared under the ground again. And so on, the runners kept seeing the Gopher at intervals, each time a little worse off than before, until they came to the last turning-place; and just as they reached it, almost in their midst appeared the most bedraggled and worn out of all the Gophers. They, seeing the red plume on his crest, almost obscured by mud and all flattened out, regarded him as surely the same old Gopher.

Finally, the original old Gopher, who had been quietly sleeping meanwhile, roused himself, and besoaking himself from the tip of his nose to the end of his short tail, wallowed about in the dirt until he was well plastered with mud, half closing his eyes, and crawled out before the astonished multitude at the end of the goal, a sorry-looking object indeed, far ahead of the runners, who were rapidly approaching. A great shout was raised by those who were present, and the runners of K'iákime for the first time lost all of their winnings, and had the swiftness, or at least all their confidence, taken out of them, as doth the wind lose its swiftness when its legs are broken.

Thus it was in the days of the ancients. By the skill and cunning of the Gopher—who, by digging his many holes and pitfalls, is the opponent of all runners, great and small—was the race won against the swiftest runners among the youth of our ancients. Therefore, to this day the young runners of Zuñi, on going forth to prepare for a race, take with them the sacred yellow pollen and red paint ; and they make for the gophers, round about the race-course in the country, beautiful little plumes, and they speak to them speeches in prayer, saying : " Behold, O ye Gophers of the plains and the trails, we race! And that we may have thy aid, we give ye these things, which are unto ye and your kind most precious, that ye will cause to fall into your holes and crannies and be hidden away in the dark and the dirt the sticks that are kicked by our opponents."

Thus shortens my story.

HOW THE RATTLESNAKES CAME TO
BE WHAT THEY ARE

KNOW you that long, long ago there lived at Yathlpew'nan, as live there now, many Rattlesnakes ; but then they were men and women, only of a Rattlesnake kind.

One day the little children of one of the houses there wished to go out to play at sliding down the sand-banks south of the Bitter Pond on the other side of our river. So they cried out to their parents : " Let us go, O mother, grandmother, father ! and take our little sister to play on the sunny side of the sand-banks."

" My children," said the mother, " go if you wish, but be very careful of your little sister ; for she is young. Carry her gently on your shoulders, and place her where she will be safe, for she is very small and helpless."

" Oh, yes ! " cried the children. " We love our little sister, don't we, little one ? " said they, turning to the baby girl. Then they took her up in their mantles, and carried her on their shoulders out to the sunny side of the sand-banks ; and there they began to play at sliding one after another.

The little girl, immensely delighted with their sport, toddled out from the place where they had set her down, just as one of the girls was speeding down the side of the sand-hill. The little creature ran, clapping her hands and laughing, to catch her sister as she came ; and the elder one, trying in vain to stop herself, called out to her to beware ; but she was a little thing, and knew not the meaning of her sister's warning ; and, alas ! the elder one slid down upon her, knocked her over and rolled her in the sand, crushing her so that she died, and rolling her out very small.

The children all gathered around their little sister, and cried and cried. Finally they took her up tenderly, and, placing her on their shoulders, sang as they went slowly toward home :

> " *Tchi-tola tsaaana !*
> *Tchi-tola tsaaana !*
> *Tchi-tola tsaaana !*
>
> *Ama ma hama seta !*
> *Ama ma hama seta !*"

> Rattlesnake little-little !
> Rattlesnake little-little !
> Rattlesnake little-little !
> Alas, we bear her !
> Alas, we bear her !

As they approached the village of the Rattlesnakes, the mother of the little one looked out and saw them coming and heard their song.

"O, my children ! my children !" she cried. "Ye foolish little ones, did I not tell ye to beware and to be careful, O, my children ?" Then she exclaimed—rocking herself to and fro, and wriggling from side to side at the same time, casting her hands into the air, and sobbing wildly—

" *Ayaa mash toki !*
Ayaa mash toki !
Hai ! i i i i ! " [1]

and fell in a swoon, still wriggling, to the ground.

When the old grandmother saw them coming, she too said :

" *Ayaa mash toki !*
Ayaa mash toki !
Hai ! i i i i ! "

And as one after another in that village saw the little child, so beloved, brought home thus mutilated and dead, each cried out as the others had cried :

" *Ayaa mash toki !*
Ayaa mash toki !
Hai ! i i i i ! "

and all swooned away ; and the children also who were bringing the little one joined in the cry of woe, and swooned away. And when they all returned to life, behold, they could not arise, but went wriggling along the ground, faintly crying, as Rattlesnakes wriggle and cry to this day.

So you see that once—as was the case with many, if not all, of the animals—the Rattlesnakes were a people, and a splendid people too. Therefore we kill them not needlessly, nor waste the lives even of other animals without cause.

Thus shortens my story.

---

[1] It is impossible to translate this exclamation, as it is probably archaic, and it is certainly the intention that its meaning shall not be plain. Judging from its etymology, I should think that its meaning might be :

" Oh, alas ! our little maiden !
Oh, alas ! our little maiden !
Ala-a-a-a-a-s ! "

HOW THE CORN-PESTS WERE ENSNARED

IN the days of the ancients, long, long ago, there lived in our town, which was then called the Middle Ant Hill of the World, a proud maiden, very pretty and very attractive, the daughter of one of the richest men among our people. She had every possession a Zuñi maiden could wish for, —blankets and mantles, embroidered dresses and sashes, buckskins and moccasins, turquoise earrings and shell necklaces, bracelets so many you could not count them. She had her father and mother, brothers and sisters, all of whom she loved very much. Why, therefore, should she care for anything else?

There was only one thing to trouble her. Behold! it came of much possession, for she had large corn-fields, so large and so many that those who planted and worked them for her could not look after them properly, and no sooner had the corn ears become full and sweet with the milk of their being than all sorts of animals broke into those fields and pulled down the corn-stalks and ate up the sweet ears of corn. Now, how to remove this difficulty the poor girl did not know.

Yes, now that I think of it, there was another thing that troubled her very much, fully as much as did the corn-pests,—pests of another kind, however, for there was n't an unmarried young man in all the valley of our ancients who was not running mad over the charms of this girl. Besides all that, not a few of them had an eye on so many possessions, and thought her home would n't be an uncomfortable place to live in. So they never gave the poor girl any peace, but hung round her house, and came to visit her father so constantly that at last she determined to put the two pests together and call them one, and thereby get rid, if possible, of one or the other. So, when these young men were very importunate, she would say to them, "Look you! if any one of you will go to my cornfields, and destroy or scare away, so that they will never come back again, the pests that eat up my corn, him I will marry and cherish, for I shall respect his ability and ingenuity."

The young men tried and tried, but it was of no use. Before long, everybody knew of this singular proposition.

There was a young fellow who lived in one of the outer towns, the poorest of the poor among our people ; and not only that, but he was so ugly that no woman would ever look at him without laughing.

Now, there are two kinds of laugh with women. One of them is a very good sort of thing, and makes young men feel happy and conceited. The other kind is somewhat heartier, but makes young men feel depressed and very humble. It need not be asked which kind was laughed by the women when they saw this ugly, ragged, miserable-looking young man. He had bright twinkling eyes, however, and that means more than all else sometimes.

Now, this young man came to hear of what was going on. He had no present to offer the girl, but he admired her as much as—yes, a good deal more than—if he had been the handsomest young man of his time. So just in the way that he was he went to the house of this girl one evening. He was received politely, and it was noticeable to the old folks that the girl seemed rather to like him,— just as it is noticeable to you and me today that what people have they prize less than what they have not. The girl placed a tray of bread before the young man and bade him eat ; and after he had done, he looked around with his twinkling little eyes. And the old man said, " Let us smoke together." And so they smoked.

By-and-by the old man asked if he were not thinking of something in coming to the house of a stranger. And the young man replied, it was very true ; he had thoughts, though he felt ashamed to say it, but he even wished to be accepted as a suitor for his daughter.

The father referred the matter to the girl, and she said she would be very well satisfied ; then she took the young man aside and spoke a few words to him,—in fact, told him what were the conditions of his becoming her accepted husband. He smiled, and said he would certainly try to the best of his ability, but this was a very hard thing she asked.

" I know it is," said the girl ; " that is why I ask it."

Now, the young man left the house forthwith. The next day he very quietly went down into the corn-fields belonging to the girl, and over toward the northern mesa, for that is where her corn-fields were—lucky being ! He dug a great deep pit with a sharp stick and a bone shovel. Now, when he had dug it—very smooth at the sides and top it was—he went to the mountain and got some poles, placing them across the hole, and over these poles he spread earth, and set up corn-stalks just as though no hole had been dug there ; then he put some exceedingly tempting bait, plenty of it, over the center of these poles, which were so weak that nobody, however light of foot, could walk over them without breaking through.

Night came on, and you could hear the Coyotes begin to sing ; and the whole army of pests—Bears, Badgers, Gophers, all sorts of creatures, as they came down slowly, each one in his own way, from the mountain. The Coyotes first came into the field, being swift of foot ; and one of them, nosing around and keeping a sharp lookout for watchers, happened to espy those wonderfully tempting morsels that lay over the hole.

" Ha !" said he (Coyotes don't think much what they are doing), and he gave a leap, when in he went—sticks, dirt, bait, and all—to the bottom of the hole. He picked himself up and rubbed the sand out of his eyes, then began to jump and jump, trying to get out ; but it was of no use, and he set up a most doleful howl.

He had just stopped for breath, when a Bear came along. " What in the name of all the devils and witches are you howling so for ?" said he. " Where are you ?"

The Coyote swallowed his whimpers immediately, set himself up in a careless attitude, and cried out: "Broadfoot, lucky, lucky, lucky fellow! Did you hear me singing? I am the happiest creature on the face of the earth, or rather under it."

"What about? I should n't think you were happy, to judge from your howling."

"Why! Mercy on me!" cried the Coyote, "I was singing for joy."

"How 's that?" asked the Bear.

"Why," said the Coyote, "I came along here this evening and by the merest accident fell into this hole. And what do you suppose I found down here? Green-corn, meat, sweet-stuff, and everything a corn-eater could wish for. The only thing I lacked to complete my happiness was someone to enjoy the meal with me. Jump in!—it is n't very deep—and fall to, friend. We 'll have a jolly good night of it."

So the old Bear looked down, drew back a minute, hesitated, and then jumped in. When the Bear got down there, the Coyote laid himself back, slapped his thighs, and laughed and laughed and laughed. "Now, get out if you can," said he to the Bear. "You and I are in a pretty mess. I fell in here by accident, it is true, but I would give my teeth and eyes if I could get out again!"

The Bear came very near eating him up, but the Coyote whispered something in his ear. "Good!" yelled the Bear. "Ha! ha! ha! Excellent idea! Let us sing together. Let them come!"

So they laughed and sang and feasted until they

attracted almost every corn-pest in the fields to the spot to see what they were doing. " Keep away, my friends," cried out the Coyote. " No such luck for you. We got here first. Our spoils ! "

" Can 't I come ? " " Can 't I come ? " cried out one after another.

" Well, yes,—no,—there may not be enough for you all." " Come on, though ; come on ! who cares ? "—cried out the old Bear. And they rushed in so fast that very soon the pit-hole was almost full of them, scrambling to get ahead of one another, and before they knew their predicament they were already in it. The Coyote laughed, shuffled around, and screamed at the top of his voice ; he climbed up over his grandfather the Bear, scrambled through the others, which were snarling and biting each other, and, knowing what he was about, skipped over their backs, out of the hole, and ran away laughing as hard as he could.

Now, the next morning down to the corn-field came the young man. Drawing near to the pit he heard a tremendous racket, and going to the edge and peering in he saw that it was half filled with the pests which had been destroying the corn of the maiden,—every kind of creature that had ever meddled with the corn-fields of man, there they were in that deep pit ; some of them all tired out, waiting for " the end of their daylight," others still jumping and crawling and falling in their efforts to get out.

" Good ! good ! my friends," cried the young man. " You must be cold ; I 'll warm you up a little." So he gathered a quantity of dry wood and threw it into the pit. "Be patient! be patient!" said he. "I hope I don't hurt any of you. It will be all over in a few minutes." Then he lighted the wood and burned the rascals all up. But he noticed the Coyote was not there. "What does it matter?" said he. "One kind of pest a man can fight, but not many."

So he went back to the house of the girl and reported to her what he had done. She was so pleased she hardly knew how to express her gratitude, but said to the young man with a smile on her face and a twinkle in her eye, "Are you quite sure they were all there?"

"Why, they were all there except the Coyote," said the young man; "but I must tell you the truth, and somehow he got out or did n't get in."

"Who cares for a Coyote!" said the girl. "I would much rather marry a man with some ingenuity about him than have all the Coyotes in the world to kill." Whereupon she accepted this very ugly but ingenious young man; and it is notable that ever since then pretty girls care very little how their husbands look, being pretty enough themselves for both. But they like to have them able to think and guess at a way of getting along occasionally. Furthermore, what does a rich girl care for a rich young man? Ever since then, even to this day, as you know, rich girls almost invariably pick out poor young men for their husbands, and rich young men are sure to take a fancy to poor girls.

Thus it was in the days of the ancients. The Coyote got out of the trap that was set for him by the ugly young man. That is the reason why coyotes are so much more abundant than any other corn-pests in the land of Zuñi, and do what you will, they are sure to get away with some of your corn, anyhow.

Thus shortens my story.

JACK-RABBIT AND COTTONTAIL

ANCIENTLY the Jack-rabbit lived in a sage plain, and the Cottontail rabbit lived in a cliff hard by. They saw the clouds gather, so they went out to sing. The long-legged Jack-rabbit sang for snow, thus:

> " *U pi na wi sho, U pi na wi sho,*
> *U kuk uku u kuk!* "

But the short-legged Cottontail sang for rain, like this:

> " *Hatchi ethla ho na an saia.*"

That 's what they sung—one asking for snow, the other for rain; hence to this day the Pók'ia (Jack-rabbit) runs when it snows, the Â'kshiko (Cottontail) when it rains.

Thus shortens my story.

THE RABBIT HUNTRESS AND HER ADVENTURES

IT was long ago, in the days of the ancients, that a poor maiden lived at K'yawana Tehua-tsana ("Little Gateway of Zuñi River"). You know there are black stone walls of houses standing there on the tops of the cliffs of lava, above the narrow place through which the river runs, to this day.

In one of these houses there lived this poor maiden alone with her feeble old father and her aged mother. She was unmarried, and her brothers had all been killed in wars, or had died gently; so the family lived there helplessly, so far as many things were concerned, from the lack of men in their house.

It is true that in making the gardens—the little plantings of beans, pumpkins, squashes, melons, and corn—the maiden was able to do very well; and thus mainly on the products of these things the family were supported. But, as in those days of our ancients we had neither sheep nor cattle, the hunt was depended upon to supply the meat; or sometimes it was procured by barter of the products of the fields to those who hunted mostly. Of these things this little family had barely enough for their own subsistence; hence, they could not procure their supplies of meat in this way.

Long before, it had been a great house, for many were the brave and strong young men who had lived in it; but the rooms were now empty, or at best contained only the leavings of those who had lived there, much used and worn out.

One autumn day, near winter-time, snow fell, and it became very cold. The maiden had gathered brush and firewood in abundance, and it was piled along the roof of the house and down underneath the ladder which descended from the top. She saw the young men issue forth the next morning in great numbers, their feet protected by long stockings of deerskin, the fur turned inward, and they carried on their shoulders and stuck in their belts stone axes and rabbit-sticks. As she gazed at them from the roof, she said to herself: " O that I were a man and could go forth, as do these young men, hunting rabbits ! Then my poor old mother and father would not lack for flesh with which to duly season their food and nourish their lean bodies." Thus ran her thoughts, and before night, as she saw these same young men coming in, one after another, some of them bringing long strings of rabbits, others short ones, but none of them empty-handed, she decided that, woman though she was, she would set forth on the morrow to try what luck she might find in the killing of rabbits herself.

It may seem strange that, although this maiden was beautiful and young, the youths did not give her some of their rabbits. But their feelings were not friendly, for no one of them would she accept as a husband, although one after another of them had offered himself for marriage.

Fully resolved, the girl that evening sat down by the fireplace, and turning toward her aged parents, said : " O my mother and father, I see that the snow has fallen, whereby easily rabbits are tracked, and the young men who went out this morning returned long before evening heavily laden with strings of this game. Behold, in the other rooms of our house are many rabbit-sticks, and there hang on the walls stone axes, and with these I might perchance strike down a rabbit on his trail, or, if he run into a log, split the log and dig him out. So I have thought during the day, and have decided to go tomorrow and try my fortunes in the hunt, woman though I be."

"*Naïya*, my daughter," quavered the feeble old mother ; "you would surely be very cold, or you would lose your way, or grow so tired that you could not return before night, and you must not go out to hunt rabbits, woman as you are."

"Why, certainly not," insisted the old man, rubbing his lean knees and shaking his head over the days that were gone. " No, no ; let us live in poverty rather than that you should run such risks as these, O my daughter."

But, say what they would, the girl was determined. And the old man said at last : " Very well ! You will not be turned from your course. Therefore, O daughter, I will help you as best I may." He hobbled into another room, and found there some old deerskins covered thickly with fur ; and drawing them out, he moistened and carefully softened them, and cut out for the maiden long stockings, which he sewed up with sinew and the fiber of the yucca leaf. Then he selected for her from among the old possessions of his brothers and sons, who had been killed or perished otherwise, a number of rabbit-sticks and a fine, heavy stone axe. Meanwhile, the old woman busied herself in preparing a lunch for the girl, which was composed of little cakes of corn-meal, spiced with pepper and wild onions, pierced through the middle, and baked in the ashes. When she had made a long string of these by threading them like beads on a rope of yucca fiber, she laid them down not far from the ladder on a little bench, with the rabbit-sticks, the stone axe, and the deerskin stockings.

That night the maiden planned and planned, and early on the following morning, even before the young men had gone out from the town, she had put on a warm, short-skirted dress, knotted a mantle over her shoulder and thrown another and larger one over her back, drawn on the deerskin stockings, had thrown the string of corn-cakes over her shoulder, stuck the rabbit-sticks in her belt, and carrying the stone axe in her hand sallied forth eastward through the Gateway of Zuñi and into the plain of the valley beyond, called the Plain of the Burnt River, on account of the black, roasted-looking rocks along some parts of its sides. Dazzlingly white the snow stretched out before her,—not deep, but unbroken,—and when she came near the cliffs with many little cañons in them, along the northern side of the valley, she saw many a trail of rabbits running out and in among the rocks and between the bushes.

Warm and excited by her unwonted exercise, she

did not heed a coming snow-storm, but ran about
from one place to another, following the trails of
the rabbits, sometimes up into the cañons, where
the forests of piñon and cedar stood, and where
here and there she had the good fortune sometimes
to run two, three, or four rabbits into a single hollow log. It was little work to split these logs, for
they were small, as you know, and to dig out the
rabbits and slay them by a blow of the hand on
the nape of the neck, back of the ears ; and as she
killed each rabbit she raised it reverently to her
lips, and breathed from its nostrils its expiring
breath, and, tying its legs together, placed it on the
string, which after a while began to grow heavy
on her shoulders. Still she kept on, little heeding
the snow which was falling fast ; nor did she notice
that it was growing darker and darker, so intent
was she on the hunt, and so glad was she to capture
so many rabbits. Indeed, she followed the trails
until they were no longer visible, as the snow fell
all around her, thinking all the while : " How happy
will be my poor old father and mother that they
shall now have flesh to eat ! How strong will they
grow ! And when this meat is gone, that which is
dried and preserved of it also, lo ! another snow-
storm will no doubt come, and I can go out hunting again."

At last the twilight came, and, looking around,
she found that the snow had fallen deeply, there
was no trail, and that she had lost her way. True,
she turned about and started in the direction of
her home, as she supposed, walking as fast as

she could through the soft, deep snow. Yet she reckoned not rightly, for instead of going eastward along the valley, she went southward across it, and entering the mouth of the Descending Plain of the Pines, she went on and on, thinking she was going homeward, until at last it grew dark and she knew not which way to turn.

"What harm," thought she, "if I find a sheltered place among the rocks ? What harm if I remain all night, and go home in the morning when the snow has ceased falling, and by the light I shall know my way ?"

So she turned about to some rocks which appeared, black and dim, a short distance away. Fortunately, among these rocks is the cave which is known as Taiuma's Cave. This she came to, and peering into that black hole, she saw in it, back some distance, a little glowing light. "Ha, ha !" thought she ; "perhaps some rabbit-hunters like myself, belated yesterday, passed the night here and left the fire burning. If so, this is greater good fortune than I could have looked for." So, lowering the string of rabbits which she carried on her shoulder, and throwing off her mantle, she crawled in, peering well into the darkness, for fear of wild beasts ; then, returning, she drew in the string of rabbits and the mantle.

Behold ! there was a bed of hot coals buried in the ashes in the very middle of the cave, and piled up on one side were fragments of broken wood. The girl, happy in her good fortune, issued forth and gathered more sticks from the cliff-side, where dead piñons are found in great numbers, and bringing them in little armfuls one after another, she finally succeeded in gathering a store sufficient to keep the fire burning brightly all the night through. Then she drew off her snow-covered stockings of deerskin and the bedraggled mantles, and, building a fire, hung them up to dry and sat down to rest herself. The fire burned up and glowed brightly, so that the whole cave was as light as a room at night when a dance is being celebrated. By-and-by, after her clothing had dried, she spread a mantle on the floor of the cave by the side of the fire, and, sitting down, dressed one of her rabbits and roasted it, and, untying the string of corn-cakes her mother had made for her, feasted on the roasted meat and cakes.

She had just finished her evening meal, and was about to recline and watch the fire for awhile, when she heard away off in the distance a long, low cry of distress—"*Ho-o-o-o thlaia-a!*"

"Ah!" thought the girl, "someone, more belated than myself, is lost; doubtless one of the rabbit-hunters." She got up, and went nearer to the entrance of the cavern.

"*Ho-o-o-o thlaia-a!*" sounded the cry, nearer this time. She ran out, and, as it was repeated again, she placed her hand to her mouth, and cried, woman though she was, as loudly as possible : "*Li-i thlaia-a!*" ("Here!")

The cry was repeated near at hand, and presently the maiden, listening first, and then shouting, and listening again, heard the clatter of an enormous rattle. In dismay and terror she threw her hands into the air, and, crouching down, rushed into the cave and retreated to its farthest limits, where she sat shuddering with fear, for she knew that one of the Cannibal Demons of those days, perhaps the renowned Atahsaia of the east, had seen the light of her fire through the cave entrance, with his terrible staring eyes, and assuming it to be a lost wanderer, had cried out, and so led her to guide him to her place of concealment.

On came the Demon, snapping the twigs under his feet and shouting in a hoarse, loud voice : *"Ho lithlsh tâ ime !"* (" Ho, there ! So you are in here, are you ? ") *Kothl !* clanged his rattle, while, almost fainting with terror, closer to the rock crouched the maiden.

The old Demon came to the entrance of the cave and bawled out : "I am cold, I am hungry ! Let me in !" Without further ado, he stooped and tried to get in ; but, behold ! the entrance was too small for his giant shoulders to pass. Then he pretended to be wonderfully civil, and said : " Come out, and bring me something to eat."

" I have nothing for you," cried the maiden. " I have eaten my food."

" Have you no rabbits ? "

" Yes."

" Come out and bring me some of them."

But the maiden was so terrified that she dared not move toward the entrance.

" Throw me a rabbit !" shouted the old Demon.

The maiden threw him one of her precious

rabbits at last, when she could rise and go to it. He clutched it with his long, horny hand, gave one gulp and swallowed it. Then he cried out: "Throw me another!" She threw him another, which he also immediately swallowed; and so on until the poor maiden had thrown all the rabbits to the voracious old monster. Every one she threw him he caught in his huge, yellow-tusked mouth, and swallowed, hair and all, at one gulp.

"Throw me another!" cried he, when the last had already been thrown to him.

So the poor maiden was forced to say: "I have no more."

"Throw me your overshoes!" cried he.

She threw the overshoes of deerskin, and these like the rabbits he speedily devoured. Then he called for her moccasins, and she threw them; for her belt, and she threw it; and finally, wonderful to tell, she threw even her mantle, and blanket, and her overdress, until, behold, she had nothing left!

Now, with all he had eaten, the old Demon was swollen hugely at the stomach, and, though he tried and tried to squeeze himself through the mouth of the cave, he could not by any means succeed. Finally, lifting his great flint axe, he began to shatter the rock about the entrance to the cave, and slowly but surely he enlarged the hole and the maiden now knew that as soon as he could get in he would devour her also, and she almost fainted at the sickening thought. Pound, pound, pound, pound, went the great axe of the Demon as he struck the rocks.

20

In the distance the two War-gods were sitting in their home at Thla-uthla (the Shrine amid the Bushes) beyond Thunder Mountain, and though far off, they heard thus in the middle of the night the pounding of the Demon's hammer-axe against the rocks. And of course they knew at once that a poor maiden, for the sake of her father and mother, had been out hunting,—that she had lost her way and, finding a cave where there was a little fire, entered it, rebuilt the fire, and rested herself; that, attracted by the light of her fire, the Cannibal Demon had come and besieged her retreat, and only a little time hence would he so enlarge the entrance to the cave that he could squeeze even his great over-filled paunch through it and come at the maiden to destroy her. So, catching up their wonderful weapons, these two War-gods flew away into the darkness and in no time they were approaching the Descending Plain of the Pines.

Just as the Demon was about to enter the cavern, and the maiden had fainted at seeing his huge face and gray shock of hair and staring eyes, his yellow, protruding tusks, and his horny, taloned hand, they came upon the old beast, and, each one hitting him a welt with his war-club, they " ended his daylight," and then hauled him forth into the open space. They opened his huge paunch and withdrew from it the maiden's garments, and even the rabbits which had been slain. The rabbits they cast away amongst the soap-weed plants that grew on the slope at the foot of the cliff. The garments they spread out on the snow, and by their knowledge cleansed and made them perfect, even more perfect than they had been before. Then, flinging the huge body of the giant Demon down into the depths of the cañon, they turned them about and, calling out gentle words to the maiden, entered and restored her; and she, seeing in them not their usual ugly persons, but handsome youths (as like to one another as are two deer born of the same mother), was greatly comforted; and bending low, and breathing upon their hands, thanked them over and over for the rescue they had brought her. But she crouched herself low with shame that her garments were but few, when, behold! the youths went out and brought in to her the garments they had cleaned by their knowledge, restoring them to her.

Then, spreading their mantles by the door of the cave, they slept there that night, in order to protect the maiden, and on the morrow wakened her. They told her many things, and showed her many things which she had not known before, and counselled her thus: "It is not fearful that a maiden should marry; therefore, O maiden, return unto thy people in the Village of the Gateway of the River of Zuñi. This morning we will slay rabbits unnumbered for you, and start you on your way, guarding you down the snow-covered valley, and when you are in sight of your home we will leave you, telling you our names."

So, early in the morning the two gods went forth; and flinging their sticks among the soap-weed plants, behold! as though the soap-weed plants were rabbits, so many lay killed on the snow before these mighty hunters. And they gathered together great numbers of these rabbits, a string for each one of the party; and when the Sun had risen clearer in the sky, and his light sparkled on the snow around them, they took the rabbits to the maiden and presented them, saying: "We will carry each one of us a string of these rabbits." Then taking her hand, they led her out of the cave and down the valley, until, beyond on the high black mesas at the Gateway of the River of Zuñi, she saw the smoke rise from the houses of her village. Then turned the two War-gods to her, and they told her their names. And again she bent low, and breathed on their hands. Then, dropping the strings of rabbits which they had carried close beside the maiden, they swiftly disappeared.

Thinking much of all she had learned, she continued her way to the home of her father and mother; and as she went into the town, staggering under her load of rabbits, the young men and the old men and women and children beheld her with wonder; and no hunter in that town thought of comparing himself with the Maiden Huntress of K'yawana Tehua-tsana. The old man and the old woman, who had mourned the night through and sat up anxiously watching, were overcome with happiness when they saw their daughter returning; and as she laid the rabbits at their feet, she said: "Behold! my father and my mother, foolish have I been, and much danger have I passed through, because I forgot the ways of a woman and assumed the ways of a man. But two wondrous youths have taught me that a woman may be a huntress and yet never leave her own fireside. Behold! I will marry, when some good youth comes to me, and he will hunt rabbits and deer for me, for my parents and my children."

So, one day, when one of those youths who had seen her come in laden with rabbits, and who had admired her time out of mind, presented himself with a bundle at the maiden's fireside, behold! she smilingly and delightedly accepted him. And from that day to this, when women would hunt rabbits or deer, they marry, and behold, the rabbits and deer are hunted.

Thus shortens my story.

THE UGLY WILD BOY WHO DROVE THE BEAR AWAY FROM SOUTH-EASTERN MESA

IN the days of the ancients there lived with his old grandmother, not far from K'iákime, east, where the sweet wafer-bread is pictured on the rocks, a frightfully ugly boy. The color of his body and face was blue. He had a twisted nose, crooked scars of various colors ran down each side of his face, and he had a bunch of red things like peppers on his head ; in fact, in all ways he resembled the *Héhea*, or the wild men of the Sacred Dance who serve as runners to the priest-clowns.

Now, one season it had rained so much that the piñon trees were laden with nuts, and the datilas were heavy with fruit, and the gray grass and red-top were so heavy with seeds that even when the wind did not blow they bent as if in a breeze.

In vain the people of K'iákime went to the Southeastern Mesa, where the nut trees and datilas and grass grew. They could not gather the nuts and the fruit and the seeds, because of the ugly old Bear who claimed the country and its products for his own, and waxed fat thereon. Some of the people were killed by him, others were maimed, and all the rest were driven away.

One day the ugly little boy said to his grandmother: "O grandmother, I am going out to gather datilas and piñon nuts on the Southeastern Mesa."

"Child, child!" cried the grandmother, "do not go; do not, by any means, go! You know very well there is an ugly Bear there who will either kill you or maim you frightfully."

"I don't care for all that!" cried the boy; "I am going!" Whereupon he went.

He followed the trail called the Road of the Pending Meal-sack, and he climbed the crooked path up Shoyakoskwe (Southeastern Mesa), and advanced over the wide plateau. No sooner had he begun to pluck the sweet datila fruit and eat of it, and had cracked between his teeth an occasional piñon nut, than " *Wha-a-a-a!* " snarled the old Bear; and he came rushing out of the nearest thicket toward the boy.

" *U shoma kutchi kihe!* " shouted the boy. "Friend, friend, don't bite me! It'll hurt! Don't bite me! I came to make a bargain with you."

"I'd like to know why I should n't bite you!" growled the Bear. "I'll tear you to pieces. What have you come to my country for, stealing my fruit and nuts and grass-seed?"

"I came to get something to eat," replied the boy. "You have plenty."

"Indeed, I have not. I will let you pick nothing. I will tear you to pieces!" said the Bear.

"Don't, don't, and I will make a bargain with you," said the boy.

"Who should talk of bargains to me?" yelled the Bear, cracking a small pine-tree to pieces with his paws and teeth, so great was his rage.

" These things are no more yours than mine,"
said the boy, " and I 'll prove it."

" How ? " asked the Bear.

" They are mine ; they are not yours ! " cried
the boy.

" They are mine, I tell you ! They are not
yours ! " replied the Bear.

" They are mine ! " retorted the boy.

And so they might have wrangled till sunset, or
torn one another into pieces, had it not been for a
suggestion that the boy made.

" Look here ! I 'll make a proposition to you,"
said he.

" What 's that ? asked the Bear.

" Whoever is certain of his rights on this plateau
and the things that grow on it must prove it by not
being scared by anything that the other does," said
the boy.

" Ha, ha ! " laughed the Bear, in his big, coarse
voice. " That is a good plan, indeed. I am perfectly willing to stand the test."

" Well, now, one of us must run away and
hide," said the boy, " and then the other must
come on him unaware in some way and frighten
him, if he can."

" All right," said the Bear. " Who first ? "

" Just as you say," said the boy.

" Well, then, I will try you first," said the Bear,
" for this place belongs to me." Whereupon he
turned and fled into the thicket. And the boy
went around picking datilas and eating them, and
throwing the skins away. Presently the Bear

came rushing out of the thicket, snapping the trees and twigs, and throwing them about at such a rate that you would have thought there was a sand-storm raging through the forest.

> *" Ku hai yaau !*
> *Ku pekwia nu !*
> *Ha ! ha ! ha ! haaaa !"*

he exclaimed, rushing at the boy from the rear.

The boy stirred never so much as a leaf, only kept on champing his datilas.

Again the Bear retired, and again he came rushing forth and snarling out : "*Ha ! ha ! ha ! hu ! hu ! hu !*" in a terrific voice, and grabbed the boy ; but never so much as the boy's heart stirred.

" By my senses !" exclaimed the Bear ; "you are a man, and I must give it up. Now, suppose you try me. I can stand as much frightening as you, and, unless you can frighten me, I tell you you must keep away from my datila and piñon patch."

Then the boy turned on his heel and fled away toward his grandmother's house, singing as he went :

> *"Kuyaina itoshlakyanaa !*
> *Kuyaina itoshlakyanaa !"*

> He of the piñon patch frightened shall be !
> He of the piñon patch frightened shall be !

" Oh ! shall he ?" cried his grandmother. " I declare, I am surprised to see you come back alive and well."

" Hurry up, grandmother," said the boy, " and paint me as frightfully as you can."

"All right, my son; I will help you!" So she blackened the right side of his face with soot, and painted the left side with ashes, until he looked like a veritable demon. Then she gave him a stone axe of ancient time and magic power, and she said: "Take this, my son, and see what you can do with it."

The boy ran back to the mountain. The Bear was wandering around eating datilas. The boy suddenly ran toward him, and exclaimed:

> "*Ai yaaaa !*
> *He ! he ! he ! he ! he ! he ! he ! tooh !*"—

and he whacked the side of a hollow piñon tree with his axe. The tree was shivered with a thundering noise, the earth shook, and the Bear jumped as if he had been struck by one of the flying splinters. Then, recovering himself and catching sight of the boy, he exclaimed: "What a fool I am, to be scared by that little wretch of a boy!" But presently, seeing the boy's face, he was startled again, and exclaimed: "By my eyes, the Death Demon is after me, surely!"

Again the boy, as he came near, whacked with his magic axe the body of another tree, calling out in a still louder voice. The earth shook so much and the noise was so thunderous that the Bear sneezed with agitation. And again, as the boy came still nearer, once more he struck a tree a tremendous blow, and again the earth thundered and trembled more violently than ever, and the Bear almost lost his senses with fright and thought surely the Corpse Demon was coming this time. When, for the fourth time, the boy struck a tree, close to the Bear, the old fellow was thrown violently to the ground with the heaving of the earth and the bellowing of the sounds that issued forth. Picking himself up as fast as he could, never stopping to see whether it was a boy or a devil, he fled to the eastward as fast as his legs would carry him, and, as he heard the boy following him, he never stopped until he reached the Zuñi Mountains.

"There!" said the boy; "I'll chase the old rogue no farther. He's been living all these years on the mountain where more fruit and nuts and grass-seed grow than a thousand Bears could eat, and yet he's never let so much as a single soul of the town of K'iákime gather a bit."

Then the boy returned to his grandmother, and related to her what had taken place.

"Go," said she, "and tell the people of K'iá-kime, from the top of yonder high rock, that those who wish to go out to gather grass-seed and datilas and piñon nuts need fear no longer."

So the boy went out, and, mounting the high rock, informed and directed the people as follows:

"Ye of the Home of the Eagles! Ye do I now inform, whomsoever of ye would gather datilas, whomsoever of ye would gather piñon nuts, whomsoever of ye would gather grass-seed, that bread may be made, hie ye over the mountains, and gather them to your hearts' content, for I have driven the Bear away!"

A few believed in what the boy said; and some,

because he was ugly, would not believe it and would not go ; and thus were as much hindered from gathering grass-seed and nuts for daily food as if the Bear had been really there. You know people nowadays are often frightened by such a kind of Bear as this.

Thus it was in the days of the ancients. And therefore the Zuñi Mountains to this day are filled with bears ; but they rarely descend to the mesas in the southwest, being fully convinced from the experience of their ancestor that the Corpse Demon is near and continues to lie in wait for them. And our people go over the mountains as they will, even women and children, and gather datila fruit, piñon nuts, and grass-seed without hindrance.

Thus shortens my story.

THE REVENGE OF THE TWO BROTH-
ERS ON THE HÁWIKUHKWE, OR
THE TWO LITTLE ONES[1] AND
THEIR TURKEYS

(THE ORIGIN OF THE PRIESTS AND CHIEFS OF
THE DANCE OF VICTORY)

LONG, long ago, there lived on Twin Mountain,
Áhaiyúta and his younger brother, with their
grandmother. They had a large flock of Turkeys
of which they were very fond, but were not so
attentive to them as they should have been. Said
the grandmother to the boys, late one morning:
"Let your poor Turkeys out, for they will starve,
poor birds, if you do not let them out oftener."

"But they will run away, grandmother," said the
two boys, who did not fancy herding them much
of the time.

"Why should they run away?" asked the vexed
grandmother, who had a sorry enough time manag-
ing the two heedless boys. "Rest assured they
will come back when roosting-time comes, for such
is their custom."

So the Twain ran down and reluctantly let their
Turkeys go. The Turkeys were many—dirty old
hens, piping, long-legged youngsters, and noisy old

[1] This term refers to the two Gods of War, Áhaiyúta and Mátsailéma,
who, as has been seen in previous tales, were accounted immortal twin
youths of small size.

cocks; but they were all more noisy when they were let out, and not long was it before they were straying far beyond the border of woods and toward Háwikuh.

Not long after noon the flock of Turkeys strolled, gobbling and chirping, into the valley north of Háwikuh[1] where many of the people of that pueblo had corn-fields. Some young men who were resting from their hoeing heard the calls of the Turkeys, and, starting up, saw across the valley a larger flock than they had ever been wont to find. Of course they were crazy. They started up and ran as fast as they could toward the pueblo, calling out as they went what they had discovered, so that all the people in the fields began to gather in. As soon as they came within the pueblo, they sought out the Priests of the Bow and told them what they had discovered.

Very quickly ran the priests to the tops of the houses, and they began to call out to their people: "Ye we would this day make wise, for our sons tell us of many Turkeys in the valley over the hill; so hasten ye to gather together good bows and arrows, boomerangs, and strings, that ye may be made happy and add unto your flocks and make more plentiful the plumes in your feather boxes."

In a very short time the people were rushing out of their doorways all prepared for the chase,

[1] Háwikuh, or Aguico of the Spaniards, a pueblo now in ruins across the valley northwestward from Ojo Caliente, the southwestern farming town of the Zuñis.

and they ran after the young men and leaders as though in a race of the kicked stick.

Now, the sage-bushes and grasses grow tall to this day in the valley north of Háwikuh, and so they grew in the days long, long ago that I tell of. It thus happened that the poor Turkeys who were racing after grasshoppers, and peeping, and calling, and gobbling, did not know that the Háwikuh people were after them until they heard some old hens calling out in alarm from behind. Even then they were unable to get away, for the people were around them shouting and hurling crooked sticks, and shooting sharp arrows at them in all directions. Soon they began to fall on every side, especially the long-legged young ones, who so tangled their legs in the grasses that they could not keep up with their mothers, and were easily overtaken by the hunters of Háwikuh; and the old hens who stayed behind to look after the young ones were no better, and the cocks who stayed back to look after the old hens were even worse off, for the people sought them most because their feathers were so much brighter.

So it happened in a very short time that more than half the flock were killed and others were falling when a half-grown Long-leg started as fast as he could alone toward Twin Mountain.

It was growing late, and Áhaiyúta and his younger brother and their old grandmother were on top of their house shading their eyes and watching for the return of the Turkeys, when they saw the solitary young Long-leg coming, all out of breath and his wings dragging, over the hill below Master Cañon.

" Ha !" said the younger brother ; " look ! there comes a Long-legs,—and what is he shouting ?— Jump up, brother, jump up ! Do you hear that ?"

" *I-wo-loh-kia-a—a—a !* " called the Turkey, so that they could just hear him ; and as that means " Murder ! Murder !" you may think to yourself how much they were excited ; but they were not so much alarmed as the old grandmother, " for," said they, one to the other, " it is nothing but a young-ster, anyway, and they are always more scared than the old ones."

Nevertheless, they hastened down to meet him, and as they approached they saw that he was ter-ribly frightened, so they anxiously waited until he breathed more easily and would stand still ; then they asked : " What is it ? Where is it ? Why do you come alone, crying ' Murder, Murder !'"

" Alas ! my fathers," exclaimed the Turkey. " Alas ! I, alone, am left to tell of it ; ere I left they were thrown down all around me."

" Who did this ?" angrily demanded the boys.

" The people of Háwikuh," exclaimed the Tur-key, glancing apprehensively around.

" Ha ! we shall yet win back our loss," ejaculated the boys to one another ; and then they turned to the Turkey. " Are they all murdered and gone ?" they asked.

" Yes, alas ! yes ; I alone am left," moaned the young Turkey.

" Oh, no !" broke in the elder brother, " there

will yet many return, for this is but a Long-leg, and
surely when he could save himself others and older
ones could." Even then they heard some of the
Turkeys calling to one another, out of breath over
the low hills. "*U-kwa-tchi!*" ("Did n't I tell
you!") exclaimed Áhaiyúta, and they started toward the mountain.

One by one, or in little bunches, the Turkeys
came fleeing in, scared, weary, and bedraggled;
and the boys knew by this, and that only a
few after all returned, that the Long-leg had not
been for nothing taught to fear. They betook
themselves to their house. There they sat down
to eat with their grandmother, and after the eating was finished, they poked little sticks into the
blazing fire on the hearth, and cried out to their
grandmother : " Tomorrow, grandmother, we will
gather fagots."

" Foolish, foolish boys!" croned the old grandmother.

" Aye, tomorrow we will gather sprouts.
Where do they grow thickest and straightest,
grandmother?"

" Now, you boys had better let sprouts and war
alone," retorted the grandmother.

" But we must win back our losing," cried the
boys, with so much vehemence that the grandmother
only shook her head and exclaimed : " *A-ti-ki!*
(" Blood!") Strange creatures, my grandchildren,
both!" whereupon the two boys poked one the
other and laughed.

" Well," added the grandmother, " I have warned

you ; now act your own thoughts " ;—and the boys looked at her as earnestly as though they knew nothing of what she would say. " Fine warriors, indeed, who do not know where to look for arrow-sticks ! But if you will go sprouting, why, over there in the Rain-pond Basin are plenty of sprouts, and then north on Scale Ridge grow more, and over in Oak Cañon are fine oak-sprouts, more than ten boys like you could carry, and above here around Great Mountain are other kinds, and everywhere grow sprouts enough, if people were n't beasts passing understanding ; and, what 's more, I could tell you boys something to your advantage if you would ever listen to your old grandmother, but—"

" What is it ? What is it ? " interrupted the boys excitedly, just as if they knew nothing of what she would say.

" Why, over there by the Rain-pond Basin lives your grandfather—"

" Who 's that ? Who 's that ? " interrupted the boys again.

" I 've a mind not to tell you, you shameless little beasts, another word," jerked out the old grandmother, sucking her lips as if they were marrow-bones, and digging into the pudding she was stirring as though it were alive enough to be killed,—" just as though I were not telling you as fast as I could ; and, besides, anything but little beasts would know their grandfather—why, the Rainbow-worm, of course ! " [1]

---

[1] One of the " measuring-worms " which is named the rainbow, on account of his streaked back and habit of bending double when travelling.

" The Rainbow-worm our grandfather, indeed ! " persisted the boys ; and they would have said more had not their grandmother, getting cross, raised the pudding-stick at them, and bid them " shut up ! " So they subsided, and the old woman continued : " Yes, your grandfather, and for shame !— You may sit there and giggle all you please, but your grandfather the Rainbow-worm is a great warrior, I can tell you, and if you boys will go sprouting, why, I can tell you, you will fare but with poverty the day after, if you do not get him to help you, that's all ! "

" Indeed," replied the boys, quite respectfully.

" Yes, that I tell you ; and, moresoever, over there beyond at the wood border, in a pond, is your other grandfather, and he is a great warrior, too."

" Indeed ! " exclaimed the boys, as though they did not know that already, also.

" Yes, and you must go to see him, too ; for you can't get along without him any more than without the other. Now, you boys go to sleep, for you will want to get up very early in the morning, and you must go down the path and straight over the little hills to where your grandfathers live, and not up into the Master Cañon to gather your sticks, for if you do you will forget all I've told you. You are creatures who pass comprehension, you two grandchildren of mine."

So the two boys lay down in the corner together under one robe, like a man and his wife, for they did not sleep apart like our boys. But, do you know, those two mischievous boys giggled and kicked one another, and kept turning about, just as though they never dreamed of the morning. Then they fell to quarrelling about who could turn over the quicker.

" I can," said the elder brother.

" You can 't ! "

" I can ! "

" No, you can 't ! "

"Yes, I can, and I 'll show you"; and he was about to brace himself for the trial when the old grandmother strode over with her pudding-stick, lifting it in the air, with her usual expression of " Blood ! my grandchildren both," when they quieted down and pretended to sleep; but still they kept giggling and trying to pull the cover off each other.

" Stop that gaping and fooling, will you ? And go to sleep, you nasty little cubs ! " cried the irritated old woman; and laughing outright at their poor old grandmother, they put their arms around each other and fell asleep.

Next morning the sun rose, till he shone straight over the mountain, but still the two boys were asleep. The old grandmother had gone out to water her garden, and now she was sitting on the house-top shading her eyes and looking down the trail she had told the boys to follow, to see them come out of the shadow.

After she had strained her poor old eyes till they watered, she grew impatient : " Did I ever see such boys ! Now they 've gone and played me another trick. They'll rue their pranks some day." Then she thought she would go down and get some mush for breakfast. As she climbed down the ladder, she heard a tremendous snoring. " Ho, ho!" exclaimed the old grandmother; and striding across the room she shook the boys soundly. " Get up, get up! you lazy creatures; fine sprouters, you!"

The boys rolled over, rubbed their eyes, and began to stretch.

" Get up, get up! the day is warmed long ago; fine warriors, you!" reiterated the old woman, giving them another shaking.

The boys sat up, stretched, gaped, rubbed their eyes, and scratched their heads—the dirtiest little fellows ever seen—but they were only making believe. Their arms were crusty with dirt, and their hair stood out like down on a wild milkweed after a rain-storm, and yet these boys were the handsomest children that ever lived—only they were fooling their old grandmother, you see.

" You'd better be down at the spring washing your eyes at sunrise, instead of scratching your heads here with the sun shining already down the sky-hole"; croaked the old woman.

" What! is the sun out?" cried the boys in mock surprise; but they knew what time it was as well as the old crone did.

" Out! I should say it was! You boys might as well go to sleep again. A fine bundle of sticks you could get today, with the sun done climbing up already"

So the boys pretended to be in a great hurry and, grabbing up their bows and quivers, never stopped to half dress nor heeded the old woman's offer of food, but were jumping down the crags like mountain goats before the old woman was up the ladder.

"*Atiki!*" exclaimed the grandmother; "these beasts that cause meditation!" Then she climbed the terrace and watched and watched and watched; but the boys liked nothing better than to worry their old grandmother, so they ran up Master Cañon and into the woods and so across to Rain-pond Basin, leaving the old woman to look as she would.

"*Uhh!*" groaned the old woman; "they are down among the rocks playing. Fine warriors, they!" and with this she went back to her cooking.

By-and-by the boys came to the edge of the basin where the pod plant grew. Sure enough, there was the Rainbow-worm, eating leaves as though he were dying of hunger—a great fat fellow, as big as the boys themselves; for long, long ago, in the days I tell you of, the Rainbow-worm was much bigger than he is now.

"Hold on," said the younger brother. "Let's frighten the old fellow."

So they sneaked up until they were close to the grandfather, and then they began to tickle him with a stalk. Amiwili—that was his name—twitched his skin and bit away faster and faster at the leaves, until Áhaiyúta shouted at the top of his voice, "*Ha-u-thla!*" which made the old man jump and turn back so quickly that he would have broken his back had he a back-bone.

"*Shoma!*" he exclaimed. "It's my grandchildren, is it? I am old and a little deaf, and you frightened me, my boys."

"Did we frighten you, grandfather? That's too bad. Well, never mind; we've come to you for advice."

"What's that, my grandchildren?" looking out of his yellow eyes as though he were very wise, and standing up on his head and tail as though they had been two feet.

"Why, you see," said the boys, "we had a big drove of Turkeys, and we let them out to feed yesterday, but the fools got too near Háwikuh and the people there killed many, many of them; so we have decided to get back our winnings and even the game with them, the shameless beasts!"

"Ah ha!" exclaimed old Amiwili. "Very well!" and he lay down on his belly and lifted his head into the air like a man resting on his elbows. "Ah ha!" said he, with a wag of his head and a squint of his goggle. "Ah ha! Very well! I'll show them that they are not to treat my grandchildren like that. I'm a warrior, every direction of me—and there are a great many directions when I get angry, now, I can tell you! I'm just made to use up life," said he, with another swagger of his head.

"Listen to that!" said Mátsailéma to his brother.

"To use up life, that's what I'm for," added

the old man, with emphasis ; " I 'll show the Háwi-kuhkwe ! "

" Will you come to the council ? " asked the two boys.

"*Shuathla*," swaggered the old man—which is a very old-fashioned word that our grandfathers used when they said : " Go ye but before me."

So the boys skipped over to the pool at the wood border. There was their old grandfather, the Turtle, with his eyes squinted up, paddling round in the scum, and stretching his long neck up to bite off the heads of the water-rushes.

" Let 's have some fun with the old Shield-back," said the boys to one another. " Just you hold a moment, brother elder," said Mátsailéma as he fitted an arrow to the string and drew it clean to the point. *Tsi-i-i-i thle-e-e !* sang the arrow as it struck the back of the old Turtle ; and although he was as big as the Turtles in the big Waters of the World now are, the force and fright ducked him under the scum like a chip, and he came up with his eyes slimy and his mouth full of spittle, and his legs flying round too fast to be counted. When he spied the two boys, he cursed them harder than their grandmother did, but they hardly heard him, for their arrow glanced upward from his back and came down so straight that they had to run for their lives. " *Atiki !* troublesome little beasts, who never knew what shame nor dignity was ! " exclaimed the old fellow.

" Don't be angry with us, grandpa," said the boys. " You must be deaf, for we called and

called to you, but you only paddled round and
ate rushes; so we thought we would fire an arrow
at you, for you know we could n't get at you."

"Oh, that 's it! Well, what may my grandchildren be thinking of, in thus coming to see me?
It cannot be for nothing," reflected the old man,
as he twisted his head up toward them and pushed
the scum with his tail.

"Quite true, grandfather; we 've started out
sprouting, and had to come to our grandfather
for advice."

"Why, what is it then?" queried the old
Shield-back.

"You see, we have a flock of Turkeys—"

"Yes, I know," interrupted the old man, "for
they came down here to drink yesterday and broke
my morning nap with their '*quit quit quittings !*'"

"Well," resumed the boys, "they went toward
the Háwikuhkwe, and the shameless beasts, that
they are, turned out and killed very nearly all of
them, and we 're going to even matters with them;
that 's why we are out sprouting."

"Ah ha!" cried the old man, paddling up nearer
to the bank. "Good! Well, that 's right, my
grandchildren; you show that you are the wise
boys that you are to come to me. I 'm a great
warrior, I am, for though I have neither bow nor
arrow, yet the more my enemies have, the worse
for themselves, that 's all. You two just wait until
tomorrow," and he stretched his head out until
it looked as though he kept a snake in his
shell.

"Will you help us?" asked the boys. (They knew very well he would like nothing better.)

"Of course, my grandchildren."

"Will you come to the council?"

"Of course, my grandchildren two. How many will be there?" called the old fellow.

"The house shall be as full as a full stomach," retorted the boys, jousting each other.

"*Thluathlá!*" gruffly said Etawa, for that was the Turtle's name.

So the boys started for Oak-wood Cañon, and, arrived there, soon had a large bundle of branches cut down with their big flint knives, and four stout, dry oak-sticks. They shouldered their "sprouts" and started home, and, although they had bundles big enough to almost hide them, they trotted along as though they had nothing. On their way they picked up a lot of obsidian, and went fast enough until they were near their home, and then they were "very tired"—so tired that the old grandmother, when she caught sight of them, pitied them, and hurried down to stir some mush for them. She buried some corn-cakes in the ashes, too, and roasted some prairie-dogs in the same way; so that when those two lying little rascals came up and seemed so worn-out, she hurried so fast to get their food ready that it made her sinews twitch.

When the boys had eaten all they could and cracked a few prairie-dog bones, they fell to breaking the sprouts. They worked with their stone chips very fast, and soon had barked all they wanted. These they straightened by passing them through their horns[1] and placed them before the fire. While the shafts were drying, they broke up the obsidian, and laying chips of it on a stone covered with buckskin, quickly fashioned them into sharp arrow-heads with the points of other stones, and these they fastened to the ends of the shafts, placing feathers of the eagle on the other ends, until they had made enough for four big bundles. Then they made a bow of each of the four oak-sticks, and stood them up to dry against the wall.

As it grew dark they heard something like a dry leaf in a little wind.

"Ah!" said one to the other, "our grandfather comes"; and sure enough presently Amiwili poked his yellow eyes in at the door, but quickly drew back again.

"*Kutchi!*" said he, "your fire is fearful; it scares me!"

"The grandfather cometh!" exclaimed the boys. "Come in; sit down."

"Very well. Ah! you are stretching shafts, are you?" said the old Worm, crawling around behind the boys and into the darkest corner he could find.

"Yes," replied they. "Why do you not come out into the light, grandpa?"

---

[1] Fragments of mountain-sheep horn are used to this day by the Zuñis for the same purpose. They are flattened by heat and perforated with holes of varying size. By introducing the shaft to be straightened, and rubbing with a twisting motion the inner sides of the crooked portions, they are gradually straightened out, afterward to be straightened by hand from time to time as they dry before the fire.

"*Kutchi!* I fear the fire; it hurts my eyes, and makes me feel as the sun does after a rain-storm and I have no leaves to crawl into."

"Very well," said the boys. "Grandmother, spread a robe for him in the corner." Then they busied themselves straightening some of the arrows and trying their bows. Just as they were pulling one toward the entrance way, they heard old Etawa thumping along, and immediately the old fellow called out: "Hold on; don't thump me against one of those sticks of yours; they jar a fellow so!"

"Oh, it's you, is it, grandfather? Well, we're only trying our new bows; come in and sit down." So the old fellow bumped along in and took his place by the fire, for he did not care whether it was hot or cold.

"Are the councillors here?" asked he, wagging his head around.

"Why, certainly," said the two boys; "and now our council is so full we had better proceed to discuss what we had better do."

When the old Turtle discovered that the boys had been playing him a joke, he was vexed, but he did n't show it. "Amiwili here?" asked he. "*Tchukwe!* We four will teach those Há-wikuhkwe!"

"Yes, indeed!" croaked the Rainbow-worm.

"Well," said the boys, "at daybreak tomorrow morning, before it is light, we shall start for Háwikuh-town."

"Very well," responded Amiwili. "Come to my place first, and let me know when you start."

"And," added Etawa, "come to my place next and let me know. When you boys get to Háwikuh and alarm the people, if they get too thick for you, come back to my house as fast as you can, and you, Mátsailéma, take me up on your back. Then you two run toward your other grandfather's house. I'll show these Háwikuhkwe that I can waste life as much as anybody, even if I have no arrows to shoot at them."

"Yes," added the Rainbow-worm, "and when you come up to my house, just run past me and I'll take care of the rest of them. I'm made to use up life, I am," swaggered he.

"And I," boasted the old Turtle. "Come, brother, let us be going, for we have a long way to travel, and our legs are short." So, after feasting, the two started away.

As soon as they had gone, the two boys went to their corner and lay down to rest, first filling their quivers with arrows, and laying their water-shield [1] out on the floor. They were presently quiet, and then began to snore; so their old grandmother went into another room and brought out a new bowl which she filled with water. Then she retired into the room again, and when she came out she was dressed in beautiful embroidered mantles and

---

[1] The *kia-al-lan*, or water-shield, is represented in modern times by a beautiful netting of white cotton threads strung on a round hoop, with a downy plume suspended from the center. This, with the dealings of Áhaiyúta and Mátsailéma with arrows of lightning, and the simile of their father the Sun, leaves little doubt that they are, in common with mystic creations of the Aryans, representatives of natural phenomena or their agents. This is even more closely suggested by the sequel.

skirts and decorated with precious ornaments of shell and turquoise.

The noise she made awoke Áhaiyúta, who punched his younger brother, and said: "Wake up, wake up! Here's grandmother dressed as though she were going to a dance!"

Then the younger brother raised his voice to a sharp whisper (they knew perfectly well what the old grandmother was intending to do): "What for?"

"Here!" said the old woman, turning toward the bed. "Go to sleep! What are you never-weary little beasts doing now? For shame! You pretend you are going out to war tomorrow!"

"Why are you dressed so, grandmother?" ventured the younger.

"What *should* I be dressed for but to make medicine for you two? Now, mind, you must not watch me. I shall make the medicine and place it in these two cane tubes, and you must shoot them into the middle of the plaza of Háwikuh as soon as you get there. That will make the people like women; for the canes will break and make the medicine fly about like mist, and whomsoever gets his skin wet by it, will become no more of a warrior than a woman. Go to sleep, I say, you pests!"

But the boys had no intention of sleeping. To be sure, they stretched themselves out and slyly laid their arms across their eyes. The old grandmother did not notice this at first. She began to wash her arms in the bowl of water. Then she rubbed them so hard that the *yepna* ("substance of flesh") was rolled off in little lumps and fell into the water. This she began to mix carefully with the water, when Áhaiyúta whispered to the other: "Brother younger, just look! Old grandmother's arms look as bright as a young girl's. Look, look!" said he, still louder, for the other had already begun to giggle; but when the old woman turned to talk sharply at them, they turned over, the rascals, as dutifully as though they had never joked with their poor old grandmother. Soon they were indeed sleeping.

Then the grandmother proceeded to fill the canes with the fluid, and then she fastened these to the ends of two good arrows. "There!" she exclaimed, with a sigh; and after she had chanted an incantation over the canes, she laid some food near the boys and softly left the room, to sleep.

The boys never minded the things they had to do in the morning, but slept soundly until the coming of day, when they arose, took their bows and quivers, knives, war-clubs, arrows, and water-shield, and quietly stole away.

It was not long ere they approached the house of Amiwili. He was fairly gorging the leaves of all the lizard plants he could lay hold of, and already looked so full that he must have felt like a ball. But he munched away so busily that he would n't have looked at the boys had it been light enough.

"How did our grandfather come unto the morning?" asked they.

" *Thluathlá !* " (" Get out !") was all the old Worm vouchsafed them between his cuds ; and they sped on.

Soon they reached the home of the old Turtle. This old grandfather was more leisurely. " You will return at the height of the sun," said he. " Now mind what I told you last night. I 'll wait right here on the bank for you."

" Very well," laughed the boys, for little they cared that they were on the war-path.

By-and-by they neared the town of Háwikuh. It was twilight, for the morning star was high. The boys sat down a moment and sang an incantation,—the same our fathers and children, the *Ápithlan Shíwani,* sing now. Then the younger brother ran round the pueblo to scout. Two or three people were getting up, as he could see, for nearly everybody slept on the roofs, it was so warm.

" *Iwolohkia-a-a !* " cried he, at the top of his voice ; and as the people were rousing he drew one of the cane arrows full length in his bow, and so straight and high did he shoot, that it fell *thl-i-i-i-i !* into the middle of the plaza, splitting and scattering medicine-water in every direction, so that the people all exclaimed, as they rubbed their eyes : " Ho ! it is raining, and yet the sky is clear ! And did n't some one cry ' Murder, murder !' "

When Áhaiyúta's arrow struck, it scattered more medicine-water upon them, until they thought they must be dreaming of rain ; but just then Mátsailéma shouted, " *Ho-o-o !* Murder !" again, and everybody started to hunt bows and arrows. Then the boy ran to the hiding-place of his brother in the grass on the trail toward the wood border, and just as he got there, some of the people who were shouting and gabbling to one another ran out to see him.

" Ha !" they shouted, " there they are, on the northern trail."

So the Háwikuhkwe all poured down toward them, but when they arrived there they found no enemy. While the people were looking and running about, *tsok tsok*, and *tsok tsok*, and *tsok tsok*, the arrows of Áhaiyúta, and Mátsailéma struck the nearest ones, for they had crawled along the trail and were waiting in the grass. They never missed. Every man they struck fell, but many, many came on, and when these saw that there were only two, their faces were all the more to the front with haste. Still the two boys shot, shot, shot at them until many were killed or wounded before the remainder decided to flee.

" Come, brother, my arrows are gone," said the younger brother. " Quick ! put on the water-shield, and let us be off !" Now, the people were gaining on them faster and faster, but Áhaiyúta threw water like thick rain from his shield strapped over his back, so that the enemies' bow-strings loosened, and they had to stop to tighten them again and again.

Whenever the Háwikuhkwe pressed them too closely, the water-shield sprinkled them so thoroughly that when they nocked an arrow the sinew bow-string stretched like gum, and all they could do was to stop and tighten their bow-strings again. Thus the boys were able to near the home of their grandfather, the big Turtle, now and then shooting at the leaders with their warring arrows and rarely missing their marks.

But as they came near, the people were gathering more and more thickly in their rear, so that Mátsailéma barely had time to take his grandfather —who was waiting on the bank of the pond— upon his back.

" Now, run you along in front and we 'll follow behind," said old Etawa, as he put one paw over the left shoulder and the other under the right arm, and clasped his legs tightly around the loins of Mátsailéma so as to hug close to his back.

"Grandfather, *kutchi!* You are as heavy as a rock and as hard as one, too," said the younger brother. "How can I dodge those stinging beasts?"

"That 's all the better for you," said the old Turtle, loosening his grip a little; "take it easy."

"They 're coming! They 're coming!" shouted Áhaiyúta from ahead. "Hurry, hurry, brother younger; hurry!" But Mátsailéma could n't get along any faster than he could.

Presently the old Turtle glanced around and saw that the people were gaining on them and already drawing their bows. "Duck your head down and never mind them. Now, you 'll see what I can do!" said he, pulling into his shell.

Thle-e-e, thle-thle-thle-e-e, rattled the arrows

against old Etawa's shell, and the warriors were already shouting, " *Ho-o-o-awiyeishikia !* "—which was their cry of victory,—when they began to cry out in other tones, for *tsuiya !* their arrows glanced from old Turtle's shell and struck themselves, so that they dropped in every direction. " Terror and blood ! but those beings can shoot fast and hard !" shouted they to one another, but they kept pelting away harder and faster, only to hit one another with the glancing arrows.

" Hold !" cried one in advance of the others. " Head them off ! Head them off ! We 're only shooting ourselves against that black shield of theirs, and the other loosens our bow-strings."

But just then Áhaiyúta reached the home of his other grandfather, Amiwili. Behold ! he was all swollen up with food and could hardly move—only wag his head back and forth.

" Are you coming ?" groaned the old fellow. " Quick, get out of the way, all of you ! Quick, quick !"

Áhaiyúta jumped out of the way just as Mátsailéma cried out : " *Ha hua !* I can run no farther ; I must drop you, grandfather,"—but he saw Áhaiyúta jump to one side, so he followed, too.

Old Amiwili reared himself and, opening his mouth, *waah ! weeh !* right and left he threw the lizard leaves he had been eating, until the Háwikuh-kwe were blinded and suffocated by them, and, dropping their bows and weapons, began to clutch their eyes from blindness and pain. And old Amiwili coughed and coughed till he had blown nearly all his substance away, and there was nothing left of him but a worm no bigger than your middle finger.

"Drop me and make your winnings," cried the old Turtle. "I guess I can take care of myself," he chuckled from the inside of his shell; and it was short work for the boys to cast down all their enemies whom Amiwili had blown upon, and the others fled terrified toward Háwikuh.

"Ha, ha!" laughed the two boys as they began to take off the scalps of the Háwikuhkwe. "These caps are better than half a flock of Turkeys."

"Who 'll proclaim our victory to our people?" said they, suddenly stopping; and one would have thought they belonged to a big village and a great tribe instead of to a lone house on top of Twin Mountain, with a single old granny in it; but then that was their way, you know.

"I will! I will!" cried the old Turtle, as he waddled off toward Twin Mountain and left the boys to skin scalps.

When he came to the top of the low hill south of Master Cañon, he stuck a stick up in the air and shouted.

"*Hoo-o! Hawanawi-i-i-i!*" which is the shout of victory; and, not seeing the old woman, he cried out two or three times.

"*Hoo-o! Iwolohkia-a-a!*" which, as you know, means "Murder! Murder!" The old woman heard it and was frightened. She threw an old robe over her shoulders, and, grabbing up the fire-poker, started down as fast as her limping old limbs would let her, and nearly tumbled over when she heard old Etawa shout again, "*Iwolohkia!*"

"Ha!" said she; "I'll teach the shameless Turkey killers, if I am an old woman;" and she shook her fire-poker in the air until she came up to where the old Turtle was waiting.

Here, just as she came near, the old Turtle pretended not to see her, but stood up on his legs, and, holding his pole with one hand, cried out, "*Hoo-o! Hawanawi-i-i-i!*" which was the shout of victory, as I told you before.

"What is it?" cried the old woman, as she limped along up and said: "*Ah! ahi!*" ("My poor old legs!")

"Victory!" said the proud Turtle, scarcely deigning to look at her.[1]

"Who has this day renewed himself?" she inquired.

"Thy grandchildren," answered the old Turtle.

"Have they won?" asked the old woman, as she said: "Thanks this day!"

"Many caps," replied the Turtle.

"Will they celebrate?"

"Yes."

"Who will purify and pass them?" asked the granny.

"Why, you will."

"Who will bathe the scalps?"

"Why, I will."

[1] The ridiculousness of the dialogue which follows may readily be understood when it is explained that each office in the celebration of victory has to be performed by a distinct individual of specified clans according to the function

"Who will swing the scalps round the pueblo?"

"Why, you will."

"Who will adopt them?"

"Why, you will."

"Who will bring out the feast?"

"Why, you will."

"Who will be the priest of initiation?"

"Why, I will."

"Who will be the song-master?"

"Why, I will."

"Who will be the dancers?"

"Why, I will."

"Who will draw the arrows and sacrifice them?"

"Why, I will."

"Who will strive for the sacrificed arrows?"

"Why, I will."

"Who will lead the dance of victory?"

"Why, I will."

"Who will be the dancers?"

"Why, I will."

"Who will go to get the women to join the dance?"

"Why, I will."

"What women will dance?"

"Why, you will."

"Who will take them to preside at the feast of their relatives-in-law?"

"Why, you will."

"Who will be their relatives-in-law?"

"Why, you will."

"Who will be the priests of their Father Society?"

"Why, I will."

And they might have talked that way till sunset had not the voices of the two boys, singing the song of victory, been heard coming over the hill. There they were, coming with two great strings of scalps as big as a bunch of buckskins.

"Oh! poor me! How shall I swing all those scalps round the pueblo?" groaned the poor old woman as she limped off to dress for the ceremony.

"Why, swing them," answered the old Turtle, as he stretched himself up with the importance of being master of ceremonies.

So the boys brought the scalps up and the old Turtle strung them thickly on a long pole.

So day after day they danced and sang, to add strands to the width of the boys' badges. And the old Turtle was master-priest of ceremonies and people, low priest, song-master, and dancers; sacrificer of arrows and striver after the arrows. He would beat the drum and sing a little, then run and dance out the measure; but it was very hard work.

And the old woman was mother of the children and sisters, and their clan, and somebody's else clan, matron of ceremonials, and maidens of ceremonials—all at the same time;—but it was very hard work, consequently they did n't get along very well.

That's the reason why today we have so many song-masters and singers, dance leaders and dancers, priests and common people, father clans and mother clans, in the great Ceremony of Victory.

Thus it happened with Áhaiyúta and Mátsailéma and their old grandmother, and their grandfathers the Rainbow-worm and the old Turtle. That is the reason why rainbow-worms are no bigger than your finger now, because their great grandfather blew all his substance away at the Háwikuhkwe. That's the reason why the great Turtles in the far-away Waters of the World are so much bigger than their brothers and sisters here, and have so many marks on their shells, where the arrows glanced across the shield of their great grandfather. For old Etawa was so proud after he had been the great master of ceremonies that he despised his old pond, and went off to seek a new home in the Western Waters of the World, and his grandchildren never grew any bigger after he went away, and their descendants are just as small as they were.

And thus shortens my story.

THE YOUNG SWIFT - RUNNER WHO
WAS STRIPPED OF HIS CLOTHING
BY THE AGED TARANTULA

A LONG, long time ago, in K'iákime, there lived a young man, the son of the priest-chief of the town. It was this young man's custom to dress himself as for a dance and run entirely around Thunder Mountain each morning before the sun rose, before making his prayers. He was a handsome young man, and his costume was beautiful to behold.

Now, below the two broad columns of rock which stand at the southeastern end of Thunder Mountain, and which are called Ak'yapaatch-ella,— below these, in the base of the mountain, an old, old Tarantula had his den. Of a morning, as the young man in his beautiful dress sped by, the old Tarantula heard the horn-bells which were attached to his belt and saw him as he passed, this young Swift-runner, and he thought to himself : "Ah, ha ! Now if I could only get his fine apparel away from him, what luck it would be for me ! I will wait for him the next time."

Early the next morning, just as the sun peeped over the lid of the world, sure enough the old Tarantula heard the horn-bells, and, thrusting his head out of his den, waited. As the young man approached, he called out to him : " Hold, my young friend ; come here ! "

"What for?" replied the youth. "I am in a great hurry."

"Never mind that; come here," said the old Tarantula.

"What is it? Why do you detain me?" rejoined the youth.

"It is for this reason," said the old Tarantula. "Would n't you like to look at yourself today?— for if you would, I can show you how."

"How?" asked the young man. "Make haste, for I am in a hurry."

"Well, in this way," was the reply. "Take off your clothing, all of it; then I will take off mine. You place yours in a heap before me; I will place mine in a heap before you. Then I will put on your apparel as you wear it, and then you will see what a handsome fellow you are."

The young man thought about it and concluded that it would be a very good thing to do. So he began drawing off his clothing—his beautiful painted moccasins, red and green; his fine white leggings, knitted with cunning stitches and fringed down the front, like the leggings worn by the Master of the Dances at New Year; his delicately-embroidered skirt, and mantle, and coat, all of white cotton and marked with figures in many colors; his heavy anklets of sacred white shell; his blue turquoise earrings, like the sky in blueness, and so long that they swept his shoulders; his plaited headband of many-colored fibers, and his bunch of blue, red, and yellow macaw feathers, which he wore in his hair-knot at the back of his head,—all these things, one after another, he took off and laid before the ugly old Tarantula.

Then that woolly, hairy, clammy creature hauled off his clothing—gray-blue, ugly, and coarse;—gray-blue leggings, gray-blue skirt and breech-cloth, gray-blue coat and mantle, nothing but gray-blue, woolly and hairy, ugly and dirty. When the old Tarantula had done this, he began to put on the handsome garments that the young man had placed before him, and, after he had dressed himself in these, he perched himself up on his crooked hind-legs, and said: "Look at me, now. How do I look?"

"Well, so far as the clothing is concerned, handsome," said the young man.

"Just wait till I get a little farther off," said the old Tarantula, and he straightened himself up and walked backward toward the door of his den. Presently he stopped and stood still, and said: "How do I look now?"

"Handsomer," said the young man.

"Just wait till I get a little farther"; and again he walked backward, which is a way Tarantulas have, and stood up straight, and said: "How do I look now?"

"Handsomer still," said the young man.

"Ah, ha! Just wait till I get a little farther"; —and now he backed to the very door of his den, and stood upon the lip of the entrance, and said: "Now, then, how do I look?"

"Perfectly handsome," said the young man.

"Ah, ha!" chuckled the old Tarantula, and he

turned himself around and plunged headforemost into his hole.

"Out upon him!" cried the young man, as he stood there with his head bowed, and thinking. "Out upon the old rascal! That is the trick he serves me, is it? Fearful!" said he. "What shall I do now? I can't go home naked, or half naked. Well, but I suppose I will have to," said he to himself. And, bending down, he reached for the hairy gray-blue breech-cloth that had been left there by the old Tarantula, and the skirt, and put them on, and took his way swiftly homeward.

When he reached home the sun was high, which never had happened before, so that the old people had been thinking, "Surely, something must have happened to our young man that he comes not as early as usual." And when he came, they said: "What has happened that has detained you so?"

"Ha!" replied the youth; "the old Tarantula that lives under the Ak'yapaatch-ella has stripped me of my garments, and with them has run away into his hole."

"We thought something of the kind must have happened," said his old father.

"Send for your warrior priest," said the other old ones. "Let us see what he thinks about this, and what shall be done."

So the priest-chief sent for his warrior priest, and when the latter had come, he asked: "Why is it that you have sent for me?"

"True, we have sent for you," said the father,

"because Old Tarantula has stripped my son of his
handsome apparel, which is sacred and precious,
and we therefore hold it a great loss to him and
us. How do you think we can recover what has
been stolen ? "

The warrior priest thought a moment, and said :
" I should think we would have to dig him out, for
it is n't likely he will show himself far from his den
again."

So the warrior priest went out on the tops of the
houses, and called to his people :

" I instruct ye this day, oh, my people and children ! Listen to my instruction ! Our child, in
running to and from his prayers this very morning
was intercepted by Old Tarantula, who, through
his skill and cunning, succeeded in stripping our
child of his handsome apparel. Therefore, I instruct ye, make haste ! Gather together digging-
sticks and hoes ; let us all go and dig out the old
villain ; let the whole town turn out, women as well
as men and children. My daughters, ye women of
this town, take with ye basket-bowls and baskets
and other things wherewith ye gather material for
plaster, with which to convey away the sand and
earth that is dug up by the men. Thus much I
instruct ye ! Make haste all ! " Whereupon he
descended, and, after eating, led the way toward
the den of Old Tarantula.

When the people had also eaten and followed,
they began to work swiftly at tunnelling into the
hole of the Tarantula ; and thus they worked and
worked from morning till night, but did not over-

take him, until at last they reached the solid rock foundations of the mountain. They had filled their baskets and basket-bowls with the sand, and cast it behind them, and others had cast it behind them, and so on until a large hillock of earth and sand had been raised, but still they had not overtaken Old Tarantula. Now, when they had reached the solid rock foundations of the mountain, they saw that the hole yawned like a cave before them, and that it was needless to follow farther. They gave up in despair, saying: "What more can we do? Let us go home. Let us give it up, since we must." And they took their ways homeward.

Now, in the evening the old ones of the town were very thoughtful, and they gathered together and talked the matter over, and finally it was suggested by someone in answer to the query, "What can we do to recover our son's lost garments?" "Suppose that we send for the Great Kingfisher? He is wise, crafty, swift of flight; he dashes himself from on high, even into the water, and takes him therefrom whatsoever he will, swift though it be, without fail. Suppose we send for him, our grandfather?"

"Ah, ha! that's it," replied others. "Send for him straightway."

So the master warrior priest called to Young Swift-runner, and sent him to the Hill of the Great Kingfisher.

"What is it?" asked Kingfisher, when he heard someone at the entrance of his house.

"Come quickly! In council the old ones of our town await you," said the young man.

So Great Kingfisher followed, and, arriving at the council, greeted them and asked: "What is it you would have of me?"

Said they: "Old Tarantula has stripped our young man, Swift-runner, of his beautiful garments, and how to recover them we know not. We have dug away the den, even to the foundation of the mountain, but beyond this it extends. What to do we know not. So we have sent for you, knowing your power and ability to quickly snatch even from under the waters whatsoever you will."

"Ah, ha! I will take a step toward this thing," said Great Kingfisher, "but it is a difficult task you place before me. Old Tarantula is exceedingly cunning and very keen of sight, moreover. I will, however, take a step, and if I have good luck will be able to bring back to you something of what he has stolen." He then made his adieu, and went back to his house at the Hill of the Kingfisher.

Very early the next morning he took his swift way to the Ak'yapaatch-ella, and there where the columns of rock fork he lay himself down between them, like a little finger between two other fingers, merely thrusting his beak over the edge, and looking at the opening of Old Tarantula's hole.

The plumes of sunlight were but barely gleaming on the farther edge of the world when Old Tarantula cast his eyes just out of the edge of his hole, and looked all around. Eyes like many eyes had he, wonderfully sharp and clear. With these he looked all around, as might have been expected. He discovered Great Kingfisher, little-so-ever of him showing, and called out: "*Heee! Wóloi weee!*" ("Ho, ho! skulker skulking. Ho, ho! skulker skulking!") Instantly Great Kingfisher shook out his wings, and *thluooo*, descended like a breath of strong wind; and *thlu-u-u-kwa*, finished his flight like a loosed arrow; but he merely brushed the tips of the plumes in Old Tarantula's head-knot, and the creature doubled himself up and headfore-most plunged into his hole. Once in, "Ha, ha!" said he. "Good for him! Good! Good! Let's have a dance, and sing," said he, talking to himself; and thereupon he pranced up, jigged about his dark, deep room, singing this song:

> "*Ohatchik'ya ti Tákwà,*
> *Ai yaa Tákwà!*
> *Ohatchik'ya lii Tákwà,*
> *Ohatchik'ya lii Tákwà!*
> *Ai yaa Tákwà!*
> *Ai yaa Tákwà!*
> *Tákwà, Tákwà!*"

Thus singing, he danced,—surely a song that nobody but he could dance to, if it be a song, but he danced to it. And when he had finished jigging about, he looked at his fluttering garments, and said: "Ha, ha! Just look at my fine dress! Now am I not handsome? I tell you I am handsome! Now, let's have another dance!" And again he sang at the top of his wheezing voice, and pranced round on his crooked hind legs, with his fine garments fluttering.

But Great Kingfisher, with wings drooping and beak gaped down at the corners,—as though being hungry he had tried to catch a fish and had n't caught him,—took his way back to the council; and he said to the people there: " No use! I failed utterly. As I said before, he is a crafty, keensighted old fellow. What more have I to say?" He made his adieus, and took his way back to the Hill of the Kingfisher.

Again the people talked with one another and considered; and at last said some: " Inasmuch as he has failed, let us send for our grandfather, Great Eagle. He, of all living creatures with wings, is swiftest and keenest of sight, strong of grasp, hooked of beak, whatever getting holding, and getting whatever he will."

They sent for the Eagle. He came, and when made acquainted with their wishes turned quickly, and said, in bidding them adieu: " I think that possibly I can succeed, though surely, as my brother has said, Old Tarantula is a crafty, keensighted creature. I will do my best."

Early the next morning he took his way, before sunrise, to the peak of the Mountain of the Badgers, a long distance away from Ak'yapaatch-ella, but still as no distance to the Eagle. There he stood, with his head raised to the winds, turning first one eye, then the other, on the entrance of Old Tarantula's den, until Old Tarantula again thrust out his woolly nose, as might have been expected. He

23

discovered the Eagle, and was just shouting "Ho, skulker, skulking!" when the Eagle swept like a singing stone loosed from the sling straight at the head of Old Tarantula. But his wings hissed and buzzed past the hole harmlessly, and his crooked talons reached down into the dark, clutching nothing save one of the plumes in Old Tarantula's head-dress. Even this he failed to bring away.

The Old Tarantula tumbled headlong into his lower room, and exclaimed: "Ha, ha! Goodness save us! What a startling he gave me! But he did n't get me! No, he did n't get me! Let's have a dance! Jig it down! What a fine fellow I am!" And he began to prance about, and jig and sing as he had sung before:

> "*Ohatchik'ya ti Tákwà,*
> *Ai yaa Tákwà!*
> *Ohatchik'ya lii Tákwà,*
> *Ohatchik'ya lii Tákwà!*
> *Ai yaa Tákwà!*
> *Ai yaa Tákwà!*
> *Tákwà, Tákwà!*"

As soon as he paused for breath, he glanced askance at his fluttering bright garments and cried out: "Ho! what a handsome fellow I am! How finely dressed I am! Let's have another dance!" And again he danced and sang, all by himself, admiring himself, answering his own questions, and watching his own movements. But Great Eagle, crest-fallen and shame-smitten, took his way to the place of the council, reported his failure, and made his adieu.

Then again the people considered, and the old ones decided to send for Hatchutsanona (the Lesser Falcon), whose plumage is hard and smooth and speckled, gray and brown, like the rocks and sage-brush, and who, being swift as the Kingfisher, and strong as the Eagle, and small, is not only able to fly where other birds fly, but can penetrate the closest thicket when seeking his prey, for trimmed he is like a well-feathered arrow. They sent for him; he came and, being made acquainted with the facts of the case, said he could but try, though he modestly affirmed that when his elder brothers, Great Kingfisher and Great Eagle, had made such efforts, it were well-nigh needless for him to try, and repeated what they had said of the cunning and keenness of sight of Old Tarantula.

But he went early the next morning, and placed himself on the very edge of the high cliff over-hanging the columns of rock and looking into the den of Old Tarantula. There, when the sun rose, you could scarcely have seen him, even though near you might have been, for his coat of gray and brown was like the rocks and dry grass around him, and he lay very close to the ground, like an autumn leaf beaten down by the rain. By-and-by Old Tarantula thrust out his rugged face, and turned his eyes in every direction, up and down; then twisted his head from side to side. He saw nothing. He had even poked his head entirely out of his hole, and his shoulders were just visible, when Lesser Falcon bestirred himself, and Old Tarantula, alas! saw him; not in time to wholly save himself, however, for Lesser Falcon, with a sweep of his wings like the swirl of a snowdrift, shot into the mouth of Old Tarantula's den, grasped at his head, and brought away with him the macaw plumes of the youth's head-dress.

Down into his den tumbled Old Tarantula, and he sat down and bent himself double with fright and chagrin. He wagged his head to and fro, and sighed: " Alas! alas! my beautiful head-dress; the skulking wretch! My beautiful head-dress; he has taken it from me. What is the use of bothering about a miserable bunch of macaw feathers, anyway? They get dirty, they get bent and broken, moths eat them, they change their color; what is the use of troubling myself about a worthless thing like that? Have n't I still the finest costume in the valley?—handsome leggings and embroidered skirt and mantle, sleeves as pretty as flowers in summer, necklaces worth fifty head-plumes, and earrings worth a handful of such necklaces? Ha, ha! let him away with the old head-plumes! Let's have a dance, and dance her down, old fellow!" said he, talking to himself. And again he skipped about, and sang his tuneless song:

" *Ohatchik'ya ti Tákwà,*
Ai yaa Tákwà !
Ohatchik'ya lii Tákwà,
Ohatchik'ya lii Tákwà !
Ai yaa Tákwà,
Ai yaa Tákwà.
Tákwà, Tákwà ! "

He admired himself as much as before. "Forsooth," said he; "I could not have seen the headplume for I would have worn it in the back of my head."

The Lesser Falcon, cursing at his half-luck, took his way back to the council, and, casting the headplume at the feet of the old men, said: "Alas! my fathers; this is the best I could do, for before I had fairly taken my flight, Old Tarantula discovered me and made into his den. But this I got, and I bring it to you. May others succeed better!"

"Thou hast succeeded exceeding well, for most precious are these plumes from Summerland," said the old priest. "Thanks be to you, this day, my grandfather!" And the Lesser Falcon took his way to the thickets and hillsides.

Then the people said to one another: "What more is there to be done? We must even have recourse to the Gods, it seems." And they called Swift-runner and said to him: "Of the feathered creatures we have chosen the wisest and swiftest and strongest to aid us; yet they have failed mainly. Therefore, we would even send you to the Gods, for your performance of duty to them has been faithful from morning to morning." So they instructed him to climb to the top of Thunder Mountain and visit the home of the two Wargods, Áhaiyúta and Mátsailéma, for in those days they still dwelt on the top of Thunder Mountain with their old grandmother, at the Middle Place of Sacrifice.

The priests in the town prepared sacrificial plumes and divided their treasures for the Gods, and again calling the young man, presented them to him as their messenger, bidding him bear to the Gods their greetings.

On the morning following, he climbed the steep path and soon neared the dwelling of the Gods and their grandmother. She was on the roof of the house, while the two bad boys—always out of the way when wanted, and never ceasing to play their pranks, as was their little way, you know— were down in the lower rooms. The old grandmother bade the youth to enter, and called out to her grandchildren, the two Gods : " My children, come up, both of you, quickly. A young man has arrived to see you, bringing greetings." So they cast off their playful behavior, and with great gravity came into the room, and looking up to the tall youth, said : " Thou hast come. May it be happily. Sit down. What is it that thou wouldst have ? because for nothing no stranger comes to the house of another."

" It is true, this which you say," said the youth reverently, breathing on his hands. " O ye, my fathers ! I bring greetings from the fathers of my town below the mountain, and offerings from them."

" It is well thus, my child," replied the Gods.

" And I bring also my burden of trouble, that I may listen to your counsel, and perchance implore your aid," said the youth.

" What is it ? " said the Two ; and they listened.

Then the youth related his misfortune, telling how he had been stripped of his clothing by Old Tarantula; how the old ones, gathered in council, had sought the aid, one after another, of the wisest and swiftest of feathered beings, but with little success; how they had at last counselled his coming to them, the fathers of the people in times of difficulty and strife.

"Grandmother!" shouted the younger brother War-god. "Make haste! Make haste, grandmother! Bestir yourself! Grind flour for us. Let it be rock flour!"

The old grandmother gathered some white calcareous sandstone called *kétchïpawe*. She broke those rocks into fragments and ground them into meal; then reduced them on a finer stone to soft, impalpable powder. She made dough of this with water, and the two Gods, with wonderful skill, molded this dough, as it hardened, into figures of elk-kind,—two deer and two antelope images they made. When they had finished these, they placed them before the youth, and said: "Take these and stand them on the sacrificial rock-shelf or terrace on the southern side of our mountain, with prayer to the gods over them. Return to your home, and tell the old ones what we have directed you to do. Tell them also where we said you should place these beings, for such they will become upon the rock-shelf; and you should go to greet them in the morning and guide them with you toward the den of Old Tarantula,—Old Tarantula is very fond of hunting; nothing is so pleasing to him as to kill anything,—that thereby he may be tempted forth from his hiding-place in his den."

The youth did as he was directed, and when he had placed the figures of the deer and the antelope in a row on the shelf, and reached home, he informed the old ones of the word that had been sent to them.

His father, the old priest-chief, called the warrior priest, and said to him: "It may be possible that Old Tarantula will be tempted forth from his den tomorrow. Would it not be well for us to take the war-path against him?"

"It would, indeed, be well," said the warrior priest. And the priest-chief went to the house-top and called to the people, saying:

"O, ye, my people and children, I instruct ye today! Let the young men and the warriors gather and prepare as for war. By means of the sacred images which have been made by the Two Beloved for our son, Swift-runner, it may be that we shall succeed in tempting Old Tarantula forth from his den tomorrow. Let us be prepared to capture him. Make haste! Make ready! Thus much I instruct ye."

In great haste, as if under the influence of joyful tidings indeed, the people prepared for war, gathered together in great numbers, testing the strength of their bows, and with much racket issued forth from the town under Thunder Mountain, spreading over all the foot-hills. And toward daylight the youth alone took his way toward the sacrificial rock-shelf on the side of the mountain. When he arrived there, behold! the two Antelopes and the two Deer were tamely walking about, cropping the grass and tender leaves, and as he approached, they said: "So, here you are."

"Now, this day, behold, my children!" said he in his prayer. "Even for the reason that we have made ye beings, follow my instructions, oh, do! Most wickedly and shamefully has Old Tarantula, living below Ak'yapaatch-ella, robbed me of my sacred fine apparel. I therefore call ye to aid me. Go ye now toward his home, that he may be tempted forth by the sight of ye."

Obediently the Deer and Antelope took their way down the sloping sides of the foot-hills toward Old Tarantula's den. As they neared the den the youth called out from one of the valleys below, "*Hu-u-u-u-u-u!* Hasten! There go some deer and antelope! Whoever may be near them, understand, there go some deer and antelope!"

Old Tarantula was talking to himself, as usual, down in his inner room. He heard the faint sound. "Ha!" cried he, "what is this humming? Somebody calling, no doubt." He skipped out toward the doorway just as the young man called the second time. "Ah, ha!" said he. "He says deer are coming, does n't he? Let us see." And presently, when the young man called the third time, he exclaimed: "That's it! that is what he is calling out. Now for a hunt! I might as well get them as anyone else."

He caught up his bow, slipped the noose over

the head of it, twanged the string, and started.
But just as he was going out of his hole, he said to
himself: "Good daylight! this never will do; they
will be after me if I go out. Oh, pshaw! Nonsense! they will do nothing of the kind. What
does it matter? Have n't I bow and arrows with
me?" He leaped out of his hole and started off
toward the Deer. As he gained an eminence, he
cried: "Ah, ha! sure enough, there they come!"
Indeed, he was telling the truth. The Deer still
approached, and when the first one came near he
drew an arrow strongly and let fly. One of them
dropped at once. "Ah, ha!" cried he, "who says I
am not a good hunter?" He whipped out another
arrow, and fired at the second Deer, which dropped
where it had stood. With more exclamations of delight, he shot at the Antelope following, which fell;
and then at the last one, which fell as the others had.

"Now," said he, "I suppose I might as well take
my meat home. Fine game I have bagged today."
He untied the strap which he had brought along
and tied together the legs of the first deer he had
shot. He stooped down, raised the deer, knelt on
the ground and drew the strap over his forehead,
and was just about to rise with his burden and
make off for his den when, *klo-o-o-o-o!* he fell
down almost crushed under a mass of white rock.
"Goodness! what's this? Mercy, but this is startling!" He looked around, but he saw nothing of
his game save a shapeless mass of white rock.
"Well, I will try this other one," said he to himself. He had no sooner placed the other on his

back than down it bore him, another mass of white rock! "What can be the matter? The devil must be to pay!" said he. Then he tried the next, with no better success. "Well, there is one left, anyway," said he. He tied the feet of the last one together, and was about to place the strap over his forehead, when he heard a mighty and thundering tread and great shouting and a terrible noise altogether, for the people were already gathering about his den. He made for the mouth of it with all possible speed, but the people were there before him; they closed in upon him, they clutched at his stolen garments, they pulled his earrings out of his ears, slitting his ears in doing so, until he put up his hands and cried: "Death and ashes! Mercy! Mercy! You hurt! You hurt! Don't treat me so! I'll be good hereafter. I'll take the clothing off and give it back to you without making the slightest trouble, if you will let me alone." But the people closed in still more angrily, and pulled him about, buffeted him, tore his clothing from him, until he was left nude and bruised and so maimed that he could hardly move.

Then the old priests gathered around, and said one of them: "It will not be well if we let this beast go as he is; he is too large, too powerful, and too crafty. He has but to think of destruction; forsooth, he destroys. He has but to think of over-reaching; it is accomplished. It will not be well that he should go abroad thus. He must be roasted; and thus only can we rid the world of him as he is."

So the people assembled and heaped up great quantities of dry firewood; and they drilled fire from a stick, and lighted the mass. Then they cast the struggling Tarantula amid the flames, and he squeaked and sizzled and hissed, and swelled and swelled and swelled, until, with a terrific noise, he burst, and the fragments of his carcass were cast to the uttermost parts of the earth. These parts again took shape as beings not unlike Old Tarantula himself.

Thus it was in the days of the ancients. And therefore today, though crooked are the legs of the tarantula, and his habit of progress backward, still he is distributed throughout the great world. Only he is very, very much smaller than was the Great Tarantula who lived below the two rocky columns of Thunder Mountain.

Thus shortens my story.

ÁTAHSAIA, THE CANNIBAL DEMON

IN the days of the ancients, when the children of our forefathers lived in Héshokta ("Town of the Cliffs"), there also lived two beautiful maidens, elder and younger, sisters one to the other, daughters of a master-chief.

One bright morning in summer-time, the elder sister called to the younger, "*Háni!*"

"What sayest thou?" said the *háni.*

"The day is bright and the water is warm. Let us go down to the pool and wash our clothes, that we may wear them as if new at the dance to come."

"Ah, yes, sister elder," said the *háni;* "but these are days when they say the shadows of the rocks and even the sage-bushes lodge unthinkable things, and cause those who walk alone to breathe hard with fear."

"*Shtchu!*" exclaimed the elder sister derisively. "Younger sisters always are as timid as younger brothers are bad-tempered."

"Ah, well, then; as you will, sister elder. I will not quarrel with your wish, but I fear to go."

"*Yaush!* Come along, then," said the elder sister; whereupon they gathered their cotton mantles and other garments into bundles, and, taking along a bag of yucca-root, or soap-weed, started together down the steep, crooked path to where the pool lay at the foot of the great mesa.

Now, far above the Town of the Cliffs, among

the rocks of red-gray and yellow—red in the form of a bowlder-like mountain that looks like a frozen sand-bank—there is a deep cave. You have never seen it? Well! to this day it is called the "Cave of Átahsaia," and there, in the times I tell of, lived Átahsaia himself. Uhh! what an ugly demon he was! His body was as big as the biggest elk's, and his breast was shaggy with hair as stiff as porcupine-quills. His legs and arms were long and brawny,—all covered with speckled scales of black and white. His hair was coarse and snarly as a buffalo's mane, and his eyes were so big and glaring that they popped out of his head like skinned onions. His mouth stretched from one cheek to the other and was filled with crooked fangs as yellow as thrown-away deer-bones. His lips were as red and puffy as peppers, and his face as wrinkled and rough as a piece of burnt buckskin. That was Átahsaia, who in the days of the ancients devoured men and women for his meat, and the children of men for his sweet-bread. His weapons were terrible, too. His finger-nails were as long as the claws of a bear, and in his left hand he carried a bow made of the sapling of a mountain-oak, with two arrows ready drawn for use. And he was never seen without his great flint knife, as broad as a man's thigh and twice as long, which he brandished with his right hand and poked his hair back with, so that his grizzly fore-locks were covered with the blood of those he had slaughtered. He wore over his shoulders whole skins of the mountain lion and bear clasped with buttons of wood.

Now, although Átahsaia was ugly and could not speak without chattering his teeth, or laugh without barking like a wolf, he was a very polite demon. But, like many ugly and polite people nowadays, he was a great liar.

Átahsaia that morning woke up and stuck his head out of his hole just as the two maidens went down to the spring. He caught sight of them while his eyes travelled below, and he chuckled. Then he muttered, as he gazed at them and saw how young and fine they were: "*Ahhali! Yaatchi!*" ("Good lunch! Two for a munch!") and howled his war-cry, "*Ho-o-o-thlai–a !*" till Teshaminkia, the Echo-god, shouted it to the maidens.

"Oh!" exclaimed the *háni*, clutching the arm of her elder sister; "listen !"

"*Ho-o-o-thlai-a!*" again roared the demon, and again Teshaminkia.

"Oh, oh! sister elder, what did I tell you! Why did we come out today!" and both ran away; then stopped to listen. When they heard nothing more, they returned to the spring and went to washing their clothes on some flat stones.

But Átahsaia grabbed up his weapons and began to clamber down the mountain, muttering and chuckling to himself as he went: "*Ahhali! Yaatchi!*" ("Good lunch! Two for a munch!").

Around the corner of Great Mesa, on the high shelves of which stands the Town of the Cliffs, are two towering buttes called Kwilli-yallon (Twin Mountain). Far up on the top of this mountain there dwelt Áhaiyúta and Mátsailéma.

You don't know who Áhaiyúta and Mátsailéma were? Well, I will tell you. They were the twin children of the Sun-father and the Mother Waters of the World. Before men were born to the light, the Sun made love to the Waters of the World, and under his warm, bright glances, there were hatched out of a foam-cup on the face of the Great Ocean, which then covered the earth, two wonderful boys, whom men afterward named *Ua nam Atch Piahk'oa* ("The Beloved Two who Fell"). The Sun dried away the waters from the high-lands of earth and these Two then delivered men forth from the bowels of our Earth-mother, and guided them eastward toward the home of their father, the Sun. The time came, alas! when war and many strange beings arose to destroy the children of earth, and then the eight Stern Beings changed the hearts of the twins to *sawanikia*, or the medicine of war. Thenceforth they were known as Áhaiyúta and Mátsailéma ("Our Beloved," the "Terrible Two," "Boy-gods of War").

Even though changed, they still guarded our ancients and guided them to the Middle of the World, where we now live. Gifted with hearts of the medicine of war, and with wisdom almost as great as the Sun-father's own, they became the invincible guardians of the Corn-people of Earth, and, with the rainbow for their weapon and thunderbolts for their arrows,—swift lightning-shafts pointed with turquoise,—were the greatest warriors of all in the days of the new. When at last they had conquered most of the enemies of men, they taught to a chosen few of their followers the songs, prayers, and orders of a society of warriors who should be called their children, the Priests[1] of the Bow, and selecting from among them the two wisest, breathed into their nostrils (as they have since breathed into those of their successors) the *sawanikia.* Since then we make anew the semblance of their being and place them each year at midsun on the top of the Mountain of Thunder, and on the top of the Mountain of the Beloved, that they may know we remember them and that they may guard (as it was said in the days of the ancients they would guard) the Land of Zuñi from sunrise to sunset and cut off the pathways of the enemy.

Well, Áhaiyúta, who is called the elder brother, and Mátsailéma, who is called the younger, were living on the top of Twin Mountain with their old grandmother.

Said the elder to the younger on this same morning : " Brother, let us go out and hunt. It is a fine day. What say you ? "

" My face is in front of me," said the younger, " and under a roof is no place for men," he added, as he put on his helmet of elk-hide and took a quiver of mountain-lion skin from an antler near the ladder.

" Where are you two boys going now ? " shrieked the grandmother through a trap-door from below. " Don't you ever intend to stop worrying me by

---

[1] Here and hereafter I use this term *priest* reluctantly, in lack of a better word, but in accordance with Webster's second definition.—F. H. C.

going abroad when even the spaces breed fear like thick war ?"

" O grandmother," they laughed, as they tightened their bows and straightened their arrows before the fire, " never mind us ; we are only going out for a hunt," and before the old woman could climb up to stop them they were gaily skipping down the rocks toward the cliffs below.

Suddenly the younger brother stopped. " Ahh !" said he, " listen, brother ! It is the cry of Átahsaia, and the old wretch is surely abroad to cause tears !"

" Yes," replied the elder. " It is Átahsaia, and we must stop him ! Come on, come on ; quick !"

" Hold, brother, hold ! Stiffen your feet right here with patience. He is after the two maidens of Héshokta ! I saw them going to the spring as I came down. This day he must die. Is your face to the front ?"

" It is ; come on," said the elder brother, starting forward.

" Stiffen your feet with patience, I say," again exclaimed the younger brother. " Know you that the old demon comes up the pathway below here ? He will not hurt them until he gets them home. You know he is a great liar, and a great flatterer ; that is the way the old beast catches people. Now, if we wait here we will surely see them when they come up."

So, after quarrelling a little, the elder brother consented to sit down on a rock which overlooked the pathway and was within bow-shot of the old demon's cave.

Now, while the girls were washing, Átahsaia ran as fast as his old joints would let him until the two girls heard his mutterings and rattling weapons.

" Something is coming, sister !" cried the younger, and both ran toward the rocks to hide again, but they were too late.   The old demon strode around by another way and suddenly, at a turn, came face to face with them, glaring with his bloodshot eyes and waving his great jagged flint knife.   But as he neared them he lowered the knife and smiled, straightening himself up and approaching the frightened ones as gently as would a young man.

The poor younger sister clung to the elder one, and sank moaning by her side, for the smile of Átahsaia was as fearful as the scowl of a triumphant enemy, or the laugh of a rattlesnake when he hears any old man tell a lie and thinks he will poison him for it.

" Why do you run, and why do you weep so ? " asked the old demon.   " I know you.   I am ugly and old, my pretty maidens, but I am your grand-father and mean you no harm at all.   I frightened you only because I felt certain you would run away from me if you could."

" Ah ! " faltered the elder sister, immediately getting over her fright.   " We did not know you and therefore we were frightened by you.   Come, sister, come," said she to the younger.   " Brighten your eyes and thoughts, for our grandfather will not hurt us.   Don't you see ? "

But the younger sister only shook her head and sobbed.   Then the demon got angry.   " What are you blubbering about?" he roared, raising his knife and sweeping it wildly through the air. "Do you see this knife? This day I will cut off the light of your life with it if you do not swallow your whimpers!"

"Get up, oh, do get up, *háni!*" whispered the elder sister, now again frightened herself. "Surely he will not cut us off just now, if we obey him; and is it not well that even for a little time the light of life shine—though it shine through fear and sadness—than be cut off altogether? For who knows where the trails tend that lead through the darkness of the night of death?"

You know, in the speech of the rulers of the world and of our ancients,[1] a man's light was cut off when his life was taken, and when he died he came to the dividing-place of life.

The *háni* tried to rally herself and rose to her feet, but she still trembled.

"Now, my pretty maidens, my own grand-daughters, even," said the old demon once more, as gently as at first, "I am most glad I found you. How good are the gods! for I am a poor, lone old man. All my people are gone." (Here he sighed like the hiss of a wild-cat.) "Yonder above is my home" (pointing over his shoulder), "and as I am a great hunter, plenty of venison is baking in my rear room and more sweet-bread than I can eat. Lo! it makes me homesick to eat alone, and when I saw you and saw how pretty and gentle you were, I thought that it might be you would

[1] One of the figures of speech meaning the gods.

throw the light of your favor on me, and go up
to my house to share of my abundance and drink
from my vessels. Besides, I am so old that only
now and then can I get a full jar of water up to
my house. So I came as fast as I could to ask
you to return and eat with me."

Reassured by his kind speech, the elder sister
hastened to say : " Of course, we will go with our
grandfather, and if that is all he may want of us,
we can soon fill his water-jars, can't we, *háni ?* "

" You are a good girl," said the old demon to
the one who had spoken ; then, glaring at the
younger sister : " Bring that fool along with you
and come up ; she will not come by herself ; she
has more bashfulness than sense, and less sense
than my knife, because that makes the world more
wise by killing off fools."

He led the way and the elder sister followed,
dragging along the shrinking *háni.*

The old demon kept talking in a loud voice as
they went up the pathway, telling all sorts of
entertaining stories, until, as they neared the rocks
where Áhaiyúta and Mátsailéma were waiting, the
Two heard him and said to one another : " Ahh,
they come ! "

Then the elder brother jumped up and began
to tighten his bow, but the younger brother
muttered : " Sit down, won't you, you fool !
Átahsaia's ears are like bat-ears, only bigger.
Wait now, till I say ready. You know he will not
hurt the girls until he gets them out from his
house. Look over there in front of his hole. Do

you see the flat place that leads along to that deep chasm beyond?"

"Yes," replied the elder brother. "But what of that?"

"What but that there he cuts the throats of his captives and casts their bones and heads into the depths of the chasm! Do you see the notch in the stone? That's where he lets their blood flow down, and for that reason no one ever discovers his tracks. Now, stiffen your feet with patience, I say, and we will see what to do when the time comes."

Again they sat and waited. As the old demon and the girls passed along below, the elder brother again started and would have shot had not Mát-sailéma held him back. "You fool of a brother elder, but not wiser, No! Do you not know that your arrow is lightning and will kill the maidens as well as the monster?"

Finally, the demon reached the entrance to his cave, and, going in, asked the girls to follow him, laying out two slabs for them to sit on. "Now, sit down, my pretty girls, and I will soon get something for you to eat. You must be hungry." Going to the rear of the cave, he broke open a stone oven, and the steam which arose was certainly delicious and meaty. Soon he brought out two great bowls, big enough to feed a whole dance. One contained meat, the other a mess resembling sweet-bread pudding. "Now, let us eat," said the demon, seating himself opposite, and at once diving his horny fingers and scaly hand half up to the wrist in the meat-broth.   The elder sister began to take bits of the food to eat it, when the younger made a motion to her, and showed her with horror the bones of a little hand.   The sweet-bread was the flesh and bones of little children.   Then the two girls only pretended to eat, taking the food out and throwing it down by the side of the bowls.

"Why don't you eat?" demanded the demon, cramming at the same time a huge mouthful of the meat, bones and all, into his wide throat.

"We are eating," said one of the girls.

"Then why do you throw my food away?"

"We are throwing away only the bones."

"Well, the bones are the better part," retorted the demon, taking another huge mouthful, by way of example, big enough to make a grown man's meal.   "Oh, yes!" he added; "I forgot that you had baby teeth."

After the meal was finished, the old demon said: "Let us go out and sit down in the sun on my terrace.   Perhaps, my pretty maidens, you will comb an old man's hair, for I have no one left to help me now," he sighed, pretending to be very sad.   So, showing the girls where to sit down, without waiting for their assent he settled himself in front of them and leaned his head back to have it combed.   The two maidens dared not disobey; and now and then they pulled at a long, coarse hair, and then snapped their fingers close to his scalp, which so deceived the old demon that he grunted with satisfaction every time.   At last their knees were so tired by his weight upon them that they said they were done, and Átahsaia, rising, pretended to be greatly pleased, and thanked them over and over. Then he told them to sit down in front of him, and he would comb their hair as they had combed his, but not to mind if he hurt a little for his fingers were old and stiff. The two girls again dared not disobey, and sat down as he had directed. Uhh! how the old beast grinned and glared and breathed softly between his teeth.

The two brothers had carefully watched everything, the elder one starting up now and then, the younger remaining quiet. Suddenly Mátsailéma sprang up. He caught the shield the Sun-father had given him,—the shield which, though made only of nets and knotted cords, would ward off alike the weapons of the warrior or the magic of the wizard. Holding it aloft, he cried to Áhaiyúta: "Stand ready; the time is come! If I miss him, pierce him with your arrow. Now, then—"

He hurled the shield through the air. Swiftly as a hawk and noiselessly as an owl, it sailed straight over the heads of the maidens and settled between them and the demon's face. The shield was invisible, and the old demon knew not it was there. He leaned over as if to examine the maidens' heads. He opened his great mouth, and, bending yet nearer, made a vicious bite at the elder one.

"Ai, ai! my poor little sister, alas!" with which both fell to sobbing and moaning, and crouched, expecting instantly to be destroyed.

But the demon's teeth caught in the meshes of the invisible shield, and, howling with vexation, he began struggling to free himself of the encumbrance. Áhaiyúta drew a shaft to the point and let fly. With a thundering noise that rent the rocks, and a rush of strong wind, the shaft blazed through the air and buried itself in the demon's shoulders, piercing him through ere the thunder had half done pealing. Swift as mountain sheep were the leaps and light steps of the brothers, who, bounding to the shelf of rock, drew their war-clubs and soon softened the hard skull of the old demon with them. The younger sister was unharmed save by fright; but the elder sister lay where she had sat, insensible.

" Hold!" cried Mátsailéma, " she was to blame, but then—" Lifting the swooning maiden in his strong little arms, he laid her apart from the others, and, breathing into her nostrils, soon revived her eyes to wisdom.

" *This day have we, through the power of sawanikia, seen* [1] *for our father an enemy of our children men. A beast that caused unto fatherless children, unto menless women, unto womenless men (who thus became through his evil will), tears and sad thoughts, has this day been looked upon by the Sun and laid low. May the favors of the gods thus meet us ever.*"

Thus said the two brothers, as they stood over the gasping, still struggling but dying demon; and as they closed their little prayer, the maidens, who

---

[1] To "see" an enemy signifies, in Zuñi mythology, to take his life.

now first saw whom they had to thank for their
deliverance, were overwhelmed with gladness, yet
shame. They exclaimed, in response to the prayer:
"*May they, indeed, thus meet you and ourselves!*"
Then they breathed upon their hands.

The two brothers now turned toward the girls.
"Look ye upon the last enemy of men," said they,
"whom this day we have had the power of *sawanikia* given us to destroy; whom this day the father
of all, our father the Sun, has looked upon, whose
light of life this day our weapons have cut off;
whose path of life this day our father has divided.
Not ourselves, but our father has done this deed,
through us. Haste to your home in Héshokta and
tell your father these things; and tell him, pray,
that he must assemble his priests and teach them
these our words, for we divide our paths of life
henceforth from one another and from the paths of
men, no more to mingle save in spirit with the
children of men. But we shall depart for our
everlasting home in the mountains—the one to the
Mountain of Thunder, the other to the Mount of
the Beloved—to guard from sunrise to sunset the
land of the Corn-priests of Earth, that the foolish
among men break not into the Middle Country of
Earth and lay it waste. Yet we shall require of
our children the plumes wherewith we dress our
thoughts, and the forms of our being wherewith men
may renew us each year at midsun. Henceforth
two stars at morning and evening will be seen, the
one going before, the other following, the Sun-
father—the one Áhaiyúta, his herald; the other

Mátsailéma, his guardian ; warriors both, and fathers of men. May the trail of life be finished ere divided ! Go ye happily hence."

The maidens breathed from the hands of the Twain, and with bowed heads and a prayer of thanks started down the pathway toward the Town of the Cliffs. When they came to their home, the old father asked whence they came. They told the story of their adventure and repeated the words of the Beloved.

The old man bowed his head, and said : " It was Áhaiyúta and Mátsailéma ! " Then he made a prayer of thanks, and cast abroad on the winds white meal of the seeds of earth and shells from the Great Waters of the World, the pollen of beautiful flowers, and the paints of war.

" It is well ! " he said. " Four days hence I will assemble my warriors, and we will cut the plume-sticks, paint and feather them, and place them on high mountains, that through their knowledge and power of medicine our Beloved Two Warriors may take them unto themselves."

Now, when the maidens disappeared among the rocks below, the brothers looked each at the other and laughed. Then they shouted, and Áhaiyúta kicked Átahsaia's ugly carcass till it gurgled, at which the two boys shouted again most hilariously and laughed. " That 's what we proposed to do with you, old beast ! " they cried out.

" But, brother younger," said Ahaiyúta, " what shall be done with him now ? "

" Let 's skin him," said Mátsailéma.

So they set to work and skinned the body from foot to head, as one skins a fawn when one wishes to make a seed-bag. Then they put sticks into the legs and arms, and tied strings to them, and stuffed the body with dry grass and moss; and where they set the thing up against the cliff it looked verily like the living Átahsaia.

"Uhh! what an ugly beast he was!" said Mátsailéma. Then he shouted: "*Wahaha, hihiho!*" and almost doubled up with laughter. "Won't we have fun with old grandmother, though. Hurry up; let's take care of the rest of him!"

They cut off the head, and Áhaiyúta said to it: "*Thou hast been a liar, and told a falsehood for every life thou hast taken in the world; therefore shalt thou become a lying star, and each night thy guilt shall be seen of all men throughout the wide world.*" He twirled the bloody head around once or twice, and cast it with all might into the air. *Wa muu!* it sped through the spaces into the middle of the sky like a spirt of blood, and now it is a great red star. It rises in summer-time and tells of the coming morning when it is only midnight; hence it is called *Mokwanosana* (Great Lying Star).

Then Mátsailéma seized the great knife and ripped open the abdomen with one stroke. Grasping the intestines, he tore them out and exclaimed: "*Ye have devoured and digested the flesh of men over the whole wide world; therefore ye shall be stretched from one end of the earth to the other, and the children of those ye have wasted will look upon ye every night and will say to one another:*

'*Ah, the entrails of him who caused sad thoughts to our grandfathers shine well tonight!*' *and they will laugh and sneer at ye.*" Whereupon he slung the whole mass aloft, and *tsolo!* it stretched from one end of the world to the other, and became the Great Snow-drift of the Skies (Milky Way). Lifting the rest of the carcass, they threw it down into the chasm whither the old demon had thrown so many of his victims, and the rattlesnakes came out and ate of the flesh day after day till their fangs grew yellow with putrid meat, and even now their children's fangs are yellow and poisonous.

"Now, then, for some fun!" shouted Mátsailéma. "Do you catch the old bag up and prance around with it a little; and I will run off to see how it looks."

Áhaiyúta caught up the effigy, and, hiding himself behind, pulled at the strings till it looked, of all things thinkable, like the living Átahsaia himself starting out for a hunt, for they threw the lion skins over it and tied the bow in its hand.

"Excellent! Excellent!" exclaimed the boys, and they clapped their hands and *wa-ha-ha-ed* and *ho-ho-ho-ed* till they were sore. Then, dragging the skin along, they ran as fast as they could, down to the plain below Twin Mountain.

The Sun was climbing down the western ladder, and their old grandmother had been looking all over the mountains and valleys below to see if the two boys were coming. She had just climbed the ladder and was gazing and fretting and saying:

" Oh! those two boys! terrible pests and as hard-
hearted and as long-winded in having their own
way as a turtle is in having his! Now, something has happened to them; I knew it would,"
when suddenly a frightened scream came up from
below.

" *Ho-o-o-ta! Ho-o-o-ta!* Come quick! Help!
Help!" the voice cried, as if in anguish.

"Uhh!" exclaimed the old woman, and she
went so fast in her excitement that she tumbled
through the trap-door, and then jumped up, scolding and groaning.

She grabbed a poker of piñon, and rushed out of
the house. Sure enough, there was poor Mátsailéma running hard and calling again and again
for her to hurry down. The old woman hobbled
along over the rough path as fast as she could,
and until her wind was blowing shorter and
shorter, when, suddenly turning around the crags,
she caught sight of Áhaiyúta struggling to get
away from Átahsaia.

" *O ai o!* I knew it! I knew it!" cried the
old woman; and she ran faster than ever until
she came near enough to see that her poor grandson was almost tired out, and that Mátsailéma had
lost even his war-club. "Stiffen your feet,—my
boys,—wait—a bit," puffed the old woman, and,
flying into a passion, she rushed at the effigy
and began to pound it with her poker, till the
dust fairly smoked out of the dry grass, and the
skin doubled up as if it were in pain.

Mátsailéma rolled and kicked in the grass, and

Áhaiyúta soon had to let the stuffed demon fall down for sheer laughing. But the old woman never ceased. She belabored the demon and cursed his cannibal heart and told him that was what he got for chasing her grandsons, and that, and this, and that, whack! whack! without stopping, until she thought the monster surely must be dead. Then she was about to rest when suddenly the boys pulled the strings, and the demon sprang up before her, seemingly as well as ever. Again the old woman fell to, but her strokes kept getting feebler and feebler, her breath shorter and shorter, until her wind went out and she fell to the ground.

How the boys did laugh and roll on the ground when the old grandmother moaned: "Alas! alas! This day—my day—light is—cut off—and my wind of life—fast going."

The old woman covered her head with her tattered mantle; but when she found that Átahsaia did not move, she raised her eyes and looked through a rent. There were her two grandsons rolling and kicking on the grass and holding their mouths with both hands, their eyes swollen and faces red with laughter. Then she suddenly looked for the demon. There lay the skin, all torn and battered out of shape.

"So ho! you pesky wretches; that's the way you treat me, is it? Well! never again will I help you, never!" she snapped, "nor shall you ever live with me more!" Whereupon the old woman jumped up and hobbled away.

But little did the brothers care. They laughed till she was far away, and then said one to the other: "It is done!"

Since that time, the grandmother has gone, no one knows where. But Áhaiyúta and Mátsailéma are the bright stars of the morning and evening, just in front of and behind the Sun-father himself. Yet their spirits hover over their shrines on Thunder Mountain and the Mount of the Beloved, they say, or linger over the Middle of the World, forever to guide the games and to guard the warriors of the Land of Zuñi. Thus it was in the days of the ancients.

Thus shortens my story.

THE HERMIT MÍTSINA

WHEN all was new, and the gods dwelt in the ancient places, long, long before the time of our ancients, many were the gods—some destined for good and some for evil or for the doing of things beneath understanding. And those of evil intent, so painfully bad were they to become that not in the company and council of the precious beloved of the *Kâkâ* (the Order of the Sacred Drama) could they be retained.

Thus it happened, in the times of our ancients, long, long ago, that there dwelt all alone in the Cañon of the Pines, southeast of Zuñi, Mítsina the Hermit. Of evil understanding he ; therefore it had been said to him (by the gods) : " Alone shalt thou dwell, being unwise and evil in thy ways, until thou hast, through much happening, even become worthy to dwell amongst us." Thus it was that Mítsina lived alone in his house in the Cañon of the Pines.

Sometimes when a young man, dressed in very fine apparel (wearing his collars of shell, and turquoise earrings, and other precious things which were plentiful in the days of our ancients), would be out hunting, and chanced to go through the Cañon of the Pines and near to the house of Mítsina, he would hear the sounds of gaming from within ; for, being alone, the hermit whiled away his time in playing at the game of sacred arrows (or cane-cards).

Forever from the ceiling of his house there hung suspended his basket-drum, made of a large wicker bowl, over the mouth of which was stretched tightly a soft buckskin, even like the basket-drums which we use in the playing of cane-cards today, and which you know are suspended with the skin-side downward from the ceilings of the gaming rooms in the topmost houses of our town. Though the one he had was no better than those we have today, save that it was larger and handsomer perhaps, yet he delighted to call it his cloud canopy, bethinking himself of the drum-basket of his former associates, the gods, which is even the rounded sky itself, with the clouds stretched across it. Forever upon the floor of his house there lay spread a great buffalo robe, the skin upward dressed soft and smooth, as white as corn-flour, and painted with the many-colored symbols and counting marks of the game, even as our own. But he delighted to call it his sacred terraced plain,[1] bethinking himself of the robe-spread of the gods, which is even the outspread earth itself, bordered by terraced horizons, and diversified by mountains, valleys, and bright places, which are

---

[1] The words " terrace," " sacred terrace," "terraced plain" (*awithlu-iane, awithluian-pewine*), and the like, wherever they occur, refer to the figurative expression for the earth in the Zuñi rituals addressed to the gods, where they are used as more nearly conforming to the usage of the gods. The symbol of the earth on the sacred altars is a terraced or zigzag figure or decoration, and the same figure appears in their carvings and other ornamental work. The disgraced god Mítsina applied the term to the robe spread out as the bed for his game. It may be stated in further explanation that the country in which the Zuñis have wandered and lived for unnumbered generations, and where they still dwell, is made

the symbols and game marks whereby the gods themselves count up the score of their game.

Hearing these sounds of the game in passing, the young man would naturally draw near and listen. Though all alone, every time he made a good throw Mítsina would exclaim "*Her-r-r-r !*" and as the canes struck the skin of the drum-basket above, *tcha-le-le*, *tcha-le-le*, it would sound; and *ke-le-le* they would rattle as they fell on the robe below. "Ha! ha!" old Mítsina would exclaim, as if triumphantly to some opponent in the game,—"*Kohakwa iyathtokyai !*" as much as to say: "Good for you, old fellow! The white-corn symbol fell uppermost!"

"Oh!" the young man would exclaim as he listened. "Oh!"—and, wishing to learn more about the matter, he would stealthily climb up the ladder and peer down through the sky-hole. Old Mítsina would catch sight of him, be sure of that, and greet him most cordially, calling to him: "Come in, come in, my fine young fellow, come in; let's have a game!"

Now, he had practised so long that he had

up largely of mesas, or flat-top mountains or elevations, rising one above another and showing as terraces on the horizon. Beheld at great distances, or in the evening, these mountain terraces are mere silhouettes and serve to exaggerate the zigzag spaces of light between them. As the conventional sacred emblem for the earth is a terrace, outspread or upreaching, as the case may be, so the conventional sacred emblem for the sky is an inverted terrace.

To the gods the whole earth is represented as having seemed so small that they invariably spoke of it as the terraced plain, and in their playing of this game they are supposed to have used it as the bed for the game, as the Zuñi people used the outspread buffalo robe for the purpose, acquired more skill than anyone else throughout the world—at least among mortals ; so that when any of the young men chanced to play with him, he invariably lost, poor fellow ! Hanging on the pole along the north side of Mítsina's house were the necklaces, embroidered mantles, and turquoises, and all sorts of treasures which he had won in this way ; and as many on the western side, on the southern side as many, and on the eastern side also.

When the young man came in, Mítsina would continue : " My good friend, sit right down over there. Have you your canes today ? " If the young man said " Yes," he would say : " Ha ! very well." Or, if he said " No," " Never mind," Mítsina would say ; " here are some," producing a very fine set of polished canes. The young man, being thus pressed, would stake perhaps his necklace or his earrings, and the game would begin. Losing them, he would stake his clothing, his bows and ar-rows—in fact, everything he had about him. You know how it is with gamesters when they have lost a great deal and wish to get it back again ? Well, so it was then. When the young man had lost everything, he would bow his head on his hand, and sit thinking. Then old Mítsina, with a jolly, devil-may-care manner, would say : " Bet your left thigh. I 'll put all you have lost and more, too, on that." The young man would say to himself, with a sigh of relief : " What an old fool you are ! " and reply : " All right ! I will take your bet." Alas ! the one thigh he bet is lost ; then the other goes the same way ; then one of his sides and arms ; losing which, he bet the other, and so on, until he had bet away his whole body, including his head. Then in utter despair he would exclaim : " Do with me as thou wilt. I am thy slave." And old Mítsina with the same devil-may-care manner would catch him up, take him out to the back of his house and wring his neck that he might not go back and report his losses to his people.

Again, some other well-equipped young man would be passing that way, and hearing the sound made by the solitary player, and being attracted thereby, would be drawn in the same way into the game, would lose everything, and old Mítsina would wring his neck and keep his treasures.

Thus it was in the days of the ancients. Great were the losses of the young men, and many of them perished.

Well, one day little Áhaiyúta and Mátsailéma— the War-gods of peace times—who dwelt, as you know, where their shrine now stands on Face Mountain, with their old grandmother,—went out hunting rabbits and prairie-dogs. It chanced that in following the rabbits along the cliffs of a side cañon they came into the Cañon of the Pines, near where the house of Mítsina stood. Presently they heard the sounds of his game. " Hu, hu ! " the old fellow would exclaim as he cast his canes into the air. *Ke-le-le-le* they would rattle as they fell on the skin.

" Uh ! " exclaimed Áhaiyúta, the elder. " Brother younger, listen."

The younger listened. " By my eyes ! " exclaimed he, " it is someone playing at cane-cards. Let 's go and have a peep at him." So they climbed the ladder and peered in through the sky-hole.

Presently, old Mítsina espied them, and called out : " Ha ! my little fellows ; glad to see you to-day ! How are you ? Come in, come in ! I am dying for a game ; I was playing here all by myself."

The two little War-gods clambered down the ladder, and old Mítsina placed blankets for them, invited them most cordially to sit down, and asked if they would like to play a game. Nothing loth they, seeing all the fine things hanging round his room ; so out from their girdles they drew their cane-cards, for those, as you know, they always carried with them.

Perhaps I have not told you that even the basket-drum old Mítsina played with was fringed with the handsome long turquoise earrings which he had won, and even under the robe on which he played there were piled one over another, in a great flat heap, the finest of the necklaces gathered from those whom he had defeated in playing and then slain.

" What would you like to put up ?" asked the old fellow, pointing around his room—particularly to the basket-drum fringed with turquoises—and lifting the robe and showing just enough of the necklaces underneath it to whet the appetites of the little War-gods.

"We've nothing fine enough to bet for these things," said they ruefully.

"O ho!" cried Mítsina. "No matter, no matter at all, my boys. Bet your bows and arrows and clothing; if you like, bet everything you have on, and I'll put up that poleful there on the north side of my room."

"Good! good! tell him all right," whispered the younger brother to the elder.

So the elder agreed, chuckling to himself, for it was rarely that a man was found who could beat the little War-gods in a game. And they began their playing. How the turquoises rattled as they threw their canes! How the canes jingled and thumped as they fell on the robe!

The game was merry and long, and well played on both sides; but the poor little War-gods lost. Their countenances fell; but old Mítsina, with a merry twinkle in his eyes, exclaimed: "Oh pshaw! never mind, never mind!"

"Yes," said the two War-gods, "but how in the world are we ever going back to our grandmother in this plight?"—glancing down over their bare bodies, for they had bet even the clothing off their backs. "What else can we bet? How can we win back what we have lost?"

"Bet your left thighs," said the old hermit.

They thought a moment, and concluded they would do so. So the game was staked again and begun and the canes rattled merrily; but they lost again. Then old Mítsina suggested that they bet their other thighs. They did so and again lost.

Then he suggested they should bet their left sides, hoping forthwith to get hold of their hearts, but the young War-gods were crafty. The elder one exclaimed : "All right !" but the younger one said : "Goodness ! as for you, you can bet your left side if you want to, but I'll bet my right, for my heart is on my left side, and who ever heard of a man betting away his heart !"

"Just as you like," said Mítsina, "but if you'll bet your bodies up to your necks I will stake all you have lost and all I have besides," said he, looking around on his fine possessions.

"Done !" cried the War-gods. And again they played and again lost. Then they had nothing left but their heads and ears and eyes to bet. Finally they concluded to bet these also, for said they to one another : "What good will our heads do us, even though they be the crown-pieces of our being, without the rest ?"

They played again, but the poor fellows lost their heads also. "Alas ! alas ! do as thou wilt with us," exclaimed the little War-gods, with rueful countenances.

Old Mítsina, locking them up in a small recess of his house, went out and gathered before his front door a great quantity of dry wood. Then he tied the little fellows hand and foot, and laid them near by,—not near enough to burn them up, but near enough so that they would scorch,— and lighted the fire, to have the pleasure of roasting them. When they began to brown and sizzle a little they writhed and howled with pain, but they

were tough and quite bad, as you know, and this did
not kill them.

Who can hide a thing from the eyes of the
gods? The elder brothers of these two foolish
little War-gods, Áhaiyúta and Mátsailéma, those
who dwelt on Thunder Mountain, became aware of
what was going on. "Come, brother younger,"
said the elder, strapping on his quiver and taking
his bow in hand, "come, let us off to old Mítsina's house and teach him a lesson!" So, in a
twinkling they were climbing down the mountain,
speeding across the wide valley, and threading
their way through the Cañon of the Pines.

Mítsina had grown tired of watching the poor
little War-gods and had gone in to have another
little game, and there he was pitching his cane-
cards and talking to himself, as usual. The two
gods hauled their unfortunate brothers away from
the fire, and, climbing the ladder, peered in. Mítsina espied them, and as usual invited them in to a
game. With as jolly an air as his own they accepted his challenge and sat down. Mítsina
offered to bet all his fine things hanging on the
north side of the house. "What will you put up,
my little fellows?" asked he.

"If you will include those ugly little devils that
we saw sizzling before the fire when we came in,
we will bet you everything we have with us,"
said they.

"Good! good! haul them in!" shouted Mítsina.

The War-gods scrambled out of the house,
and, by no means gently, dragged their wretched

little brothers in by the heels and dumped them down on the floor to show their indifference, sat down, and began to play. They bet their weapons, holding up the knife of war which they carried, the point of lightning itself fatal in power,—splitter of mountains and overcomer of demons and men alike.

Old Mítsina, when told of the power of the weapons, became doubtful as to his company, but presently fell to and played with a will. He lost. Then he put up all the rest of his goods hanging on the other side of the room. Again he lost, and again, even the turquoises hanging from the basket-drum, the necklaces under his robe, and the things he played with, and getting wild with excitement, sure that his luck would return, followed out the plan he had so often suggested to others, and bet away his thighs, then his sides and arms, then his head and ears, excepting his eyes, and last of all his very eyes themselves. Each time the young War-gods won. The old gambler let his hands fall by his sides, and dropped his head on his breast, sick with humiliation and chagrin.

" Now, my brother," said the elder to the younger, " what shall we do with this beast ? "

" I don't know," said the other. " We can't kill him ; yet, if we leave him to go his own way, he will gamble and gamble without ceasing, and make no end of trouble. Suppose we make a good man of him."

" How ? " asked the other.

" Pluck out his eyes."

" Capital ! " exclaimed the first. So, while one of them held the old fellow down, the other gouged out his eyes, and with pain and horror he utterly forgot in unconsciousness (swooned away).

The two elder War-gods set their younger brothers on their feet, and all four of them joined in clearing out the treasures and magnificent possessions which Mítsina through all these years had won from his victims ; and these they took away with them that by their sacred knowledge they might change them into blessings for the faithful of their children among men, and thus return, as it were, what had been lost. Then away they went, leaving old Mítsina still as witless as a dead man, to his fate.

By-and-by the old man came to his senses, and raising himself up, tried to look around, but, forsooth, he could not see.

" What in the world has happened ? What a fearful pain I have in my temples ! " said he. " What is the matter ? Is it night ? "

Then gradually his situation came to him. He uttered a groan of pain and sorrow, and, putting out his hand, felt the wall and raised himself by it. Then he crept along, feeling his way to the window, not yet quite certain whether he had been dreaming all this and it was still night, or whether he had really lost everything and been bereft of his eyes by those midgets. When he put his hand into the window, however, he felt the warm sunlight streaming in, and knew that it was still day, and that it was all true.

In feeling there he chanced to touch a little package of pitch which had been laid in the window. He felt it all over with both hands, but could not quite tell what it was. Then he put it against his cheek, but was still uncertain; then he rubbed it, and smelt of it. "Pitch! pitch! as I live!" said he. "I have often lighted this when it was dark, and been able to see. Now, maybe, if I light it this time, I shall be able to see again." He felt his way all round the room to the fireplace, and after burning his fingers two or three times in feeling for coals, he found a sliver and held it in the coals and ashes until he heard it begin to sputter and crackle. Then he lighted the pitch with it. Eyeless though he was, the fumes from this medicine of the woodlands restored to him a kind of vision. "Good!" cried the old fellow, "I see again!" But when he looked around, he saw nothing as it had been formerly; and his thoughts reverted to the great City of the Gods (*Kothlu-ellakwin*); and, as it were, he could see the way thither. So he turned toward his door, and with a sigh gave up his old place of abode, relinquished all thought of his possessions, gave up his former bad inclinations, and turned westward toward the City of the Gods and Souls.

As he went along holding his light before him and following it, he sang a mournful song. The Birds, hearing this song, flocked around him, and as he went on singing, exclaimed to one another: "Ha! ha! the old wretch; he has lost his eyes! Served him right! Let's put out his light for him."

Now, before that time, strange as it may seem, the Eagles and even the Crows were as white as the foam on warring waters. The Eagles were so strong that they thrust the other birds away, and began to pounce down at Mítsina's light, trying to blow it out with their wings. *Thluh ! thluh !* they would flap into the light ; but still it would not go out ; and they only singed their feathers and blackened their wings and tails with smoke. In looking at one another they saw what a sad plight they were in. " Good gracious, brothers !" exclaimed some of them to the others, " we have made a fine mess of our white plumage !" And they gave it up.

Then the Crows rushed in and flapped against the light, but they could not put it out ; and although they grew blacker and blacker, they would not give it up. So they became as black as crows are now ; and ever since then eagles have been speckled with brown and black, and crows have been black, even to the tips of their beaks. And whenever in the Sacred Drama Dance of our people old Mítsina appears, he sings the doleful song and carries the light of pitch pine. He goes naked, with the exception of a wretched old cloth at his loins ; and he wears a mask with deep holes for eyes, blood streaming from them.

Thus shortens my story.

HOW THE TWINS OF WAR AND CHANCE, ÁHAIYÚTA AND MÁTSAI-LÉMA, FARED WITH THE UNBORN-MADE MEN OF THE UNDERWORLD[1]

TRANSLATOR'S INTRODUCTION

HERETOFORE I have withheld from publication such single examples of Zuñi folk-lore as the following, in order that the completer series might be brought forth in the form of an unbroken collection, with ample introductory as well as supplementary chapters, essential to the proper understanding by ourselves of the many distinctively Zuñi meanings and conceptions involved in the various allusions with which any one of them teems. Yet, to avoid encumbering the present example with any but the briefest of notes, I must ask leave to refer the reader to the more general yet detailed chapters I have already written in the main, and with which, I have reason to hope, I will ere long be able to present the tales in question. Meanwhile, I would refer likewise to the essay I have recently prepared for the Thirteenth Annual Report of the Bureau of American Ethnology, on *Zuñi Creation Myths* in their relation to primitive dance and other dramaturgic ceremonies.

Ever one of my chief story-tellers was Waíhusiwa,—of the priestly kin of Zuñi. He had already told me somewhat more than fifty of the folk tales, long and short, of his people, when one night I asked him for " only one more story of the grandfathers." Wishing to evade me, he replied with more show than sincerity:

[1] Reprinted from the *Journal of American Folk-Lore*, vol. v., No. 16, pp. 49–56.

" There is a North, and of it I have told you *té-la-p'-na-we*.[1] There is a West; of it also I have told you *té-la-p'-na-we*. There are the South and East; of them likewise have I told you *té-la-p'-na-we*. Even of the Above have I not but lately told you of the youth who made love to his eagle and dwelt apace in the Sky-world ? And of the great World-embracing Waters ? You have been told of the hunter who married the Serpent-maiden and journeyed to the Mountain of Sunset. Now, therefore, my word-pouch is as empty as the food-pack of a lost hunter, and—"

" Feel in the bottom of it, then," interposed old Pál-owahtiwa, who was sitting near, " and tell him of the Underworld."

"*Hi-ta !* [Listen !] brother younger," said Waíhusiwa, nonplussed but ever ready. " Did you ever hear tell of the people who could not digest, having, forsooth, no proper insides wherewithal to do so ? Did you ever hear of them, brother younger ?"

"Nay, never; not even from my own grandfathers," said I. " *Sons éso* to your story; short be it or long."[2]

" *Sons éso tse-ná !* " (" Cool your ' *sons éso !* ' and wait till *I* begin.")—F. H. C.

ZUÑI INTRODUCTION

It seems—so the words of the grandfathers say —that in the Underworld were many strange things and beings, even villages of men, long ago.

---

[1] From *té-na-la-a*, " time or times of," and *pé-na-we*, words or speeches (tales) : " tales of time."

[2] The invariable formula for beginning a folk tale is, by the raconteur: " *Són ah-tchi !* " (" Let us take up ")—*té-la-p'-ne*, or " a folk tale," being understood. To this the auditors or listeners respond: "*É-so !* " (" Yea, verily.") Again, by the raconteur: "*Sons i-nó-o-to-na ! Tem*," etc. (" Let us (tell of) the times of creation ! When," etc.) Again, by the listeners: " *Sons éso ! Te-ä-tú !* " (" Yea, let us, verily ! Be it so.")

But the people of those villages were unborn-made,
—more like the ghosts of the dead than ourselves,
yet more like ourselves than are the ghosts of the
dead, for as the dead are more finished of being
than we are, they were less so, as smoke, being
hazy, is less fine than mist, which is filmy ; or as
green corn, though raw, is soft like cooked corn
which is done (like the dead), and as both are softer
than ripe corn which, though raw, is hardened by
age (as we are of meat).

And also, these people were, you see, dead in
a way, in that they had not yet begun to live, that
is, as we live, in the daylight fashion.

And so, it would seem, partly like ourselves,
they had bodies, and partly like the dead they had
no bodies, for being unfinished they were unfixed.
And whereas the dead are like the wind, and take
form from within of their own wills (*yän'te-tseman*),
these people were really like the smoke,[1] taking
form from without of the outward touching of
things, even as growing and unripe grains and
fruits do.

---

[1] The Zuñi classification of states of growth or being is as elaborate
as that of relative space in their mythology—both extremely detailed and
systematic, yet, when understood, purely primitive and simple.   The
universe is supposed to have been generated from haze (*shí-wai-a*) produced by light (of the All-container, Sun-father) out of darkness.   The
observed analogy of this in nature is the appearance of haze (both heat
and steam) preceding growth in springtime ; the appearance of the
world, of growing and living things, through mist seemingly rising out
of the darkness each morning.   In harmony with this conception of the
universe is the correlative one that every being (as to soul, at least) passes
through many successive states of becoming, always beginning as a
shí-u-na há-i (haze being), and passing through the raw or soft (*k'ya-
pi-na*), the formative (*k'yaí-yu-na*), variable (*thlím-ni-na*), fixed or done

Well, in consequence, it was passing strange what a state they were in ! Bethink ye ! Their persons were much the reverse of our own, for wherein we are hard, they were soft—pliable. Wherein we are most completed, they were most unfinished ; for not having even the organs of digestion, whereby we fare lustily, food in its solidity was to them destructive, whereas to us it is sustaining. When, therefore, they would eat, they dreaded most the food itself, taking thought not to touch it, and merely absorbing the mist thereof. As fishes fare chiefly on water, and birds on air, so these people ate by gulping down the steam and savor of their cooked things whilst cooking or still hot ; then they threw the real food away, forsooth !

THE TALE

NOW, the Twain Little-ones, Áhaiyúta and Mátsailéma,[1] were ever seeking scenes of

(ak-na), and finished or dead (ä-shĭ-k'ya) states ; whilst the condition of the surpassing beings (gods) may be any of these at will (i-thlim-na, or thlim-nah-na, etc.). There are many analogies of this observed by the Zuñi, likening, as he does, the generation of being to that of fire with the fire-drill and stick. The most obvious of these is the appearance, in volumes, of " smoke-steam " or haze just previously to ignition, and its immediate disappearance with ignition. Further, the succession of beings in the becoming of a complete being may be regarded as an orderly personification of growth phenomena as observed in plants and seeds ; for example, in corn, which is characterized by no fewer than thirteen mystic names, according to its stages of growth. This whole subject is much more fully and conclusively set forth in the writings to which I have already referred.

[1] For the mythic origin of these two chief gods under the Sun, as his right- and left-hand being, their relation to chance, war, games, etc., I again refer the reader to the *Zuñi Creation Myths*.

contention ; for what was deathly and dreadful to others was lively and delightful to them ; so that cries of distress were ever their calls of invitation, as to a feast or dance is the call of a priest to us.

On a day when the world was quiet, they were sitting by the side of a deep pool. They heard curious sounds coming up through the waters, as though the bubbles were made by moans of the waters affrighted.

" Uh ! " cried the elder. " What is that ? "

The younger brother turned his ear to the ground and listened.

" There is trouble down there, dire trouble, for the people of the Underworld are shrieking war-cries like daft warriors and wailing like murder-mourners. What can be the matter ? Let us descend and see ! "

" Just so ! " said Áhaiyúta.

Then they covered their heads with their cord-shields [1]— turned upside down — and shut their eyes and stepped into the deep pool.

" Now we are in the dark," said they, " like the dark down there. Well, then, by means of the dark let us go down "—for they had wondrous power, had those Twain ; the magic of in-knowing-how thought had they.

---

[1] *Pi-a-la-we* (cord or cotton shields), evidently an ancient style of shield still surviving in the form of sacrificial net-shields of the Priesthood of the Bow. But the shields of these two gods were supposed to have been spun from the clouds which, supporting the sky-ocean, that in turn supported the sky-world (as this world is believed to be supported by under-waters and clouds), were hence possessed of the power of floating—upward when turned up, downward when reversed.

Down, like light through dark places, they went ; dry through the waters ; straight toward that village in the Underworld.

" Whew ! the poor wretches are already dead," cried they, "and rotting " — for their noses were sooner accustomed to the dark than their eyes, which they now opened.

" We might as well have spared ourselves the coming, and stayed above," said Áhaiyúta.

" Nay, not so," said Mátsailéma. " Let us go on and see how they lived, even if they are dead."

" Very well," said the elder ; and as they fared toward the village they could see quite plainly now, for they had made it dark (to themselves) by shutting their eyes in the daylight above, so now they made it light (to themselves) by opening their eyes in the darkness below and simply looking,—it was their way, you know.

" Well, well ! " said Mátsailéma, as they came nearer and the stench doubled. " Look at the village ; it is full of people ; the more they smell of carrion the more they seem alive ! "

" Yes, by the chut of an arrow ! " exclaimed Áhaiyúta. " But look here ! It is food we smell— cooked food, all thrown away, as we throw away bones and corn-cobs because they are too hard to eat and profitless withal. What, now, can be the meaning of this ? "

" What, indeed ! Who can know save by knowing," replied the younger brother. " Come, let us lie low and watch."

So they went very quietly close to the village, crouched down, and peered in. Some people inside were about to eat. They took fine food steaming hot from the cooking-pots and placed it low down in wide trenchers ; then they gathered around and sipped in the steam and savor with every appearance of satisfaction ; but they were as chary of touching the food or of letting·the food touch them as though it were the vilest of refuse.

"Did you see that?" queried the younger brother. "By the delight of death,[1] but—"

"Hist!" cried the elder. "If they are people of that sort, feeding upon the savor of food, then they will hear the suggestions of sounds better than the sounds themselves, and the very demon fathers would not know how to fare with such people, or to fight them, either!"

Hah! But already the people had heard! They set up a clamor of war, swarming out to seek the enemy, as well they might, for who would think favorably of a sneaking stranger under the shade of a house-wall watching the food of another? Why, dogs growl even at their own offspring for the like of that!

"Where? Who? What is it?" cried the people, rushing hither and thither like ants in a shower. "Hah! There they are! There! Quick!" cried they, pointing to the Twain, who were cutting away to the nearest hillock. And immediately they fell to singing their war-cry.

---

[1] *Hĕ-lu-ha-pa ;* from *hĕ-lu,* or *ĕ-lu,* "hurrah," or "how delightful!"— and *hä-pa,* a corpse-demon, death.

" *Ha-a !   Sús-ki !*
Ó-ma-ta
Há-wi-mo-o !
Ó-ma-ta,
Ó-ma-ta   Há-wi-mo ! " [1]

sang they as they ran headlong toward the Two, and then they began shouting :

" Tread them both into the ground ! Smite them both ! Fan them out ! *Ho-o ! Ha-a ! Há-wi-mo-o ó-ma-ta!* "

But the Twain laughed and quickly drew their arrows and loosed them amongst the crowd. *P'it ! tsok !* sang the arrows through and through the people, but never a one fell.

" Why, how now is this ? " cried the elder brother.

" We 'll club them, then ! " said Mátsailéma, and he whiffed out his war-club and sprang to meet the foremost whom he pummelled well and sorely over the head and shoulders. Yet the man was only confused (he was too soft and unstable to be hurt); but another, rushing in at one side, was hit by one of the shield-feathers and fell to the ground like smoke driven down under a hawk's wing.

" Hold, brother, I have it ! Hold ! " cried Áhaiyúta. Then he snatched up a bunch of dry plume-grass and leaped forward. *Swish !* Two ways he swept the faces and breasts of the pursuers.

[1] This, like so many of the folk-tale songs, can only be translated etymologically or by extended paraphrasing. Such songs are always jargonistic, either archaic, imitative, or adapted from other languages of tribes who possibly supplied incidents to the myths themselves ; but they are, like the latter, strictly harmonized with the native forms of expression and phases of belief.

Lo ! right and left they fell like bees in a rainstorm, and quickly sued for mercy, screeching and running at the mere sight of the grass-straws.

"You fools !" cried the brothers. " Why, then, did ye set upon us ? We came for to help you and were merely looking ahead as becomes strangers in strange places, when, lo ! you come running out like a mess of mad flies with your '*Ha-a sús-ki ó-ma-ta !*' Call us coyote-sneaks, do you ? But there ! Rest fearless ! We hunger ; give us to eat."

So they led the Twain into the court within the town and quickly brought steaming food for them.

They sat down and began to blow the food to cool it, whereupon the people cried out in dismay : " Hold ! Hold, ye heedless strangers ; do not waste precious food like that ! For shame ! "

"Waste food ? Ha ! This is the way *we* eat ! " said they, and clutching up huge morsels they crammed their mouths full and bolted them almost whole.

The people were so horrified and sickened at sight of this, that some of them sweated furiously,— which was their way of spewing — whilst others, stouter of thought, cried: " Hold ! hold ! Ye will die ; ye will surely sicken and die if the stuff do but touch ye ! "

"Ho ! ho ! " cried the Twain, eating more lustily than ever. " Eat thus and harden yourselves, you poor, soft things, you ! "

Just then there was a great commotion. Everyone rushed to the shelter of the walls and houses, shouting to them to leave off and follow quickly.

"What is it?" asked they, looking up and all around.

" Woe, woe! The gods are angry with us this day, and blowing arrows at us. They will kill you both! Hurry!" A big puff of wind was blowing over, scattering slivers and straws before it; that was all!

" Brother," said the elder, "this will not do. These people must be hardened and be taught to eat. But let us take a little sleep first, then we will look to this."

They propped themselves up against a wall, set their shields in front of them, and fell asleep. Not long after they awakened suddenly. Those strange people were trying to drag them out to bury them, but were afraid to touch them now, for they thought them dead stuff, more dead than alive.

The younger brother punched the elder with his elbow, and both pretended to gasp, then kept very still. The people succeeded at last in rolling them out of the court like spoiling bodies, and were about to mingle them with the refuse when they suddenly let go and set up a great wail, shouting "War! Murder!"

" How now?" cried the Twain, jumping up. Whereupon the people stared and chattered in greater fright than ever at seeing the dead seemingly come to life!

"What's the matter, you fool people?"

" *Akaa kaa*," cried a flock of jays.

" Hear that!" said the villagers. " Hear that, and ask what's the matter! The jays are coming;

whoever they light on dies—run you two! *Aïi!*
Murder!" And they left off their standing as
though chased by demons. On one or two of the
hindmost some jays alighted. They fell dead as
though struck by lightning!

"Why, see that!" cried the elder brother—
"these people die if only birds alight on them!"

"Hold on, there!" said the younger brother.
"Look here, you fearsome things!" So they
pulled hairs from some scalp-locks they had, and
made snares of them, and whenever the jays flew
at them they caught them with the nooses until
they had caught every one. Then they pinched
them dead and took them into the town and
roasted them. "This is the way," said they, as
they ate the jays by morsels.

And the people crowded around and shouted:
"Look! look! why, they eat the very enemy—
say nothing of refuse!" And although they
dreaded the couple, they became very conciliatory
and gave them a fit place to bide in.

The very next day there was another alarm.
The Two ran out to learn what was the matter.
For a long time they could see nothing, but at
last they met some people fleeing into the town.
Chasing after them was a cooking-pot with ear-
rings of onions.[1] It was boiling furiously and

---

[1] The onion here referred to is the dried, southwestern leek-clove, which
is so strong and indigestible that, when eaten raw and in quantity, gives
rise to great distress, or actually proves fatal to any but mature and
vigorous persons. This, of course, explains why it was chosen for its
value as a symbol of the vigor (or "daylight perfection" and invincibility)
of the Twin gods.

belching forth hot wind and steam and spluttering mush in every direction. If ever so little of the mush hit the people they fell over and died.

"*He !*" cried the Twain ;

> " *Té-k'ya-thla-k'ya*
> *Í-ta-wa-k'ya*
> *Àsh'-she-shu-kwa !*

—As if food-stuff were made to make people afraid!" Whereupon they twitched the ear-rings off the pot and ate them up with all the mush that was in the pot, which they forthwith kicked to pieces vigorously.

Then the people crowded still closer around them, wondering to one another that they could vanquish all enemies by eating them with such impunity, and they begged the Twain to teach them how to do it. So they gathered a great council of the villagers, and when they found that these poor people were only half finished, . . . they cut vents in them (such as were not afraid to let them), . . . and made them eat solid food, by means of which they were hardened and became men of meat then and there, instead of having to get killed after the manner of the fearful, and others of their kind beforetime, in order to ascend to the daylight and take their places in men born of men.

And for this reason, behold! a new-born child may eat only of wind-stuff until his cord of viewless sustenance has been severed, and then only by sucking milk or soft food first and with much distress.

Behold! And we may now see why, like new-born children are the very aged; childish withal— *á-ya-vwi*[1]; — not only toothless, too, but also sure to die of diarrhœa if they eat ever so little save the soft parts and broths of cooked food. For are not the babes new-come from the *Shi-u-na*[2] world; and are not the aged about to enter the *Shi-po-lo-a*[3] world, where cooked food unconsumed is never heeded by the fully dead?

Thus shortens my story.

[1] Dangerously susceptible, tender, delicate.
[2] Hazy, steam-growing.
[3] Mist-enshrouded.

THE COCK AND THE MOUSE

NOTE.—While on their pilgrimage to the "Ocean of Sunrise" in the summer of 1886, three Zuñis—Pálowahtiwa, Waíhusiwa, and Héluta—with Mr. Cushing, were entertaining their assembled friends at Manchester-by-the-Sea with folk tales, those related by the Indians being interpreted by Mr. Cushing as they were uttered. When Mr. Cushing's turn came for a story he responded by relating the Italian tale of "The Cock and the Mouse" which appears in Thomas Frederick Crane's *Italian Popular Tales*. About a year later, at Zuñi, but under somewhat similar circumstances, Waíhusiwa's time came to entertain the gathering, and great was Mr. Cushing's surprise when he presented a Zuñi version of the Italian tale. Mr. Cushing translated the story as literally as possible, and it is here reproduced, together with Mr. Crane's translation from the Italian, in order that the reader may not only see what transformation the original underwent in such a brief period, and how well it has been adapted to Zuñi environment and mode of thought, but also to give a glimpse of the Indian method of folk-tale making.—*Editor*.

ITALIAN VERSION

ONCE upon a time there were a cock and a mouse. One day the mouse said to the cock: "Friend Cock, shall we go and eat some nuts on yonder tree?" "As you like." So they both went under the tree and the mouse climbed up at once and began to eat. The poor cock began to fly, and flew and flew, but could not come where the mouse was. When it saw that there was no hope of getting there, it said: "Friend Mouse, do you know what I want you to do? Throw me a nut." The mouse went and threw one and hit the cock on the head. The poor cock, with its head all broken and covered with blood, went away to an old woman. "Old aunt, give me some rags to cure my head." "If you will give me two hairs I will give you the rags." The cock went away to a dog. "Dog, give me two hairs; the hairs I will give the old woman; the old woman will give me rags to cure my head." "If you will give me a little bread," said the dog, "I will give you the hairs." The cock went away to a baker. "Baker, give me bread; I will give bread to the dog; the dog will give hairs; the hairs I will carry to the old woman; the old woman will give me rags to cure my head." The baker answered: "I will not give you bread unless you give me some wood." The cock went away to the forest. "Forest, give me some wood; the wood I will carry to the baker; the baker will give me some bread; the bread I will give to the dog; the dog will give me hairs; the hairs I will carry to the old woman; the old woman will give me rags to cure my head." The forest answered: "If you will bring me a little water, I will give you some wood." The cock went away to a fountain. "Fountain, give me water; water I will carry to the forest; forest will give wood; wood I will carry to the baker; baker will give bread; bread I will give dog; dog will give hairs; hairs I will give old woman; old woman will give rags to cure my head." The fountain gave him water; the water he carried to the forest; the forest gave him wood; the wood he carried to the baker; the baker gave him bread; the bread he gave to the dog; the dog gave him the hairs; the hairs he carried to the old woman; the old woman gave him the rags; and the cock cured his head.

ZUÑI VERSION

THUS it was in the Town of the Floods Abounding,[1] long ago. There lived there an old woman, so they say, of the *Italia-kwe*,[2] who, in the land of their nativity, are the parental brothers of the Mexicans, it is said. Now, after the manner of that people, this old woman had a *Tâkâkâ* Cock which she kept alone so that he would not fight the others. He was very large, like a turkey, with a fine sleek head and a bristle-brush on his breast like a turkey-cock's too, for the *Tâkâkâ*-kind were at first the younger brothers of the Turkeys, so it would seem.

Well, the old woman kept her Cock in a little corral of tall close-set stakes, sharp at the top and wattled together with rawhide thongs, like an eagle-cage against a wall, only it had a little wicket also fastened with thongs. Now, try as he would, the old *Tâkâkâ* Cock could not fly out, for he had no chance to run and make a start as turkeys do in the wilds, yet he was ever trying and trying, because he was meat-hungry—always anxious for worms ;—for, although the people of that village had abundant food, this old woman was poor and lived mainly on grain-foods, wherefore, perforce, she fed the old *Tâkâkâ* Cock with the refuse of her own eatings. In the morning the old woman would come and throw this refuse food into the corral cage.

Under the wall near by there lived a Mouse. He had no old grandmother to feed him, and he was particularly fond of grain food. When, having eaten

[1] Venice.   [2] " Italy-people."

his fill, the old Cock would settle down, stiff of neck and not looking this side nor that, but sitting in the sun *ká-tá-ká-tok-ing* to himself, the little Mouse would dodge out, steal a bit of tortilla or a crumb, and whisk into his hole again. Being sleepy, the *Tákáká* Cock never saw him, and so, day after day the Mouse fared sumptuously and grew over-bold. But one day, when corn was ripe and the Cock had been well fed and was settling down to his sitting nap, the Mouse came out and stole a particularly large piece of bread, so that in trying to push it into his hole he made some noise and, moreover, had to stop and tunnel his doorway larger.

The Cock turned his head and looked just as the Mouse was working his way slowly in, and espied the long, naked tail lying there on the ground and wriggling as the Mouse moved to and fro at his digging.

"Hah! By the Grandmother of Substance, it is a worm!" cackled the Cock, and he made one peck at the Mouse's tail and bit it so hard that he cut it entirely off and swallowed it at one gulp.

The Mouse, squeaking "Murder!" scurried down into his sleeping-place, and fell to licking his tail until his chops were all pink and his mouth was drawn down like a crying woman's; for he loved his long tail as a young dancer loves the glory of his long hair, and he cried continually: "*Weh tsu tsu, weh tsu tse, yam hok ti-i-i!*" and thought: "Oh, that shameless great beast! By the Demon of Slave-creatures, I'll have my payment of him! For he is worse than an owl or a night-hawk. They eat us all up, but he has taken away the very mark of my mousehood and left me to mourn it. I 'll take vengeance on him, will I !"

So, from that time the Mouse thought how he might compass it, and this plan seemed best : He would creep out some day, all maimed of tail as he was, and implore pity, and thus, perchance, make friends for a while with the *Tâkâkâ* Cock. So he took seed-down, and made a plaster of it with nut-resin, and applied it to the stump of his tail. Then, on a morning, holding his tail up as a dog does his foot when maimed by a cactus, he crawled to the edge of his hole and cried in a weak voice to the *Tâkâkâ :*

> " *Ani, yoa yoa ! Itâ-ak'ya Mosa,*
> *Motcho wak'ya,*
> *Oshe wak'ya,*
> *Ethl hâ asha ni ha. Ha na, yoa, ha na !* "

> Look you, pity, pity ! Master of Food Substance,
> Of my maiming,
> Of my hunger,
> I am all but dying. Ah me, pity, ah me !

Whereupon he held up his tail, which was a safe thing to do, you see, for it no longer looked like a worm or any other eatable.

Now, the *Tâkâkâ* was flattered to be called a master of plenty, so he said, quite haughtily (for he had eaten and could not bend his neck, and felt proud, withal), "Come in, you poor little thing, and eat all you want. As if I cared for what the like of you could eat!" So the Mouse went in and ate very little, as became a polite stranger, and thanking the Cock, bade him good-day and went back to his hole.

By-and-by he came again, and this time he brought part of a nutshell containing fine white meat. When he had shouted warning of his coming and entered the corral cage, he said: "Comrade father, let us eat together. Of this food I have plenty, gathered from yonder high nut-tree which I climb every autumn when the corn is ripe and cut the nuts therefrom. But of all food yours I most relish, since I cannot store such in my cellar. Now, it may be you will equally relish mine; so let us eat, then, together."

"It is well, comrade child," replied the Cock; so they began to eat.

But the Cock had no sooner tasted the nut than he fairly chuckled for joy, and having speedily made an end of the kernel, fell to lamenting his hard lot. "Alas, ah me!" he said. "My grandmother brings me, on rare days, something like to this, but picked all too clean. There is nought eatable so nice. Comrade little one, do you have plenty of this kind, did you say?"

"Oh, yes," replied the Mouse; "but, you see, the season is near to an end now, and when I want more nuts I must go and gather them from the tree. Look, now! Why do you not go there also? That is the tree, close by."

"Ah me, I cannot escape, woe to me! Look at my wings," said the Cock, "they are worn to bristles—and as to the beard on my breast, my chief ornament, alas! it is all crumpled and uneven, so much have I tried to fly out and so hard have I pushed against the bars. As for the door, my grandmother claps that shut and fastens it tightly with thongs, be you sure, as soon as ever she finishes the feeding of me!"

"Ha! ha!" exclaimed the Mouse. "If that's all, there's nothing easier than to open that. Look at my teeth; I even crack the hard nuts with these scrapers of mine! Wait!" He ran nimbly up the wicket and soon gnawed through the holding-string. "There! comrade father; push open the door, you are bigger than I, and we will go nutting."

"Thanks this day," cried the Cock, and shoving the wicket open, he ran forth cackling and crowing for gladness.

Then the Mouse led the way to the tree. Up the trunk he ran, and climbed and climbed until he came to the topmost boughs. "Ha! the nuts are fine and ripe up here," he shouted.

But the *Tákáká* fluttered and flew all in vain; his wings were so worn he could not win even to the lowermost branches. "Oh! have pity on me, comrade child! Cut off some of the nuts and throw them down to me, do! My wings are so worn I cannot fly any better than the grandmother's old dog, who is my neighbor over there."

"Be patient, be patient, father!" exclaimed the Mouse. "I am cracking a big one for you as fast as I can. There, catch it!" and he threw a fat

27

nut close to the Cock, who gleefully devoured
the kernel and, without so much as thanks, called
for more.

"Wait, father," said the Mouse. "There!
Stand right under me, so. Now, catch it; this is
a big one!" Saying which the Mouse crawled
out until he was straight over the Cock. "Now,
then," said he, "watch in front!" and he let fall
the nut. It hit the Cock on the head so hard that
it bruised the skin off and stunned the old *Tâkâkâ*
so that he fell over and died for a short time,
utterly forgetting.

"*Té mi thlo kô thlo kwa!*" shouted the Mouse,
as he hurried down the tree. "A little waiting,
and lo! What my foe would do to me, I to him
do, indeed!" Whereupon he ran across, before
ever the Cock had opened an eye, and gnawed his
bristles off so short that they never could grow
again. "There, now!" said the Mouse. "Lo!
thus healed is my heart, and my enemy is even as
he made me, bereft of distinction!" Then he ran
back to his cellar, satisfied.

Finally the Cock opened his eyes. "Ah me,
my head!" he exclaimed. Then, moaning, he
staggered to his feet, and in doing so he espied
the nut. It was smooth and round, like a brown
egg. When the Cock saw it he fell to lamenting
more loudly than ever: "Oh, my head! *Tâ-kâ-
kâ-kâ-â-â!*" But the top of his head kept bleeding and swelling until it was all covered over with
welts of gore, and it grew so heavy, withal, that
the *Tâkâkâ* thought he would surely die. So off

to his grandmother he went, lamenting all the way.

Hearing him, the grandmother opened the door, and cried: "What now?"

"Oh, my grandmother, ah me! I am murdered!" he answered. "A great, round, hard seed was dropped on my head by a little creature with a short, one-feathered tail, who came and told me that it was good to eat and—oh! my head is all bleeding and swollen! By the light of your favor, bind my wound for me lest, alas, I die!"

"Served you right! Why did you leave your place, knowing better?" cried the old woman. "I will not bind your head unless you give me your very bristles of manhood, that you may remember your lesson!"

"Oh! take them, grandmother!" cried the Cock; but when he looked down, alas! the beard of his breast, the glory of his kind, was all gone. "Ah me! ah me! What shall I do?" he again cried. But the old woman told him that unless he brought her at least four bristles she would not cure him, and forthwith she shut the door.

So the poor Cock slowly staggered back toward his corral, hoping to find some of the hairs that had been gnawed off. As he passed the little lodge of his neighbor, the Dog, he caught sight of old *Wahtsita's* fine muzzle-beard. "Ha!" thought he. Then he told the Dog his tale, and begged of him four hairs—"only four!"

"You great, pampered noise-maker, give me some bread, then, fine bread, and I will give you the hairs." Whereupon the Cock thought, and went to the house of a Trader of Foodstuffs; and he told him also the tale.

"Well, then, bring me some wood with which I may heat the oven to bake the bread," said the Trader of Foodstuffs.

The Cock went to some Woods near by. "Oh, ye Beloved of the Trees, drop me dry branches!" And with this he told the Trees his tale; but the Trees shook their leaves and said: "No rain has fallen, and all our branches will soon be dry. Beseech the Waters that they give us drink, then we will gladly give you wood."

Then the Cock went to a Spring near by,—and when he saw in it how his head was swollen and he found that it was growing harder, he again began to lament.

"What matters?" murmured the Beloved of the Waters.

Then he told them the tale also.

"Listen!" said the Beings of Water. "Long have men neglected their duties, and the Beloved of the Clouds need payment of due no less than ourselves, the Trees, the Food-maker, the Dog, and the Old Woman. Behold! no plumes are set about our border! Now, therefore, pay to them of thy feathers—four floating plumes from under thy wings—and set them close over us, that, seen in our depths from the sky, they will lure the Beloved of the Clouds with their rain-laden breaths. Thus will our stream-way be replenished and the Trees watered, and their Winds in the Trees will drop thee dead branches wherewith thou mayest make payment and all will be well."

Forthwith the *Tákákà* plucked four of his best plumes and set them, one on the northern, one on the western, one on the southern, and one on the eastern border of the Pool. Then the Winds of the Four Quarters began to breathe upon the four plumes, and with those Breaths of the Beloved came Clouds, and from the Clouds fell Rain, and the Trees threw down dry branches, and the Wind placed among them Red-top Grass, which is light and therefore lightens the load it is among. And when the Cock returned and gathered a little bundle of fagots, lo! the Red-top made it so light that he easily carried it to the Food-maker, who gave him bread, for which the Dog gave him four bristles, and these he took to the old Grandmother.

"Ha!" exclaimed she. "Now, child, I will cure thee, but thou hast been so long that thy head will always be welted and covered with proud-flesh, even though healed. Still, it must ever be so. Doing right keeps right; doing wrong makes wrong, which, to make right, one must even pay as the sick pay those who cure them. Go now, and bide whither I bid thee."

When, after a time, the Cock became well, lo! there were great, flabby, blood-red welts on his head and blue marks on his temples where they were bruised so sore. Now, listen:

It is for this reason that ever since that time the medicine masters of that people never give cure without pay; never, for there is no virtue in medicine of no value. Ever since then cocks have had no bristles on their breasts—only little humps where they ought to be;—and they always have blood-red crests of meat on their heads. And even when a hen lays an egg and a *tákáká* cock sees it, he begins to *tá-ká-ká-á* as the ancient of them all did when he saw the brown nut. And sometimes they even pick at and eat these seeds of their own children, especially when they are cracked.

As for mice, we know how they went into the meal-bags in olden times and came out something else, and, getting smoked, became *tsothliko-ahái*, with long, bare tails. But that was before the Cock cut the tail of the *tsothliko* Mouse off. Ever since he cried in agony: "*Weh tsu yii weh tsu!*" like a child with a burnt finger, his children have been called *Wehtsutsukwe*, and wander wild in the fields; hence field-mice to this day have short tails, brown-stained and hairy; and their chops are all pink, and when you look them in the face they seem always to be crying.

Thus shortens my story.

THE GIANT CLOUD-SWALLOWER

A TALE OF CAÑON DE CHELLY

TRANSLATOR'S INTRODUCTION

DEEP down in cañons of the Southwest, especially where they are joined by other cañons, the traveller may see standing forth from or hugging the angles of the cliffs, great towering needles of stone—weird, rugged, fantastic, oftentimes single, as often—like gigantic wind-stripped trees with lesser trees standing beside them—double or treble. Seen suddenly at a turn in the cañon these giant stones startle the gazer with their monstrous and human proportions, like giants, indeed, at bay against the sheer rock walls, protecting their young, who appear anon to crouch at the knees of their fathers or cling to their sides.

Few white men behold these statuesque stones in the moonlight, or in the gray light and white mists of the morning. At midday they seem dead or asleep while standing; but when the moon is shining above them and the wanderer below looks up to them, lo! the moon stands still and these mighty crags start forth, advancing noiselessly. His back is frozen, and even in the yielding sand his feet are held fast by terror—a delicious, ghostly terror, withal! Still he gazes fascinated, and as the shadow of the moonlight falls toward him over the topmost crest, lo, again! its crown is illumined and circled as if by a halo of snow-light, and back and forth from this luminous fillet over that high stony brow, black hair seems to tumble and gather.

Again, beheld in the dawn-light, when the mists are rising slowly and are waving to and fro around the giddy columns, hiding the cliffs behind them, these vast pinnacles seem to nod and to waver or to sway themselves backward and forward, all as silently as before. Soon, when the sun is risen and the mists from below fade away, the wind blows more mist from the mesa; you see clouds of it pour from the cliff edge, just behind and above these great towers, and shimmer against the bright sky; but as soon as these clouds pass the crag-nests they are lost in the sunlight around them—lost so fast, as yet others come on, that the stone giants seem to drink them.

Of such rocks, according to their variety and local surroundings, the Zuñis relate many tales which are so ingenious and befitting that if we believed, as the Zuñis do, that in the time of creation when all things were young and soft and were therefore easily fashioned by whatever chanced to befall them—into this thing or that thing, into this plant or that plant, this animal or that, and so on endlessly through a dramatic story longer than Shakespeare or the Bible—we would fain believe also as he does in the quaint incidents of these stories of the time when all things were new and the world was becoming as we see it now.

One of these tales, a variant of others pertaining to particular standing rocks in the west, south, or east, is told of that wonder to all beholders, "El Capitan," of the Cañon de Chelly in the north. No one who has seen this stupendous rock column can fail to be interested in the following legend, or will fail to realize how, as this introduction endeavors to make plainer, the Zuñi poet and philosopher of olden times built up a story which he verily believed quite sufficient to account for the great shaft of sandstone and its many details and surroundings.—F. H. C.

Häki Suto, or Foretop Knot, he whose hair was done up over his forehead like a quail's crest, lived among the great cliffs of the north long ago, when the world was new. He was a giant, so tall that men called him *Lo Ikwithltchunona*, or the Cloud-swallower. A devourer of men was he,—men were his meat—yea, and a drinker of their very substance was he, for the cloud-breaths of the beloved gods, and souls of the dead, whence descend rains, even these were his drink. Wherefore the People of the Cliffs sought to slay him, and hero after hero perished thuswise. Wherefore, too, snow ceased in the north and the west; rain ceased in the south and the east; the mists of the mountains above were drunk up; the waters of the valleys below were dried up; corn withered in the fields; men hungered and died in the cliffs.

Then came the Twin Gods of War, Áhaiyúta and Mátsailéma, who in play staked the lives of foes and fierce creatures. "Lo! it is not well with our children, men," said they. "Let us destroy this Häki Suto, the swallower of clouds," said they.

They were walking along the trail which leads southward to the Smooth-rocks-descending.

"O, grandchildren, where be ye wending?" said a little, little quavering voice. They looked,—the younger, then the elder. There on the tip of a grass-stalk, waving her banner of down-stuff, stood their grandmother, Spinner of Meshes.

"The Spider! Our Grandmother Spider!" cried one of the gods to the other. "Ho! grandmother, was that you calling?" shouted they to her.

"Yea, children; where wend ye this noon-day?"

"A-warring we are going," said they. "Look now!

> "No beads for to broider your awning
> Have fallen this many a morning."

" Aha, wait ye ! Whom ye seek, verily I know him well," said the Spider-woman.

> " Like a tree fallen down from the mountain
> He lies by the side of the cliff-trail
> And feigns to sleep there, yet is wary.
> I will sew up his eyes with my down-cords.
> Then come ye and smite him, grandchildren."

She ran ahead. There lay Häki Suto, his legs over the trail where men journeyed. Great, like the trunks and branches of pine trees cast down by a wind-storm, were his legs arching over the pathway, and when some one chanced to come by, the giant would call out : "Good morning !" and bid him "pass right along under." " I am old and rheumatic," he would continue, oh, so politely ! " Do not mind my rudeness, therefore ; run right along under ; never fear, run right along under !" But when the hunter tried to pass, *kúutsu !* Häki Suto would snatch him up and cast him over the cliff to be eaten by the young Forehead-cresters.

The Spider stepped never so lightly, and climbed up behind his great ear, and then busily wove at her web, to and fro, up and down, and in and out of his eyelashes she busily plied at her web.

" Pesk the birds and buzz creatures !" growled the giant, twitching this way and that his eyebrows. which tickled ; but he would not stir,—for he heard the War-gods coming, and thought them fat hunters and needs must feign sleepy.

And these ? Ha ! ha ! They begin to sing, as was their fearless wont sometimes. Häki Suto never looked, but yawned and drawled as they came near, and nearer. "Never mind, my children, pass right along under, pass right along under; I am lame and tired this morning," said he.

Áhaiyúta ran to the left. Mátsailéma ran to the right. Häki Suto sprang up to catch them, but his eyes were so blinded with cobwebs that he missed them and feigned to fall, crying: "Ouch! my poor back! my poor back! Pass right along under, my children, it was only a crick in my back. Ouch! Oh, my poor back!" But they whacked him over the head and stomach till he stiffened and died. Then shouting "*So ho!*" they shoved him over the cliff.

The Navahos say that the grandmother tied him there by the hair—by his topknot—where you see the white streaks on the pillar, so *they* say; but it 's the birds that streak the pillar, and *this* is the way. When Häki Suto fell, his feet drave far into the sands, and the Storm-gods rushed in to the aid of their children, the War-gods, and drifted his blood-bedrenched carcass all over with sand, whence he dried and hardened to stone. When the young ones saw him falling, they forthwith flocked up to devour him, making loud clamor. But the Twain, seeing this, made after them too and twisted the necks of all save only the tallest (who was caught in the sands with his father) and flung them aloft to the winds, whereby one became instantly the Owl, who twists her head wholly around whensoever she pleases, and stares as though frightened and strangled; and another the Falcon became, who perches and nests to this day on the crest of his sand-covered father, the Giant Cloud-drinker. And the Falcons cry ever and ever "'Tis father; O father!" (" *Ti-tätchu ya-tätchu.*")

But, fearing that never again would the waters refreshen their cañons, our ancients who dwelt in the cliffs fled away to the southward and eastward —all save those who had perished aforetime; they are dead in their homes in the cliff-towns, dried, like their cornstalks that died when the rain stopped long, long ago, when all things were new.

Thus shortens my story.

THE MAIDEN THE SUN MADE LOVE
TO, AND HER BOYS

OR, THE ORIGIN OF ANGER

LET it be about a person who lived in the Home of the Eagles (K'iákime), under the Mountain of Thunder, that I tell you today. So let it be. It was in the ancient, long-forgotten times. It was in the very ancient times beyond one's guessing. There lived then, in this town, the daughter of a great priest-chief, but she had never, never, never since she was a little child, come forth from the doorway of the house in which she dwelt. No one there in that town had ever seen her; even her own townspeople had never seen her.

Now, day after day at noon-time, when the Sun stood in the mid-heavens, he would look down from the sky through a little window in the roof of her house. And he it was who instant was her lover, and who, descending upon the luminously yellow trail his own rays created, would talk to her. And he was her only companion, for she knew not her own townspeople, neither had she seen them since she was a child. None save only her parents ever saw her.

"Wonder what the cacique's child looks like," the people would say to one another. "She never comes out; no one has seen her since she was a little child." And so at last they schemed to get a look at her. One said : " I have it ! Let us have a dance for her. Then it may be she will deign to come forth."

The young man who spoke was chief of the dances, and why should he not suggest such a thing ? So, his friends and followers agreeing, they began to make plumes of macaw feathers — beautiful plumes they were — for the Plume dance. They set a day, and on that day, in the morning, they danced, with music and song, in the plaza before the house of the great priest-chief where the girl lived. They looked along the top of the house in vain ; the girl was not there ; only her old parents sat on the roof.

" Oh ! I 'm so thirsty !" cried the chief of the dance, for he it was who wanted to see the girl.

" Run right in and get a drink," said the girl's old ones. So the young man climbed the ladder and went into the first room. There was no water there ; then he went into the second room, but there was no water there ; then into the third room, but still he found no water. He looked all around, but saw nothing of the priest-chief's daughter. All the same, she was back in the fourth room, sitting there just as if no dance were going on in the plaza, weaving away at her beautiful trays of colored splints.

Well, the young man went back ; they finished their dance, but no one saw anything of the priest-chief's daughter ; and when the dancers all returned to their ceremonial chamber they said to one another : " Alas ! although we danced for her, she came not out to see us ! "

Now, in reality, the Sun, who was her lover, and came down each day on a ray of his own light to visit her, loved her so much he would not that she should come forth from her house and be seen of men. Therefore he set an Eagle upon the house-top in a great cage to watch her. He was a very wise old Eagle. He could understand every word that the people said. And he it was that she fed and watered from day to day. Now, the dancers in the ceremonial chamber asked : " What shall we do ? "

" Why, let us dance again," said the chief of the dances, " and if we do not succeed, yet again." They did as he said, but with no better success than before ; so at last the two Warrior Priests of the Bow grew angry, and although they were the girl's father's own warriors, they ordered the War-rior festival, or *Óinahe* dance. " Surely," said they, " she will come forth, and if not, let her perish, for how can she refuse the delight of the great *Óinahe*, where each young man dances and masks himself according to his fancy ? "

So, one night the two warriors went out and called to the people to make ready and be happy, for in four days they should dance the *Óinahe*. When they had done calling, they descended, and the people said to one another : " Surely she will come out when we dance the *Óinahe*, for she will be delighted with it, and we shall yet see her. She was very beautiful when she was a little girl."

Then both of the warriors climbed to the top of Thunder Mountain, where Áhaiyúta and his brother, Mátsailéma, the Gods of War, and their grandmother lived in the middle of the summit. As they approached the presence of the two gods, they exclaimed : " *She-e !* "

" *Hai !* " the gods replied.

" Our fathers, how is it that ye are, these many days ? " they asked, and the Twain replied : " We are happy. Come in ; sit down " ; and they placed a couple of stools for the warriors. " What is it that ye would of us ? " they continued ; " for it would be strange if ye came up to our house for nothing."

" True it is," replied the warriors. " It is in our hearts as your two chosen children—as the war-priests of our nation—that our people should be made happy as the days of the year go by ; and we therefore think over all the beautiful dances, and now and then command that the most fitting of them shall appear. Now, our children, the people of the Home of the Eagles, are anxious to see our child, the daughter of the priest-chief, who has not come forth from her house, and whom we have never seen since she was a little girl. We have thought to order your dance of the *Óinahe*, and we would that without fail our daughter should be made to come forth or else die ; therefore, our fathers, we have come to consult ye and to ask your advice."

" Aha ! " cried the Twain. " Then ye are anxious that this should be, are ye ? "

"Yes," they replied.

"Well, it shall come to pass as ye wish it, and the girl must die if she come not forth at the bidding of the *Óinahe !*"

"Aha !" ejaculated they both.   " Thanks !"

"Yea, it shall be as ye wish.   Make our days for us—name the times for preparation, and we shall be with ye to lead the *Óinahe*.   The first time our dance will come forth, and the second time our dance will come forth, and the third time our dance will come forth, but the fourth time our dance comes forth, it will happen as ye wish it.   It will certainly be finished as ye wish it.

"Well !   Thanks ; we go !" (good-by).

"Go ye," said the gods to their children ; and they went.

The Eagle was very unhappy with all this.   He knew it all, for he understood everything that was said.   Next morning he hung his head at the window with great sadness ; so the girl, after she had eaten her morning meal, took some dainty bits to the window and said : "Why are you so unhappy?   See, I have brought you some food. Eat !"

" I will not eat ; I cannot eat," replied the Eagle.

"Why not ?" asked she.   " I will not harm you ; I am happy ; I love you just as much as ever."

"Alas, alas ! my mother," said the Eagle.   "It is not with thoughts of myself that I am unhappy, but your father's two war-priests are anxious that their children shall be made happy, and their

28

children, the people of our town under the mountain, are longing to see you. They have said to one another that you never come forth ; they have never seen you. Therefore they have ordered the *Óinahe*, that you may be tempted out. They went up to the home of Áhaiyúta and his younger brother, where they live with their grandmother, on the top of Thunder Mountain, and the two gods have said to them: " It shall come to pass as ye wish it." Therefore they will dance, and on the fourth day of their dancing it shall come to pass as they wish it. Indeed, it shall happen, my poor mother, that you shall be no more. Alas ! I can do nothing ; you can do nothing ; why should I tarry longer with you ? You must loosen my bonds and let me free."

" As you like," said the girl. " I suppose it must be as you say." Then she loosened the Eagle's bonds, and, straight as the pathway of an arrow, away he flew upward into the sky—even toward the zenith where the Sun rested at noon-time, and whither he soon arrived himself.

" Thou comest," said the Sun.

" I do, my father. How art thou these many days ? " said the Eagle to the Sun.

" Happy. Here, sit down." There was a blanket already placed for him, and thereupon he sat ; but he never looked to the right nor to the left, nor yet about the Sun-father's splendid home. He said not a word. He only drooped his head, so sad was he.

" What is it, my child ? " asked the Sun. " I

suppose thou hast some errand, else why shouldst thou come? Surely it is not for nothing that thou wouldst come so far to see me."

"Quite true," answered the Eagle. "Alas! my child; alas, my mother! Day after day down in the home under the mountain the people dance that they may tempt her forth; yet she has never appeared. So her father's war-priests are angry and have at last been to see the Twain in their home on Thunder Mountain, and the Twain have commanded that soon it shall come to pass as the people wish or that our beautiful maiden shall perish. Even tomorrow it shall be; so have the Twain said; and when the fourth dance comes out it shall come to pass, and our beautiful maiden shall be no more; thus have the Twain said. I cannot enrich my mother, the daughter of the priest-chief, thy beautiful child, with words of advice, with aid of mine own will; hence come I unto thee. What shall I do?"

"What shalt thou do?" repeated the Sun. "I know it is all as thou hast said. Know I not all these things? The Twain, whose powers are surpassed only by mine own, have they not commanded that it shall be? What shalt thou do but descend at once? Tell her to bathe herself and put on her finest garments tomorrow morning. Then, when the time comes, mount her upon thy shoulders and bear her up to me. Only possibly thou wilt have the great good fortune to reach my house with her. Possibly in thy journey hither it shall come to be, alas! as the Twain have said; for have not they said it should be, and are they not above all things else powerful?"

"Well, we 'll try to come."

"But I will watch thee when thou art about to reach the mid-heavens."

"Well, I go," said the Eagle, rising.

"Very well," responded the Sun; "happily mayest thou journey." And the Eagle began to descend.

Meanwhile the daughter of the priest-chief opened the sky-hole and placed a sacred medicine-bowl half full of water on the floor where the sunlight would shine into it, and where it would reflect the sky, and there she sat looking intently down into the water. By-and-by the Eagle came in sight, and she saw his shadow in the water.

Just then the Sun drew his shield from his face. Oh! how hot it was down there on the earth. The sky was ablaze with light, and no one dared to look at it; and the sands grew so hot that they burned the moccasins of those who walked upon them. Everybody ran into the houses, and the Eagle spread his wings and gently descended, for he too was hot. And when he came near to the house, the girl let him in and welcomed him.

"Thou comest, father," said she.

He only drooped his head and flapped his wings, unable even to speak, so hot was he.

She saw that he was near to fainting. Therefore she fanned him—made cool wind for him with the basket tray and her mantle—and sprinkled cold water upon his head.

"Thou hast been to the home of our father?" she asked, when he had recovered.

"Yes," replied the Eagle.

"What has he advised that we should do?" asked she.

"This," said the Eagle; "tomorrow morning at the dawn of day thou wilt arise and bathe thyself. Then at sunrise thou shalt put on thy finest garments. The dance will come forth; and then it will come forth the second time, and the third time, and again it will come the fourth time. Then I will mount thee upon my shoulders and bear thee away toward the Sun, who will be waiting for us. It may be that we shall have the good fortune to reach his home; and it may be that we shall get only a little way when everything shall come to pass unhappily and thou wilt be no more." That is what he said to her.

It grew night. The girl collected all the basket-trays that she had made for her father's sacred plumes; these by the fire-light she spread out, and then began to divide them into different heaps.

Now, her parents, who were sitting in the next room, heard her until it was late at night, and they said to each other: "Wonder what it is that keeps our daughter up?" So the old priest-chief arose and entered her room.

"My child, art thou not at rest yet?" asked he.

"No," replied she. "I am dividing the trays I have made for thee. "These," said she, pointing to a heap of yellow ones, "shall pertain to the north-land; these, the blue, to the west-land; the red to the land of the south, the white to the east, the variegated to the upper regions, and the black to the regions below. For tomorrow, beloved father, thou shalt see me no more."

"It is well," said the father, for he was a great priest and knew the will of the gods, and to this he always said: "It is well. What, therefore, should I say?" So the old man left her.

Then as morning approached she bathed herself. And the Eagle, looking down, said: "My child, my mother, lie down and rest thyself, for we are about to undertake a long journey. Never fear; I will wake thee at the right time." So she lay down and slept. The Eagle perched himself above her and watched for the dawn.

By-and-by the great star arose. Then he knew that the Sun would soon follow it, and he said: "Mother, arise! dress thyself, for the time is near at hand."

Outside on the house-tops called the two war-priests to their children:

> "Hasten, hasten! Prepare for the dance!
> Hasten, hasten! Eat for the dance!
> Hasten, hasten, our children all!"

Then the girl went into another room and brought forth her finest dresses, and these, garment after garment, she put on—not one dress, but many. Upon her shoulders she placed four mantles of snow-white embroidered cotton. Then she said to the Eagle: "Wait a moment; I have yet to think of our children in the Home of the

Eagles." Therefore she brought forth her basket-bowls of fine meal with which she had been accustomed to powder her face. There was meal of the yellow corn, the blue corn-meal, the red corn-meal, the white corn-meal, the speckled corn-meal, and the black corn-meal. "See," said she, as she regarded the various vessels of meal; "my children, by means of these shall ye beautify flesh; by means of these be precious against evil; by means of these shall ye finish preciously your roads of life. I am to be no more. Far off and to an unknown region go I. Possibly I may reach it, and live; probably not reach it, and die. These do I leave as your inheritance. My children, good-by."[1]

Then the Eagle descended. The drum began to sound outside; the dance was coming—for the first time, mind you, not the fourth. Then said the Eagle, as he lowered himself: "Place thyself upon my back; grasp me by the shoulders." And the girl did as she was bidden. She reclined herself lengthwise on the back of the Eagle, and grasped with her left hand his shoulders. "Now, place one foot on one of my thighs and the other on the other." She placed one foot on one of his thighs and the other on the other; and the Eagle spread his tail and raised it that she might not fall off. "All ready?" asked he, as the drum of the coming dance sounded outside.

"Yes," said the girl; and they arose.

"Open the wicket!" and *shoa!* the Eagle

---

[1] The maiden here addresses mankind generally.

spread his wings and away off up into the sky he sprang with the maiden. Round and round, round and round, they circled in the sky, but those below saw nothing as they danced in the shadows of the great houses. The dancers retired. Then they came forth again. Again they retired and came forth. Then the girl said: "Father, slower. Let me sing a farewell song to my people, my children of Earth, that they may know I am going."

The Eagle spread his wings and sailed gently through the air as the maiden sang. Then the people in the plaza below heard the song, and said: "Alas, alas! ye Twain!" said they to the two gods who led the dance. "Our mother, our child, away off through the skies goes she! Ye are fools that ye have let her escape and deceive us!"

Some listened to the song and learned it. Others did not. For the third time the dancers came forth. "Once more have we to dance," said the two gods. "Where are they now?"

"In the mid-heavens," said the people.

"Take it easily, my child," said the Eagle. "Once more are they to come forth. Possibly we will yet have the great good fortune to reach the home of our father." And they sped along through the air, nearer and nearer to the home of the Sun-father, while the dancers below danced harder and harder—many so joyful that they listened not to the complainings of the people around, but danced only more vigorously.

Then the dancers retired and came out for the fourth and last time. In the van danced the two gods, their faces blackened with the paint of war, their hands bearing bows and arrows with which to destroy the daughter of the priest-chief.

Yes, they were almost there. Now, the Eagle's heart was high with hope. When the two gods below reached the center of the plaza they turned to the people and asked: "Where are they? Where have they gone?"

"There they are in the skies—almost there," replied the people.

"Humph!" responded the gods. "Suppose they *are* almost there; they shall never reach the home of our father!"

"Now, then, hurry, brother younger!" exclaimed the elder; "with which hand wilt thou draw the arrow?"

"With thy hand, my right," said the younger.

"Very well; with thy hand, my left," said the elder.[1]

So they drew their medicine-pointed arrows to the heads. *Tsi-ni-i-i!* sang the arrows as they shot through the air. Soon they reached the home of the Sun, crossed one another over his face, and shot downward more swiftly than ever toward the coming Eagle and the maiden. "Alas! my mother, my child," said the Sun as the arrows flew past him and

---

[1] The twin children of the Sun were, in the days of creation, the benignant guardians of men; but when the world became filled with envy and war, they were changed by the eight gods of the storms into warriors more powerful than all monsters, gods, or men. The elder one was right-handed, the younger, left-handed; hence the form of expression here used.

from him, "thou art no more." And the arrows shot downward on their course.

Tsook! sang the arrow of the elder god as it pierced the back of the girl and entered her heart. *Tso-ko!* sang the arrow of the younger as it struck in the middle of her back.

"Alas! my mother, my mother," cried the Eagle, "it is over, alas, alas!" said he, as she released her hold, and, fainting, he left her to fall through the air. Over and over, this way and that, fell the beautiful maiden; and as the people strained their eyes, nearer and nearer to the town neath the mountain she fell. Soon, over and over, this way and that, she came falling even with the top of the mountain.

Then the people rushed past one another out of the plaza toward the place where they thought she would strike. And just over there below the Home of the Eagles, where the Waters of the Coyote gush forth from the cliff-base, fell the beautiful maiden.

Then there were born twin children—two wee infants who rolled off into the rubbish and were concealed under sticks and stones.

Down rushed the people, and an Acoma spectator seized her body. "Mine!" cried he, triumphantly, as he raised the body above him.

"Thine!" cried the people, for they had lost the beautiful maiden.

"Ours!" cried the Acomas, one to another, who had come to witness the dances. "Great good fortune this day has smiled on us." And they bore her body away to their pueblo in the east.

Now, under the other end of Thunder Mountain was the home of the Badgers, and an old Badger who lived there was out hunting. After the people had again gathered in the city, he passed near the Waters of the Coyote and heard the voices of the infants crying among the rubbish.

"Ah!" said he, "I hear the cry of children. My little boys, my little girls," cried he, "whichever ye may be"; and he hastily searched and found them where they were rolling about and crying among the refuse. "Twins!" cried he. "Boys! Somebody has left them here. Soon he will come back to reclaim them. Let me walk away for a few moments."

So he walked all around, but found no traces of the parents, only the tracks of many men who had gathered near.

"Mine!" said he, as he trotted back; and with soft grass he rubbed them till they were free from the mud and refuse. "Thanks, thanks! Splendid! Children have I, and boys at that, and when I am older grown they will take from me the cares of the chase. Goodness! Thanks! Nothing but boys shall be my children!" So he rubbed them dry and clean with more soft grass, and they stopped crying. Then he took some dry grass and made a bundle and put them in it, and started off for his home in the Red Hills.

The old Badger-woman was up on top of their house looking around, running back and forth and jumping in and out of her doorway. "Hai!" said she; "thou comest?"

"Yes, hurry!" said the old Badger. "Come down and meet me."

"What have you?" asked the Badger-woman, as she ran down to meet him.

"What have I," said the old Badger, "but a couple of wee little children! Here, take them and carry them up to the house."

So the old woman took the bundle of grass and opened it and began to fondle the children. "O my poor little children; poor little babes!" said she.

"Ah! stop playing with them and hurry along!" commanded the old Badger.

So the old woman hurried up to their doorway as fast as possible and ran in. The old Badger followed, and she said to him: "Where in the world did you get these little children?"

"Why," replied he, "I had the greatest luck in the world. I was out hunting, you know, and found these two little fellows down in Coyote Cañon, just this side of those men's houses. They're boys, both of them. When they grow up, old wife, perhaps they can hunt for us, and then I shall rest myself from the labors of the hunt, with plenty of meat for you and me every day of the year. What are you standing there for?" said he. "Why don't you go and get them something to eat and make them a bed?"

"Oh, yes!" responded the old woman. "My poor little children!" So she made a little nest at the bottom of the hole and laid them on it. Then she ran and fetched some green-corn ears and, picking the kernels off, made some gruel of them, and fed the little fellows.   So the boy babies ate till they kicked their heels with satisfaction, and that night the old Badger-mother took one in her arms and slept with it, and the old Badger-father slept with the other.

Now, every day they grew as much as the children of men do in a year, so that in eight days they were as large and knew as much as children usually do in eight years.   There was no little animal that they could not kill unfailingly, for they were the children of the Sun, you know.   But, alas! they grew weary of killing birds around their doorway, and their old father kept telling them every morning never to go out of sight of their house; and the old woman kept watching them always for fear that they would run off and get lost, or somebody would find and claim them.   Yes, they grew impatient of this. They wanted to kill prairie-dogs and cottontails, but they could not get near enough to them.   So one night when the old Badger came home they said to him : " Father, come now ; do make us some bows and arrows so that we can hunt rabbits, and you and mother can have all that you want to eat."

" All right," replied the old man.   And the next day he went off to the Cañon of the Woods, and somehow he managed to cut down a small oak and get a lot of branches for arrows.   He brought these home, and that night with a piece of flint, little by little he managed to make each of the boys a bow and some arrows.   But when he tried to put feathers on the arrows he was very awkward (for you know badgers don't have fingers like men), so he had to take a single feather for each arrow and split it and twist it around the butt of the shaft. That very night, do you know, it snowed; yes, a great deal of snow fell, and the little fellows looked out and said to each other and to the old Badgers: "Now then, tomorrow we will go rabbit-hunting."

"O mother, make a lunch for us!" they exclaimed.

"Where are you going?" asked the old woman.

"We are going out among the hills and down on the plains where the trees grow, to hunt rabbits."

"O my poor little boys! What will you do? —you will freeze to death, for you have no clothes and no wool grows on your backs."

"Well, mother, we 're tough. We will get up tomorrow and wait until the sun shines warm—then we can go hunting."

"How in the world will you carry your food? You have no blanket to wrap it in."

"Oh, you just make some corn-cakes, " answered the boys, "and string them on a little stick, and we can take hold of the middle of the stick and carry them just as well as not."

Hi-ta ! " cried the old woman. "Listen, father." So she made the corn-cakes and strung them on little sticks, and the two boys went to bed. But they could n't sleep very well, being so impatient to go hunting rabbits, and they kept waking each other and peeping out to see how long it would be before daylight.

In the morning the old Badger got up early and collected a lot of bark which he rubbed until it was soft, and then he wove the boys each a curious pair of moccasins that would come half-way up to the knees. So the elder brother put on his moccasins and ran out into the snow. "*U-kwatchi!*" exclaimed he. "First rate!" So the other little boy put on his bark moccasins, and they took their strings of corn-cakes and bows and arrows, and started off as fast as they could. Well, they went off among the hills at the foot of Thunder Mountain. It was only a little while ere they struck a rabbit trail, and the first arrow they shot killed the rabbit. So they kept on hunting until they had a large number of rabbits and began to get tired. Although there was snow on the ground, the sun was very warm, so they soon forgot all about it until they began to grow hungry, and then they looked up and saw that it was noon-time, because the sun was resting in the mid-heavens. So they went up on top of a high hill, and carried their rabbits there one by one, to find a place where the snow was shallow. Here they brushed a space clear of the snow, and, depositing the rabbits, sat down to eat their corn-cakes, which they laid on a bundle of grass. While they sat there eating, the Sun looked down and pitied his two poor little children. "Wait a bit," said he to himself, "I 'll go down and talk to the little fellows, and help them." So by his will alone he descended, and lo! he stood there on the earth just a little way from the two boys,—grand, beautiful, sublime. Upon his body were garments of embroidered cotton; fringed leggings covered his knees, and he was girt with many-colored girdles; buckskins of bright leather protected his feet; bracelets and strings of wampum ornamented his neck and arms; turquoise earrings hung from his ears; beautiful plumes waved over his head; his long, glossy hair was held with cords of many colors, into which great plumes of macaw feathers were stuck. Fearful, wonderful, beautiful, he stood. Suddenly one of the boys looked up and saw the Sun-father standing there.

"Blood!" cried he to the other. "*Ati!* Somebody's coming!"

"Where?" asked the other. "Where?"

"Right over there!"

"*Ati!*" he exclaimed.

Then the Sun, with stately step, approached them, dazzling their eyes with his beauty and his magnificent dress. So the poor little fellows huddled together and crouched their knees close to their bodies (for they had no clothes on), and watched him, trembling, until he came near. Then one of them said faintly: "Comest thou?" as though he just remembered it.

"Yea, I do, my children," said the Sun. "How are ye these many days?"

"Happy," responded they; but they were almost frightened out of their wits, and kept looking first at the Sun-father and then at each other.

"My children," said the Sun-father tenderly, "ye are my own children; I gave ye both life." But they only gazed at him, not believing what he said.

"Ye are both mine own children," he repeated.

"Is that so?" replied they.

"Yea, that is true; and I saw ye here, and pitied ye; so I came to speak with ye and to help ye."

"*Hai!*" exclaimed they. But they still looked at each other and at the Sun-father, and did not believe him.

"Yea, ye are verily my children," continued the Sun. "I am your own father. Around Thunder Mountain there is a city of men. It is called the Home of the Eagles, and there once lived a beautiful maiden who never left her home, but was always shut in her room. Day after day at midday, just at this time, I came down and visited her in my own sunlight. And a great Eagle always stood and watched her. Now, the townspeople grew anxious to see her, so they danced day after day their most beautiful dances, hoping to entice her to come forth; but she never looked out. So her father's warriors went to the home of Áhaiyúta and his younger brother, Mátsailéma, where they lived with their grandmother, on the middle of Thunder Mountain, and the Twain said that they would go with them and compel her to come forth. Therefore, one day they went and led the dance of the Óinahe. Yet, although they danced four times, she would not come forth, but tried to escape to my home in the heavens on the back of her Eagle; so the two gods shot her, and she fell down the cañon. Then it was that ye two, my children, were born and rolled among the bushes. Now, the people ran down from the village to

29

strive for your mother's body, and an Acoma got her and carried her away to the home of his people. An old Badger found ye and brought ye home to his wife, and that is the way ye came to live in the home of the Badgers."

Still the little ones did not believe him.

"Look!" said the Sun-father. "See what I have brought ye!" Then he continued: "Wait; in eight days, in the Home of the Eagles, where your aunts live in the house of your mother's father, there will be a great dance. Go ye thither. Ye will climb up a crooked path and enter the town through a road under the houses. Do not go out at once into the plaza, but wait until the dancers come out. Then step forth, and over to the left of the plaza ye will see your grandfather's house. It is the greatest house in the city, and the longest ladder leads up to it, and fringes of hair ornament its poles. On the roof ye will see, if the day be warm, two noisy macaws, and there ye will see your mother's sisters—your own aunts. When ye go into the plaza the people will rush up to ye and say: 'Whither do ye come, friends? Will ye not join in the dance?' And ye must say ye will, and then your aunts will come down and dance for the first time, because they are the most beautiful maidens in the pueblo, and very proud. But they will take hold of your hands and dance with ye, and when they have done will ask ye to come into their house; and ye must go.

"Now, the one who sits over in the northern corner is the first sister of your mother, therefore your mother; and the one who sits next to her is your next mother, and so on. There will be eight of them, and the youngest will be like a sister unto ye. They will place stools for ye, and ye must sit down and call them aunts. They will say: 'Certainly, we are the aunts of all good boys in the cities of men who are not our enemies.' And then ye must tell them that they are your real aunts, that this is your house, that your mother used to live there—was the maiden who never went out, but always sat making beautiful basket-trays of many-colored splints. Then ye must lead them into the next room, and the next, and then into the next one, and point to the beautiful basket-trays on the walls. There on the northern wall will hang a yellow tray, on the west wall will hang a blue one, and on the south wall, a red tray, then on the east wall will hang a white tray, and fastened to the ceiling will be a tray of many colors, while a black one will stand under the floor. And then ye must point to the trays and say: 'These our mother made.' Then they will believe and embrace ye and will not want to let ye go; but after ye have sat and eaten with them, ye must come back to the home of the Badgers. And the next day ye must go to Acoma to get your mother. Just before ye arrive at the town of Acoma ye will meet an old, wrinkled hag carrying a big bundle of wood on her back. Ye must call her 'grandmother' and greet her pleasantly. She will tell ye she is the dance-priestess of Acoma. Then ye must ask her why she, a woman, comes out to gather wood, and she will reply that she gets the wood to make a light. Then ask her why she wishes a light, and she will say to ye that day after day she lights a fire in her ceremonial chamber and that when she reaches home with her wood the young men of her clan come together and give her food, and that at night she takes the wood to the ceremonial chamber and then sits on a stone seat by the side of the fireplace and builds a fire; that the young men gather in the chamber and prepare for a dance. And when they are ready she takes the bones of your mother from a niche in the west end of the chamber and distributes them among the young men, who carry them in the dance. She gives the skull to the first one, the breast-bone to the next, the ribs to another, and so on until they all have bones to carry in the dance. When the dance is over, she goes around and takes all the bones back again and replaces them in the niche. Then the young men depart for their homes, but some of them sleep there in the chamber, and then she lies down to sleep and to keep guard over the bones.

" Now, when she has told ye these things, ye must ask her if that is all. If she says ' Yes,' kill her; then skin her, and the younger brother must wave his hands over her skin and put it on, and he will look just like the old woman. And he must climb up to the town of the Acomas and enter and do just as the old woman said that she did.

" Now, after the dance is over and he has taken

back all of the bones and replaced them in the niche, he must lie down and pretend to sleep, and some of the young men will go home; others will sleep there. When they all begin to snore, he must gather all the bones, and the two dried eyes, and the heart of his mother, and bring them away as fast as ever he can to where his brother waits. And when he gets there,—lo! she will come to life again and be just as she was before she was killed by the Twain. Now, mind, ye must not leave a single bone nor any part, for if ye do, your mother will lack that when she comes to life again."

"Very well," replied the boys, "we will do as you have told us; certainly we will."

"Now, I have given ye with your birth the power to slay all game; but mind that not a single rabbit, nor deer, nor antelope, nor mountain sheep, nor elk—though he be the finest ye have ever seen—shall ye slay, for in that case ye shall perish with your mother."

So the two boys promised they would not. "Of course we will not," said the younger brother. "When one's father commands him, can he disobey?"

"Come hither," said the Sun-father to the younger brother. "Stand here." So the little boy did as he was bidden.

"Lift up thy foot." Then the Sun-father drew off the moccasin of bark and put beautiful fringed leggings upon it, and replaced the bark moccasins with buskins like his own, and tied up the leggings with many-colored garters, and dressed him as he was dressed, and placed a beautiful quiver upon his back. But the poor little boys were dark-colored, and their hair was tangled and matted over their heads. Then the Sun-father turned himself about as if to summon some unseen messenger, and created a great warm cloud of mist, with which he cleansed the boys, and lo! their skins became smooth and clear, and their hair fell down their backs in wavy masses. Then the Sun-father arranged the younger brother's hair and placed a plume therein like his own, and beautiful plumes on his head.

"There," said he to the elder; "look at thy younger brother." But the poor little fellow was covered with shame, and dared only steal glances at his brother and the Sun-father. Then the Sun-father dressed the other like the first.

"*Ti!*" exclaimed they, as they looked at each other and at the Sun-father.

"You are just like Him," they said to each other. But still they did not call him father. Then they fell to conversing.

"Why; he must be our father!" said they to each other. "Mother's face has a black streak right down the middle of it, and father's face is just like it, except that his chin is grizzly." Then they knew that the Sun was their father, and they thanked him for his goodness.

Then said the Sun-father to them: "Mind what I have told ye, my children. I must go to my home in the heavens. Happy may ye always be.

Ye are my children; I love ye, and therefore I came' to help ye. Run home, now, for your father and mother who reared ye—the Badgers— are awaiting your coming. They will not know ye, so ye must roll up your bark moccasins and take along your strings of corn-cakes together with the rabbits ye have slain."

"How can we carry them?" asked they; "for they are heavy."

Then the Sun-father turned about and passed his hands gently over the heap of dead rabbits. "Lift them now," said he to the children; and when they tried to lift them, lo! they were as light as dry grass-stalks. So they bade their father farewell and started home. When they had gone a little way they stopped to look around, but their father was nowhere to be seen.

Sure enough, when they neared home there were the two old Badgers running around their hole, and the old Badger-father was just getting ready to go out and search, for fear that they had perished from cold. He had just gone down to get some rabbit-skins and other things with which to wrap them, when the old woman, who was up above, shouted down: "Hurry, come out! Somebody is coming!"

"Look!" said one of the children to the other. "There's our poor mother waiting for us. Hurry up! Let's run, or else our father will come out searching for us."

As they approached they called out: "Poor mother, here you are in the cold waiting for us."

But she did not recognize them, and only hid her face in her paws from shame, for they were too beautiful to look upon—just like the Sun-father.

"Don't you know us, mother?" asked the Two to the old woman just as the old Badger came out.

"No!" answered she.

"Why, we are your children!"

"Ah! my children did not look like you!"

"We are they! Look here!" said they, and they showed the bark moccasins and the strings of corn-cakes.

"Our poor children!"

"Yes, our father is no other than the Sun-father, and he came down to speak to us today, and he dressed us as you see, just like himself, and he said that our mother used to live over in the Home of the Eagles, that our aunts still live there, and our grandfather, and that our mother used to live there, but the Twain killed her as she was trying to escape on the back of an Eagle. And when she fell into the Cañon of the Coyote we were born, and father here found us and you both reared us."

"Yes, that is very true," said the old Badger. "I know it all; and I know, too, that there will be a dance at the Home of the Eagles in eight days. Tomorrow there will be only seven left, and when the eighth day comes you will both go there to see it. Come up and come down," said they.

So the two entered, but they were ill at ease in their clothes, which they were not used to. And when the old mother had placed soft rabbit-skins on the floor, they doffed their clothing and carefully laid it away. Then the whole family ate their evening meal.

"Keep count for us, father, and when the time comes, let us know," said the boys.

So the days passed by until the day before the dance, and that morning the old Badger said to the Two: "Tomorrow the dance will come."

"Very well," replied they; "let us go out and hunt today, that you and mother may have something to eat." So they went forth, and in the evening came back with great numbers of rabbits; and the old mother skinned the rabbits and put some of them to cook over night, so that her children might eat before starting for the town under Thunder Mountain.

At sunrise next morning both dressed themselves carefully, put on their plumes, and started on the pathway that leads around the mountain. They passed the village of K'yátik'ia on their way, and the people marvelled greatly at their beauty and their magnificent dress. And so they followed the road through the Cañon of the Coyotes, thence by the crooked pathway and the covered road under the house into the court of K'iákime. Just as the Sun-father had told them, they found everything there. There was the great house with the tall ladder and the two macaws, and there were the young maidens, their aunts, sitting on the housetop.

And as the dancers came into the court they stepped forward, and then it was that the people first saw and hailed them. The chief of the dance

came forward and asked them whither they came
and if they would not join in the dance. So they
assented and came forward to the center of the
plaza, and as they began to dance, the young girls
arose and the dance chiefs went and escorted them
to the dance plaza.

Although they told them, " Dance here," they
did not obey. They ran right over to where the
two young men were dancing, and took hold of
their hands just as the Sun-father had told them it
would come to pass. And, in fact, everything
happened just as he had said. Yes, they all ran
down and grasped the two boys' hands, and when
the dance was over and they let go, they said to
the two handsome young strangers : " Come up ;
come in."

" It is well," said the two young men. So they
all went up into the house and sat down. Now,
all these girls were young, and they were very
much pleased with the young men. In fact the
two youngest were in love with them already ; so
they smiled and made themselves very pleasant.
Then the first brother arose and went over to the
eldest one, and said : " Mother-aunt."

" What is it ? " she replied, " for of course throughout the cities of men we, as the daughters of a
great priest, are the mothers of children,"— and
so on until they came to the last and youngest one,
whom they called " little mother-aunt," and she
also replied that, however young they might be,
still they might be counted the mothers of the
children of men.

"No, verily, ye are our parents," replied the Twain. "Beyond this room is another, and beyond that another, and beyond that yet another where lived our mother, who never went forth from her house, but sat day after day making sacred trays. And there even now, according to the colors of the parts of the world hang her trays on the wall."

And so, as the Sun had told them, they finished their story. Then the people were convinced, and sent for the grandfather, the great priest-chief, and when he came they all embraced their new children, admiring greatly their straight, smooth limbs and abundant hair. Then the grandfather dressed them in some of the beautiful ornaments their mother used to wear, and when evening approached they feasted them. And after the meal was over, as the Sun was setting, the two boys arose and said, "We must go."

"Stay with us, stay with us," the young girls and the grandfather said. "Why should you go away from your home? This is your own home."

"No; we said to our mother and father, the Badgers, that we would return to them; therefore we must go," urged the boys. So at last they consented and wished them a happy journey.

"Fear not," said the Two as they started, "for we shall yet go and get our mother. Even tomorrow we shall go to Acoma where the people dance day after day in her memory." Then they departed and returned to the place of the Badgers.

When they arrived at home, sure enough, there

were their Badger-mother and Badger-father awaiting them outside their holes.

"Oh, here you are!" they cried.

"Yes; how did you come unto the evening?"

"Happily!" replied the old ones. "Come in,
come in!" So they entered.

When they had finished eating, the elder brother said: "Mother, father, look ye! Tomorrow
we must go after our mother to Acoma. Make
us a luncheon, and we will start early in the morning. We are swift runners and shall get there in
one day; and the next day we will start back;
and the next day, quite early, we will come home
again with our mother."

"Very well," replied the Badger-father; "it is
well." But the Badger-mother said, "Oh! my poor
children, my poor boys!"

So, early next morning, the Badger-mother
rolled up some sweet corn-cakes in a blanket, for
she did not have to string them now, and together
the Twain started up the eastern trail. Their
father, the Sun, thought to help them; therefore
he lengthened the day and took two steps only
at a time, until the two boys had arrived at the
Springs of the Elks, almost on the borders of the
Acoma country. Then, with his usual speed journeyed the Sun-father toward the Land of Night;
and the two boys continued until they arrived
within sight of the town of the Acomas—away out
there on top of a mountain. Sure enough, there
was an old hag struggling along under a load of
wood, and as the two brothers came up to her

they said: "Ha, grandmother, how are you these
many days?"

"Happy," replied the old woman.

"Why is it that you, a woman, and an old
woman, have to carry wood?"

"Why, I am the priestess of the dance!" answered the old woman.

"Priestess of the dance?"

"Yes."

"What dance?"

"Why, there once lived a maiden in the Town
of the Eagles, and the two Gods of War shot her
one day from the back of an Eagle who was trying
to run away with her, and she fell; and one of my
young men was the first to grasp her, therefore we
dance with her bones every night."

"Well, why do you get this wood?" they asked.

"I light the ceremonial chamber with it."

"What do you do when you get home?"

"Why, the maidens of my clan come and baptize
me and feast me; then when the evening comes I
go and light a fire with this wood in the chamber
and wait until the young men gather; and when
everything is ready I go to a niche in the wall and
get the maiden's bones and distribute them; and
when they have finished the dance I tell them to
stop, and they replace the bones."

"What do they do then?" asked the two boys.

"Why, some of them go home, and some sleep
right there, and I lie down and sleep there, too."

"Is that all?" inquired the two boys.

"Why, yes, what more should there be?"

"Nothing more, except that I think we had better kill you now." Thereupon they struck her to the earth and killed her. Then they skinned her like a bag, and the elder brother dressed the younger in the skin, as the Sun-father had directed, and he shouldered the bundle of wood.

"How do I look?" asked he.

"Just like her, for all the world!" responded the other.

"All right," said he; "wait for me here."

"Go ahead," said the elder brother, and away the younger went. He ran with all his might till he came near to the town, and then he began to limp along and labor up the pathway just as the old woman was wont to do, so that everybody thought that he was the old woman, indeed. And sure enough it all happened just as the Sun-father had said it would. When the dance was over, some of the young men went away and others slept right there. There were so many of them, though, that they almost covered the floor. When they all began to snore, the young man arose, threw off his disguise, and stepped carefully between the sleepers till he reached the niche in the wall. Then he put his mother's bones, one by one, into his blanket, felt all around to see that he left nothing, and started for the ladder. He reached it all right and took one, two, three steps; but when his foot touched the fourth rung it creaked, and the sleeping dancers awoke and started.

"Somebody is going up the ladder!" they exclaimed to one another. Then the young man ran up as fast as ever he could, but alas! he dropped one of his mother's eyes out of the blanket. He kept on running until he reached the foot of the hill upon which the town stood; and when he came to the spring down on the plains he stopped to drink, and lo! his mother had come to life!

"*Ahwa!*" uttered the mother, "I'm tired and I don't know what is the matter with my eyes, for things don't look straight."

Then the young man looked at his mother. She was more beautiful than all the other girls had been, but one of her eyes was shrunken in. "Alas! my mother," said he, "I have dropped one of your eyes; but never mind, you can comb your hair down over it and no one will ever know the difference."

As soon as they were rested they started again, and soon came to where the elder brother stood awaiting them. When he looked at his mother, he saw that one of her eyes had been left.

"Did n't I tell you beforehand to be careful?" said he. "Poor mother; you have lost one of her eyes!"

"Well, it can't be helped; never mind, she can comb her hair down over the eye that is dry and no one will ever know the difference."

"That's so; it can't be helped. Now let's go," said the elder brother, and they all started.

When they arrived at the Waters of the Elks, the younger brother said: "Let's camp here."

"No, let's run home," returned the elder brother.

"No, let's camp. Our poor mother will get

tired, and, besides, she can see nothing of the country we are going through."

And although the elder brother urged that they should go on, the younger insisted that they should stay; therefore they camped. The next day they continued their journey until they came near to the City of the Heights, not far from their own home; and as they journeyed, the deer, the antelope, the elks, and the mountain sheep were everywhere.

"Just look at that buck!" exclaimed the younger brother, clutching his bow. "Let's shoot him."

"No, no!" said the other; "Do you not remember that our father forbade us?" So they went on until they came to some trees, and as it was noonday they sat down to eat. Now, the fine game animals circled all around and even came up near enough to smell them, and stood gazing or cropping the grass within a few steps of them.

"Just look at that splendid antelope!" cried the younger brother, and he nocked an arrow quicker than thought.

"No, no, no!" cried the elder, "you must not shoot it."

"Why not? Here our poor mother has nothing but corn-cakes to eat, with all this meat around us." And before his brother could speak another word, he drew his arrow to the head, and *tsi!* it pierced the heart of the great antelope and it fell dead.

Now, all the great animals round about grew angry when they saw this, and *tene!* they came thundering after the little party. So the two fools, forgetting all about their poor mother, jumped up and ran away as fast as they could and climbed a big tree to the very top. When they straddled a big branch and looked down, the great deer had trampled their poor mother to death. Then they gathered around the foot of the tree to batter its trunk with their sharp horns, but they could not stir it. Presently some big-horn bucks came running along. *Thle-ee-ta-a-a!* they banged their horns against the butt of the tree until it began to split and tremble, and presently bang! went the tree, and the boys fell to the ground. Then the mountain sheep and the great bucks trampled and tore and speared them with their sharp horns, and tossed them from one to another and lacerated them with their hoofs until they were like worn-out clothing— all torn to pieces except the head of the elder brother which none of them would touch. And there the head lay all through the winter; and the next spring there was nothing but a skull left of the two brothers.

Now, off in the valley that led to Thunder Mountain, just where it turns to go south, stood the village of K'yátik'ia, and down in the bottom of the valley the great priest-chief of K'yátik'ia had his fields of corn and melons and squashes. Summer came, and the squashes were all in bloom, when the rain poured down all over the country; and thus, little by little, the skull was washed until it fell into a stream and went bumping along on the waters even till it came to the fields of corn and pumpkins and melons in the planting of the priest-chief of K'yátik'ia.

30

Now, when the pumpkin and squash vines were in bloom, the priest-chief's daughter, who was as beautiful as you could look upon, went down every morning just at daylight to gather squash-flowers with which to sweeten the feast bread. The morning after the rain had passed over, very early, she said to her younger sister: "Stay here and grind meal while I run down to the squash patch to pick a lot of flowers." So she took her mantle with her and started for the fields. She had not been picking flowers long when a voice rose from the middle of the vines:

"*Ä-te-ya-ye,*
Ä-te-ya-ye.
E-lu-ya."

Here are more flowers,
Here are more flowers.
Beautiful ones.

"Ah!" said the girl, "I wonder what that is!" So she put her blanket of flowers down as soon as possible and started to hunt. As she approached the vine where the skull had been wont to lie, lo! there was a handsome young man!

"What are you doing?" asked the young man.

"Gathering flowers," said she.

"If you will promise to take me home with you, I will help you," said the young man.

"Very well," replied the girl.

"Will you surely do it?" inquired the young man.

"Yes," said she, and lo! the young man reached out his hand and there was a great heap of flowers already plucked before him! And while they were yet talking, the Sun rose; and as its first rays touched him he began to sink, until there before the girl was nothing but a hideous old skull.

"Oh, dear!" cried she; "but I promised to take it, and I suppose I must." So she took the skull up with the tips of her fingers and put it into the blanket among the flowers, and started for home. Then she entered an inner room of the house, and taking the skull carefully out of the blanket, placed some cotton in a large new water-jar, and laid the skull upon it. Then she covered the jar with a flat stone and went to work grinding meal.

When the Sun was setting, a voice came from the jar.

"Take me down, quick!" And the girl took the skull down and placed it on the floor, and as it grew dark there stood the same handsome young man as before, magnificently clothed, with precious stones and shells all about him, just as the Sun-father had dressed him. And the girl was very happy, and told him she would marry him.

Next morning, just as the Sun rose, the young man vanished, and nothing but the old white skull lay on the floor. So the girl placed it in the jar again, and taking up another water-jar went out toward the spring. Now, her younger sister went into the room and espied the jar. "I wonder what sister has covered this jar up so carefully for," said she to herself; and she stepped up to the jar and took the lid off.

"*Ati!*" cried she. "O dear! O dear!" she

screamed. For when she looked down into the jar there was a great rattlesnake coiled up over the smooth white skull.

So she ran and called her father and told him in great fright what she had seen.

"Ah!" said the father, for he was a very wise priest-chief, "thou shouldst not meddle with things. Thou shouldst keep quiet," said he. He then arose and went into the room. Then he approached the jar, and, looking down into it, said: "Have mercy upon us, my child, my father. Become as thou art. Disguise not thyself in hideous forms, but as thou hast been, be thou." And the skull rattled against the sides of the jar in assent.

"It is well that thou shouldst marry my daughter. And we will close this room that thou shalt never come forth"; and again the skull clattered and nodded in glad assent.

So when the young girl returned, the voice came forth from the jar again, and said: "Close all the windows and doors, and bring me raw cotton if thy father have it, for he has consented that I marry you and throw off my disguise."

Then the girl gladly assented, and ran to get the cotton, and brought a great quantity in the room. Then when the night came the voice called once more: "Take me down!" The girl did as she was bidden, and the young man again stood before her, more handsome than ever. So he married the girl and both were very happy.

And the next morning when the Sun rose the young man did not again change his form, but re-

mained as he was, and began to spin cotton marvellously fine and to weave blankets and mantles of the
most beautiful texture, for in nothing could he fail,
being a child of the Sun-father and a god himself.

So the days and weeks passed by, and the Sun-
father looked down through the windows in sorrow
and said : " Alas ! my son ; I have delivered thee and
yet thou comest not to speak with thy father. But
thou shalt yet come ; yea, verily, thou shalt yet
come."

So in time the beautiful daughter of the priest-
chief gave birth to two boys, like the children of
the deer. As day succeeded day, they grew larger
and wiser and their limbs strengthened until they
could run about, and thus it happened that one day
in their play they climbed up and played upon the
house-top and on the ground below. Thus it was
that the people of K'yátik'ia saw for the first time
the two little children ; and when they saw them
they wondered greatly. Of course they wondered
greatly. Our grandfathers were fools.

" Who in the world has married the priest-chief's
daughter ? " everybody asked of one another. Nobody knew ; so they called a council and made all
the young men go to it, and they asked each one
if he had secretly married the priest-chief's daughter ; and every one of them said " No," and looked
at every other one in great wonder.

" Who in the world can it be ? It may be that
some stranger has come and married her, and it
may be that he stays there." So the council decided that it would be well for him and the girl and

their two little ones to die, because they had deceived their people. Forthwith two war-priests mounted the house-tops and commanded the people to make haste and to prepare their weapons. "Straighten your arrows, strengthen the backs of your bows, put new points on your lances, harden your shields, and get ready for battle, for in four days the daughter and grandchildren of the priest-chief and the unknown husband must die!"

And when the priest-chief's daughter heard the voices of the heralds, she asked her younger sister, who had been listening, what they said. And the younger sister exclaimed: "Alas! you must all die!" and then she told her what she had heard.

Now, the young man called the old priest and told him that he knew what would happen, and the old priest said: "It is well; let the will of the gods be done. My people know not the way of good fortune, but are fools and must have their way."

Therefore for two days the people labored at their weapons, and on the morning of the third day they began to prepare for a feast of victory. Then said the young man to his wife: "My little mother, dearly beloved, on the morrow I must go forth to meet my father"; for he suddenly remembered that he had neglected his father.

When the Sun had nearly reached the mid-heavens, the young man said to his wife: "Go up and open the sky-hole. Farewell!" said he, and he suddenly became a cloud of mist which whirled round and round and shot up like a whirlwind in the rays of sunlight.

When he neared the Sun, the Sun-father said nothing, and the young man waited outside in shame. Then said the Sun-father in pretended anger: "Come hither and sit down. Thou hast been a fool. Did I not command thee and thy brother?" And the young man only bent his head and said: "It is too true."

Then the Sun-father smiled gently, and said: "Think not, neither be sad, my child. I know wherefore thou comest, and I remember how thou didst try to prevail upon thy younger brother to obey my commandments; and that it might be well I caused thee to forget me, and to come unto the past that thou hast come unto. Thou shalt be a god, and shalt sit at my left hand. Forever and ever shalt thou be a living good unto men, who will see thee and worship thee in the evening. And through thy will shall rain fall upon their lands. True, I had designed, had my children been wiser, that thou shouldst remain with them and enrich them with thy precious shells and stones, with thy great knowledge and good fortune. But those are men very unwise and ungrateful, therefore shalt thou and thy children, and even thy wife, be won from thy earth-life and sit by my left hand. Descend. Make four sacred hoops and entwine them with cotton. Make four sacred wands, such as are used in the races. Hast thou an unembroidered cotton mantle?"

"I have," replied the young man.

"It is well. This evening spread it out and place at each of its four corners one of the sacred hoops

and wands. Place all thereon that thou valuest.
Leave not a precious stone nor yet a shell to serve
as parentage for others, but place all thereon. The
people will gather around thy father's house and
storm it, and then retire and storm it again. Now,
when the people approach the house, sit ye down,
one at each of the four corners; grasp them and lift
them upward, and gradually ye will be raised. Then
when the people approach nearer, lift them upward
once more, and ye will be raised yet farther. And
when they begin to mount the ladders, lift ye again,
and yet again, and ye shall come unto my country."

So the young man descended. No change was
visible in the old priest-chief's countenance. He
had caused gay preparations to go forward for the
festival, for a priest knows that all things are well,
and he makes no change in his mind or actions.
And when he asked the young man what the Sun-
father had said to him, the only reply was: "It shall
be well. Tomorrow we go to dwell forever at the
home of the Sun-father."

Early in the morning the two Priests of War
mounted to the house-tops and called out: "Hasten,
hasten! For the time has come and the people
must gather, each carrying his weapons, for today
the children of our priest-chief must die!"

So, after the morning meal, all gathered at the
council chambers of the warriors, and a great company they were. The Sun had risen high. Brightly
painted shields glittered in his light. Long lances
stood black with paint like the charred trunks of a
burned forest; and the people raised their war-clubs

and struck them against one another until the din was like thunder.

"*Ho-o-o!*" sounded the clash of weapons and the war-cries of the people, and in the home of the priest-chief they knew they were coming. All night long they had been preparing; the young man had placed all their belongings upon the blanket, and now one by one they sat down. The wife and the husband grasped two corners, the children grasping the two others. They lifted them and slowly arose toward the ceiling. Once more, as the people came nearer, they lifted the corners and neared the sky-hole. When again they lifted the corners, they passed above the roof, and the people saw their shadows cast upon the ground.

"Quick, quick!" shouted the young men. "See the shadow; they are escaping!"

Already the arrows began to whistle past them, but the Sun cast his shield beneath them, and the arrows only glanced away or flew past. Once more they drew the corners of the mantle upward, and as they rose higher and higher, the people, old and young, began to quarrel and fell to beating one another, and to fighting among themselves. The old ones called the young ones fools for attempting the life of a god, and the young ones in turn called the old ones fools for counselling them to attempt the life of a god.

"Thus shall ye ever be," cried the young man, "for ye are fools! Your father, the Sun, had intended all things for your good, but ye were fools; therefore with me and mine will pass away your peace and your treasures."

My children, at sunset have you not seen the
little blue twinkling stars that sit at the left hand
of the Sun as he sinks into night? Thus did it
come to pass in the days of the ancients, and thus
it is that only in the east and the west where the
Sun rises and sets, even on the borders of the great
oceans, may we find the jewels whereby we decorate
our persons. And ever since then, my children, the
world has been filled with anger, and even brothers
agree, then disagree, strike one another, and spill
their own blood in foolish anger.

Perhaps had men been more grateful and wiser,
the Sun-father had smiled and dropped everywhere
the treasures we long for, and not hidden them
deep in the earth and buried them in the shores of
the sea. And perhaps, moreover, all men would
have smiled upon one another and never enlarged
their voices nor strengthened their arms in anger
toward one another.

Thus short is my story; and may the corn-stalks
grow as long as my stretches, and may the will of
the Holder of the Roads of Life shelter me from
dangers as he sheltered his children in the days of
the ancients with the shield of his sunlight.

It is all finished. *(Tenk'ia.)*

6853